# THE GULAG P-PA DIARIES

*A Bittersweet Memoir of Grand-Parenting*

*PRESTON LEWIS*

The Gulag P-Pa Diaries
by Preston Lewis

Paperback Edition

CKN Christian Publishing
An Imprint of Wolfpack Publishing

6032 Wheat Penny Avenue
Las Vegas, NV 89122

Copyright © 2020 Preston Lewis

All rights reserved. No part of this book may be reproduced by any means without the prior written consent of the publisher, other than brief quotes for reviews.

Paperback ISBN: 978-1-64734-876-2
Ebook ISBN: 978-1-64734-875-5
Library of Congress Control Number: 2020935684

# THE GULAG P-PA DIARIES

# DEDICATION

In Memory
of
Benjamin Scott Lewis,
Our First Grandson,
and in Honor of His Successors
Hannah, Cora, Miriam, Carys and Jackson

# CHAPTER ONE

*"Grandchildren are the crown of the aged."*
—*Proverbs 17:6 (English Standard Version)*

Ah, grandkids! They are the toppings on life's last ice cream sundae. Some grandchildren are the sprinkles that add color and sweetness to the dish. Others are the whipped cream that smothers the concoction with love. Some resemble the chocolate sauce that overpowers the other flavors. A few represent the cherry that crowns the dessert, drawing everyone's attention, even though the smallest part of the dessert. And a handful take after the nuts that provide a crunch of zaniness to every bite.

Ah, grandkids, God's greatest gift to humanity, all the fun and none of the responsibility you had with your own children. Perhaps American humorist Sam Levenson best summarized the relationship between grandparents and grandkids. "The reason grandparents and grandchildren get along so well," said Levenson, "is that they have a common enemy." Levenson also noted, "The simplest toy, one which even the youngest child can operate, is called a grandparent." That's true, but grandparenting also provides a second chance at getting parenting right, an opportunity for redemption for our failures in raising our own kids, when patience, tolerance and understanding were often short-circuited by the stresses of jobs, relationships and life in general. As many of us wish we had the opportunity to improve our grades as parents, grandparenting provides that prospect, primarily because we can be our grandkids' friends rather than their parents. While that provides a successful strategy for grandparents, I don't believe it is the best course for parents whose responsibilities extend far beyond friendship. That may well be the paradox of parenting versus grandparenting.

We grandparents are important enough to have our own designated day each year. While Harriet knew about it, I did not until we visited our fourth-grader one Labor Day weekend, and she invited us to her school for a breakfast reception honoring grandparents the following Friday. Only after I investigated did I realize that the event corresponded with National Grandparents Day, which falls each year on the Sunday after Labor Day. That it was established in 1978 by President Jimmy Carter seemed somehow appropriate to our family as that was the year Harriet gave birth to our daughter, who would in turn bear three of our grandchildren. Grandparents Day has an official flower "the forget-me-not", though oddly enough the flower blooms in the spring, making it difficult to give a bouquet to grandparents in the fall. Grandparents Day also has an official song as selected by the National Grandparents Day Council, "A Song for Grandma and Grandpa," written by Johnny Prill, a Grammy Award-nominated songwriter and accordion virtuoso.

Poland became the first country to recognize a grandparents day with its 1965 designation of "Grandma's Day", celebrated in January each year. "Grandpa's Day" follows on the next day in Poland.

As of this writing, seventeen countries worldwide celebrate Grandparents Day annually. West Virginian Marian McQuade is considered the originator of National Grandparents Day in the United States, convincing her governor to proclaim such an occasion in 1973. Five years later President Carter accepted the idea and signed the proclamation establishing the national day of honor for grandparents. McQuade was well qualified to promote the occasion because at her death at ninety-one, she left behind fifteen children, forty-three grandchildren and fifteen great-grandchildren.

Harriet and I were pikers by comparison, having only a son and a daughter and but five surviving grandchildren. Even so, after our first grandchildren arrived, we began to host our children's families in alternate Christmases and Thanksgivings, allowing our son and daughter to spend time with their in-laws every other year during the holiday season. Even if we hosted the families at Thanksgiving, we shared our Christmas tree with the kids and grandkids at that time. Harriet came up with the term Thanksmas to represent those years when we celebrated Christmas in November.

Perhaps our most poignant and memorable Thanksmas came five years ago when my parents joined us for our gift-opening and traditional feast. It would be the last holiday all four generations dined together at our house because my folks were approaching their nineties and soon could not venture far from their home. After exchanging gifts that year, we cleared the mess and gathered for the special dinner. We held hands in an unbroken circle of our family and gave thanks for our savior, our presents and our meal before us. Then we went through the buffet line, filling our plates with turkey and dressing and all the trimmings. My parents ate in the dining room with our son and daughter along with their spouses while Harriet and I dined at the kitchen table with our grandchildren.

Cascades of laughter came from both tables. We heard our children remembering tales of their summer vacations at Pa's and Gamma's farm or second home in the mountains of Ruidoso, New Mexico, where they created such enduring memories. For instance, take the time Pa took our son Scott and our nephew Jason for a walk in the woods. At one point Pa pointed out some black bear droppings on the trail, amazing the boys with his outdoors knowledge. They passed the spot again on the way back to the house and Pa gestured at the scat and asked which boy had stepped in it. Both kids inspected the bottom of their shoes and shrugged, then looked at their grandfather's boot, stained from his misstep. Oh, the boys celebrated then and laughed even harder at the retelling.

Then came the time when they returned from Ruidoso with the boys in the front seat with Pa while our daughter Melissa and niece Lauren sat in the back with Gamma. As they neared the state line, the boys started bragging how they would re-enter Texas first. Approaching the border, Pa slowed, pulled off of the road onto the shoulder, turned the car around and backed into Texas. Even as the boys unbuckled their seat belts and lunged toward the back, Melissa and Lauren still entered Texas first, much to the boys' dismay. Or there came the time, the boys got up before the girls at Mom's and Dad's Ruidoso home and ate all of Lauren's favorite breakfast cereal. Sure enough when Lauren sat down at the table, they gloated over how tasty their breakfast had been and how they had eaten every last bite. Only then did Gamma open a cabinet door and pull out a bowl she had poured for Lauren when she heard the boys plotting against her. Oh, how the laughter resounded as my parents and children recalled those fun times.

Meanwhile, Harriet and I dined at the cool table

with our grandkids. While Generations One and Three laughed and reminisced about their early years together, Generations Two and Four (less the baby Jackson who was napping) created memories of our own. We discussed the Christmas spirit of giving, such as the aprons Mema had made for all the girls, and how the gift of generosity tied in with Thanksgiving and the exchange between Indians and Pilgrims that gave us the November holiday. To celebrate that bicultural heritage, we selected Native American names for everyone at the table. Our four granddaughters pondered and then came up with an appropriate sobriquet for each other.

"What about Mema and P-Pa?" I asked. "Don't we get Indian names?" The quartet looked perplexed until Miss Miriam nodded. "Mema is 'Love Apron,'" she announced. Wow! Wasn't that sweet? Talk about clever and sensitive little angels, they were it! I couldn't wait to hear what loving name The Grands planned for me. "What's my Indian name?" I persisted when I should have left well enough alone. Miriam, whose unfiltered comments make her a hoot, took but a second to reply. "Big Belly," she proclaimed. So much for their angelic sensitivity! But, oh, what a funny memory! While my parents relived past memories in the dining room with their grandchildren, we sat at the kitchen table making new memories of our own.

While our heavenly immortality is forever, for most of us our earthly immortality lasts only as long as the memory of our grandchildren. They are our link to the future, and we are their connection to the past. So, Harriet and I wanted to create some fun times for them to look back on as well as teach them about their family heritage. While we did not have a second home in the mountains like my folks, we had a nice dwelling where we could host the kids. We came up with what we called "Camp

Mema/Gulag P-Pa," where we would welcome The Grands for seven to ten days and give their parents a break from child-raising, much like we had enjoyed a week's reprieve from those responsibilities when my folks took our son and daughter and our niece and nephew to New Mexico.

When I was growing up, my brother and I often spent a week or more with a special uncle and aunt each summer. My younger sibling always seemed to enjoy it more than I did because I got bored, especially since Joe and Ella Mae were childless and had no toys to keep me busy and little reading material to occupy me other than a few Ranch Romances, which I devoured summer after summer. Consequently, I wanted to make sure that The Grands were always amused while visiting us, so we revived a few toys we had left over from our children's upbringing and bought others more attuned to a new generation's tastes. By the time we finished shopping, we had more LEGO Duplo sets than we had ever purchased for our own kids, for instance.

To attend camp, Mema required that The Grands be at least two years old and able to speak clearly enough to communicate their needs, especially if they got sick. I would've stipulated that they had to be house-trained so we didn't have to mess with diapers. Unfortunately, I was overruled, despite one traumatic diaper experience a few years before. When our son and daughter-in-law moved back to Texas from Alaska, they asked us to keep their daughters Hannah and Miriam while they hunted for a home in Houston. As Harriet and I still worked then, she'd take half of the day off and I'd take the other half to tend to the girls.

Fortunately for me, at least, Miriam had her major movements during Harriet's shift, except for one afternoon when I detected an unwanted aroma seeping from Miriam's attire. When I got her on the changing table, I encountered the biggest diaper catastrophe of my life as everything was oozing out of her diaper down her legs, up her belly and virtually everywhere. To make matter worse, Miriam was just as happy as could be, smiling and laughing and gesticulating and even getting her fingers in the mess. I was torn whether she was just taunting me with this special gift or was genuinely proud of her accomplishment.

So, I lifted her up and cradled her head in my elbow, then held her hands and feet in the other hand to tote her to the bathroom where I ran the water long enough to get it not too hot and not too cold but just right. I slid her under the gentle stream and carefully washed the muddle away. Miriam jabbered as happy as a puppy with two tails the whole time. After we got her cleaned up and re-clothed, we next had to cleanse the diaper and changing table. Figuring it too expensive to call a hazmat team, I plunged in and wrapped up the dirty diaper, the stained clothing and the soiled changing linens, then took them out to the patio where I left them for later disposal while I disinfected the changing area.

When Harriet returned home, she sniffed something was amiss when she reached the patio and got a whiff of the debris. She entered the house, concerned over everyone's well-being. I had barely mentioned the word diaper before Hannah shouted, "Mema, it was horrible." Harriet helped finish the related chores, and I rejoiced to have reinforcements, though I was emotionally scarred for years. To ease the mental anguish, we subsequently established a family medal, "The Poople Heart", to be awarded in cases of heroism under bombardment. The award has been given twice for going above and beyond the call of duty in diaper management.

While I opposed diaper duties, Harriet insisted that any inconvenience would be offset by the fun we would create with The Grands. Beyond fun, we aimed to teach little ones some lessons in life, to enjoy their development and, most of all, to create memories. Except for an occasional accident, the four girl Grands met my unreasonable potty-trained criteria.

For the camp's first year, our son's daughters Hannah and Miriam were eight and three respectively and our daughter's girls Cora and Carys were five and two-and-a-half while her son Jackson was not yet three months old. To keep their parents informed that their children remained safe and secure, I offered tongue-in-cheek posts on Facebook to chronicle our adventures as it had been decades since we had cared for children so young. Our kids loved the posts and shared them with their friends, whose comments suggested they enjoyed my warped look at grandparenting and incarcerating The Grands for a week at Camp Mema/Gulag P-Pa. The positive reception by those friends and acquaintances provided the genesis for the annual Gulag P-Pa Diaries.

While the camp narrative is one of fun and joy, it masked the pain of the greatest tragedy of our lives, the loss of our first grandchild, Benjamin Scott Lewis. The passing of Benjamin challenged my faith and left me asking questions to this day. A decade and a half later, I still find it hard to talk to others without getting emotional about the little grandson we never got to hold or know. I can now in solitude, however, write and share my thoughts on the tragedy of losing a grandchild while counterbalancing the hurt of our loss with the joys of watching his five successors mature. With the surviving Grands, every day is an ice cream sundae covered with sprinkles, syrup, whipped cream, cherries and, yes, even nuts.

# CHAPTER TWO

## *YEAR ONE*

**Gulag P-Pa Diary, Day 1:**

The inmates arrived late last night. It's a motley crew. There's Hannah L, a.k.a., The Trouble Maker. She's so tricky, she's even been known to put her name on gifts intended for her kindly grandfather. P-Pa doesn't know where she would ever get an idea like that.

Then there's Cora K, a.k.a., The Plotter. She's so kind and sweet, she's just got to be plotting something, something like overthrowing the commandant.

Next is Miriam L, a.k.a. The Tattler. Somehow last night she got out of her cell and approached the guards with this message: "My cousins say there are no books in here." Then she offered to get books out of her backpack, but only she could fetch them because "my backpack is dangerous."

Then comes Carys K, a.k.a., The Mischief Maker. When things get quiet, you've got to find her. She may be tunneling out under the barbed wire or scaling the fence. The guards know to keep an eye on her.

Finally, there's Jackson K, a.k.a., The Muscle. He's a tough cookie. Don't know we will be able to manage this one, not with the four other hard cases here.

### Gulag P-Pa Diary, Day 2:

The delivery guards have all left. Now the terror begins. Us against them. The two of us against four of the most clever minds in kid history. The day began with Carys K trying to escape. When Mema and P-Pa arose, she was wandering the prison grounds, looking for a way out.

No sooner than had the delivery guards left, than Hannah L turned to Cora K and said, "You're The Plotter. What's the plan?" Fortunately, Commandant P-Pa overheard the question and is on full alert for an uprising. Then when Mema left the room for just a moment, Hannah L looked at Commandant P-Pa and said, "It's just you!" Talk about a scary moment. P-Pa's worried for his safety.

Cora K did a magic trick and made Mema disappear. Now, no one can find her. Panic is setting in. We'll starve to death. Finally, Hannah L found her, cowering in fear behind a bedroom door. What have we gotten into? The inmates are thinking the same thing. Hannah L said to Cora, "Don't make Mema disappear again or we'll all go to Gulag P-Pa. I have a plan to overthrow 'The Condamant'." (Her pronunciation)

While all of this is going on, Miriam L appears to be making a weapon or an escape vehicle from LEGO Duplos. Condamant P-Pa doesn't have enough eyes to keep up with them all. Hannah L has called a meeting of all the inmates. Trouble's brewing.

To be continued!

### Gulag P-Pa Diary, Day 2, Part 2:

The fear of an uprising finally caught up with Condamant P-Pa, who was so scared he had to take a nap to regain his strength and courage, locking himself in his own cell for security. Three of the four inmates took a nap, too, but The Condamant feared they were just playing possum while they plotted his overthrow. Hannah L watched a DVD of Little Women, a classic literary story of four girls plotting to overthrow their parents. Coincidence? P-Pa thinks not.

Troubles abound. When The Condamant provided The Trouble Maker with a glass of water, he told her he filled it with crazy juice. "Good," said Hannah L, "now I'll have more power to overthrow The Condamant."

Mema had troubles of her own. She was helping Miriam L wash her hands after a potty break when The Tattler cried, "No, no, no, that's not the way Mommy does it. She puts the soap on first, not the water." Well, duh! Everyone knows that, Mema! Then at snack time, Mema had to list everything in the pantry before Carys K decided on mandarin oranges for a little snack. Snack time is much simpler at Gulag P-Pa. It's bread and water only.

Now the L sisters are playing with LEGO Duplos. "How's your secret weapon going?" Hannah L said to Miriam L. P-Pa best abandon the Gulag Diary and see what they are up to.

**Gulag P-Pa Diary, Day 3:**

Mema and The Condamant survived a night of horror. They awoke to find house lights on that were off at bedtime. Carys K escaped her cell and was found on the couch where she apparently was planning to ambush Condamant P-Pa, but she dozed off and missed her chance.

Miriam L, The Tattler, complained about her breakfast. When Mema told her to drink all her chocolate milk against her will, The Tattler replied, "I did. The top of it is gone!" Mema answered, "The bottom needs to be gone." Miriam L finally complied. Lunch was a different story. She protested the vegetarian corn dog, saying, "My mommy fixes healthy stuff." Miss Miriam's now doing time in solitary confinement. Gulag P-Pa is getting a bad rap, but Camp Mema has a dark side as well.

Cora K has been playing with LEGO Duplos, singing lyrics, "O – B – BAH – DOO – B – OH – B – U." It must be a code. Got to be careful. After all, she is The Plotter.

Hannah L is the girl of the day at Camp Mema or inmate of the day at Gulag P-Pa. As girl of the day, the recipient gets to pick the movie, the day's Bible story to share and the activity of the day. So, this is Splash Day, where the inmates get to play in the wading pool. By contrast, Gulag P-Pa is offering Water Boarding Day, where the motto is "all the fun with only a fraction of the water," a sound policy in water-starved West Texas.

Splash Day turned into an escape attempt. Someone smuggled water guns into the wading pools and Condamant P-Pa was the main target. He was able to survive and thwart the escape. Splash Day turned into Water Gun Confiscation Day, where all water guns except those necessary to protect Condamant P-Pa were seized for the greater safety of society.

However, we have an even bigger confiscation problem now. Miriam L didn't think water guns delivered enough punch, so she went to the nuclear option, filling pails with water and chasing The Condamant around the yard until she could dump the water on him. Looks like we will have to ban all pails and buckets for the greater safety of society and The Condamant.

The travails continue!

**Gulag P-Pa Diary, Day 4:**

The terror continues. Condamant P-Pa awoke at 5 a.m. Carys K was standing by his bed, blanky in hand, apparently planning to smother him. He asked what was wrong. "Can't find Dita," she said. Nice recovery! "Dita" is short for "Perdita," a stuffed Dalmatian from the Disney movie One Hundred and One Dalmatians. The Condamant got up with flashlight and slipped among the other three sleeping inmates, finally spotting a Dalmatian on the floor. "There's Dita," he said. "No," she replied indignantly, "that's Pongo!" One stuffed Dalmatian looks like another to Condamant P-Pa in the early morning darkness. Eventually, The Condamant found the actual Dita under the covers on Carys K's bed, making him suspicious of The Mischief Maker's true motives.

Cora K is girl of the day. Today at Camp Mema is Dinosaur Day, with a new dinosaur floor puzzle and various books on dinosaurs for everyone's enjoyment. Gulag P-Pa is countering with Political Dinosaur Day, with two-hour lectures on Marx, Lenin, Mao and others. Laugh if you will, but the political dinosaur lectures put them to sleep every time. Dinosaur Day culminated with a dinosaur party, including party hats, dinosaur cake toppings and dinosaur blowouts.

To distract the inmates from plotting his demise, The Condamant got up early today (thanks Carys K) and made a trip to the store where he bought another truckload of LEGO Duplos. The inmates are building and arguing among themselves over who gets the horses and who gets the girl figures as they are outnumbered by boy figures.

Miriam L tried to start a riot for a second day in a row in the Gulag cafeteria. She was protesting the menu, cheese pizza. While the other three inmates gobbled up their pizza, The Tattler insisted, "I don't like Pizza." When The Condamant reminded her that he and Mema had gone to a pizza parlor with her on their last visit to Houston, and she had eaten a lot of pizza then. Her response: "I eat pizza at other places."

She went without lunch, then got even with Condamant P-Pa. While Carys kept Mema occupied, The Tattler exploded a bomb. P-Pa had to serve as the bomb disposal squad. Dangerous work, earning him his second "Poople Heart" with Miss Miriam. The Condamant is still in therapy from the original "Poople Heart" incident during "The Mad Bomber's" first stint at Mema's and P-Pa's house in 2010.

Besides LEGO Duplos, Hannah L has been focused on reading the dinosaur books Mema brought out for Dinosaur Day. Between her and Cora K, there's not a dinosaur question Condamant P-Pa is smart enough to think up that they can't answer. It's pretty intimidating to know that an eight- and a five-year-old are smarter than The Condamant in any subject. It must be part of the reverse psychological warfare they are waging before the uprising.

**Gulag P-Pa, Day 4, Part 2:**

Dinosaur Day ended around the kitchen table with the Grand Dinosaurs and the Wee Dinosaurs eating chicken nuggets shaped like dinosaurs. Then everyone told dinosaur stories about Hannahsaurus, Corasaurus, Miriamosaurus, Carysosaurus, Memasaurus and the most feared of all dinosaurs, the P-Pasaurus.

Hannahsaurus, according to her namesake, is light blue on the top and dark blue on the bottom and her limbs are dark blue with light blue stripes. Hannahsaurus is an omnivore with teeth sharper than the sharpest knife, even though knives didn't exist at the time. She's the fastest and bravest dinosaur of them all and likes to attack the P-Pasaurus as a hobby. On top of that, she's a showoff.

Corasaurus has orange eyes, according to her namesake. She is green skinned with sharp teeth.

She is a big attack dinosaur and a meat eater. She, too, attacks the P-Pasaurus and she never gives up. Corasaurus also runs fast if P-Pasaurus attacks.

Miriamosaurus is a pink dinosaur with blonde highlights. She is a friendly dinosaur overall but doesn't like P-Pasaurus. The Miriamosaurus eats grass and other plants when she's not throwing fits at mealtime. The Miriamosaurus likes to run, but she's not very fast, according to Hannahsaurus.

Carysosaurus, as described by her fellow dinosaurs, is a small, shy, retiring dinosaur that doesn't attack other dinosaurs except to bite their tails and then run away. The Carysosaurus has a pink tail and a red body. And, the Carysosaurus loves the P-Pasaurus.

Memasaurus is a kind, nurturing dinosaur that mothers little dinosaurs, even when they don't deserve it. She chases the other dinosaurs but never harms them when she catches them, and she always makes sure they have plenty to eat. She has no natural enemies, yet is the nemesis to the P-Pasaurus.

Finally, there's the P-Pasaurus, described by his fellow dinosaurs as the meanest, ugliest, slowest dinosaur afoot. He bedevils the Hannahsaurus, Corasaurus, Miriamosaurus and Carysosaurus, tormenting them constantly. He fears nothing except the Memasaurus, according to Corasaurus. He is green with gold highlights.

After P-Pasaurus got Hannahsaurus a piece of white bread with crust on, buttered and warmed for her seconds at supper, he told Hannahsaurus that she was undoubtedly the dumbest dinosaur of all as she was so dense she could not get up and fix her own bread. Hannahsaurus responded, "Hannahsaurus is the trickiest dinosaur of all because she got P-Pasaurus to do it for me." So, apparently P-Pasaurus is not only slow afoot but also slow of mind.

**Gulag P-Pa Diary, Day 5:**

We survived another night. Nobody wandered around that we know of, but they are a sly bunch. Their strategy appears to be to wear us out until we are so tired that we can't resist their breakout.

The inmates apparently have connections with a major Donut Cartel because someone smuggled in donuts this morning for breakfast. Three of the four inmates were excited. Miriam the Contrarian, however, was not particularly pleased. Yes, the donut smuggler had gotten a pink donut, her favorite, but the only available pink donuts had sprinkles on them. Big mistake! The runners for the Donut Cartel are in trouble if she ever finds out and gets her hands on them.

So, it wasn't a great start for the Girl of the Day! Mema and Condamant P-Pa are hoping to rebound with the activities for Creative Arts Day, covering culinary arts, literary arts and painting arts. Mema started it off with mixing and baking a Cookie Pizza for decorating with icing and M&Ms.

Then The Condamant needed help writing his next middle reader book that features a camel in 1850s Texas. So, each inmate created a line about what a camel and a horse would say. Camel Lines—Cora: That's the desert. It doesn't rain. It's so sunny; Hannah: I've never seen a camel without a hump. By the way, I'm joking; Carys: I don't know; and Miriam: Ohhhhh, no! Horse Lines—Cora: Camels always sink when they are too big. Why do you have such big feet?; Hannah: I'm no camel. I'm a horse. You can tell. Are you blind or something? Why do you have a mountain on your back?; Carys: Hay, hay, hay or hey, hey, hey (she wouldn't clarify); and Miriam: No, no, no. As you can see, there is a certain consistency in the Girl of the Day's lines and attitude as well as her mealtime demeanor, turning down a hamburger for lunch.

Then Mema organized the water coloring. She told the girls they were going to paint on the patio table to which Cora K replied, "I want to paint on paper." Yeah, Mema, find the paper. When they were done, Condamant P-Pa asked Hannah L if she was another Picasso. He had second thoughts and then said, "Do you even known who Picasso was?" To which she replied, "Yes, he was a 20th century Spanish painter and sculptor credited as a co-founder of the Cubist movement and perhaps best known for his 1937 painting Guernica, representing German bombing during the Spanish Civil War." Or, she said something like that, letting Condamant P-Pa know she knew as much or more than he did about Picasso.

**Gulag P-Pa Diary, Day 5, Part 2:**

The moment we had feared finally came late afternoon with a riot. The inmates cornered Condamant P-Pa in the hall, pounding him with their flailing little palms, then chasing him in the family room, trying to tickle him to death. Hannah L offered him a reprieve, "Say 'Calf rope'," she commanded. As he saw his life flash before his eyes, The Condamant cried out, "Calf rope."

Immediately, the pummeling stopped, and Hannah L started shouting "Now, I'm The Condamant, Condamant Hannah." Apparently, there is some rule that Condamant P-Pa had previously made years ago, evidently, that saying "calf rope" reverses the roles. Thus, Condamant P-Pa was relegated to the status of an inmate under her control.

Later, Inmate P-Pa collected his wits and approached Condamant Hannah, nonchalantly asking her to remind him what words made her

Condamant. "Calf rope," she replied, eyes widening as she realized what she had just said. "You tricked me," she cried. "Just call me Condamant P-Pa again," he replied. So much for Hannahsaurus being the trickiest thing around!

**Gulag P-Pa Diary, Day 6:**

Hope dawned with the sun this morning. Mema and Condamant P-Pa survived another night and reinforcements are on the way. If they can only survive until the cavalry arrives, but it may be iffy.

Another food riot. Mema made two tons of pancakes. And three of the four inmates loved them. The Contrarian said, "I want pancakes with chocolate chips." Mema responded, "I don't have chocolate chips." Responded the Contrarian, "My mommy has chocolate chips." Then the rioting began.

The Condamant finally got control over the inmates and established a chain gang, which he and Mema then marched to the park for some forced work on the swings, slides and other implements. Girl of the Day Carys K really enjoyed the manual labor, spending a lot of time working on the slide and the swings.

Returning to the Gulag, the inmates were forced into the dipping tanks for cleaning, then dressed up for Camp Mema and Gulag P-Pa photos in special tee-shirts designed by Michal Martin from The Condamant's office. Next, they got photos in the summer outfits Mema made for them. For the Camp Mema and new dress photos, they were all smiles. For the Gulag P-Pa mugshots, they made ugly faces. They thought the passive-aggressive behavior was funny, but The Condamant now has extortion material for when they grow older, especially when they get married.

Then it was lunch. Guess who didn't want pepperoni pizza? Yep, the Contrarian.

After lunch, the inmates were sent to solitary confinement for a while, then punished by having to help Mema make chocolate chip cookies (for those of you remembering the breakfast riot, the chocolate chips were in a mix, not freestanding. Yes, perhaps Mema could have picked the chips out of the mix and prevented the breakfast riot, but with this crew cause-and-effect is unpredictable). The Condamant expected the Contrarian to demand the removal of all chocolate chips from her cookie, but she didn't complain. For once.

Then, it was dress-up time and the inmates got dresses, shoes, purses and costume jewelry to wear. The Condamant thought they were trying to use disguises to escape, but he used the photos he had taken earlier in the day to confirm their identities and prevent a breakout.

And then, Mema's and The Condamant's prayers were answered with the arrival of reinforcements. They might survive after all as they are signing the paperwork to send the inmates to two separate maximum security facilities tomorrow. This crowd is too tough for one correctional facility for long.

**Gulag P-Pa Diary, Day 7:**

The silence is deafening. We had forgotten what quiet was like. It was so wonderful, though our ears were still ringing from a week of riots, escape attempts and confrontations with four of the most clever young minds in kid history. Bottom line, we survived, though the Camp Mema compound is a smoldering wreck that may take decades to rebuild without government aid. Even so, you might say we are suffering from post part 'em depression after one of the most fun weeks of our lives.

The four inmates left about 8:45 this morning. They were so dangerous, they had to be strapped into their seats for the security of their new guards, Scott and Celeste. With Scott and Celeste as extra guards today, we were able to avoid the insurrections that had been common in the preceding days.

The festivities official ended last night with the combined Camp Mema/Gulag P-Pa Awards Show. Each girl got a combined CM/GPP award as "Girl of the Day". The Camp Mema Awards went to Carys K for "Best Lego Engineer" (she was showing Hannah how to put some pieces together); to Miriam L for "Best Ballerina Dancer"; to Cora K for "Best Behaved"; and to Hannah L for "Best Bible Story Reader".

Gulag P-Pa awards went to Carys K for "Best Sleep Walker"; to Miriam L for "Best Contrarian"; to Cora K for "Best Joke Teller"; and to Hannah L for "Best Temporary Condamant".

In a stunning upset, heavily favored Hannah L lost the night's most prestigious award for the "Ugliest, Meanest Attendee at Gulag P-Pa" to Condamant P-Pa, who immediately protested a rigged vote and offered to give it to the most deserving recipient, but Hannah L declined, ending the award ceremony on a note of controversy.

Everyone, save for The Condamant, was proud of their awards. Carys blessed us with her wide, smile each time her name was called and even held her certificates over her head for everyone to see. Once the ballerina and contrarian categories were announced, Miriam jumped down from the couch, even before her name was called, to pick up her certificates because she knew she had no competition in her categories. Cora shyly picked up her awards, a little bit intimidated by all of the applause. As for Hannah, she predicted her Gulag P-Pa Award, apparently having slipped into The Condamant's office when he wasn't looking and seeing it on the computer screen.

Thus ended the first beloved Camp Mema and the greatly maligned Gulag P-Pa. They were quite the adventure for everyone.

**Gulag P-Pa Diary, Epilogue:**

Last week I had a lot of tongue-in-cheek fun with Gulag P-Pa posts. I realized how blessed I am to have parents who have a sense of humor, who enjoy laughing and who find humor even in difficult circumstances. Too, I am blessed to have married Harriet, who enjoys – or at least puts up with – my sense of humor. While my posts had some fun with the girls, each is a blessing in her own way.

Hannah will always hold a special place in our hearts, arriving 454 days after we lost little Benjamin, our first grandson. Her birth eased our grief and helped us look to the future rather than the past. She is a precocious reader with an appreciation of history and a great sense of humor. When I was writing my Gulag posts, she sat in my lap, reading each sentence, laughing when appropriate and making suggestions. She takes a joke well, laughing even when the joke is on her. I've tormented her with practical jokes, like putting my name over hers on gifts meant for her, and she has returned in kind. Some of my fondest memories are of the jokes she has pulled on me.

As for Cora, you will not find a more kind, sensitive and caring five-year-old anywhere. She made it clear from the beginning of her visit that she would not be going to Gulag P-Pa because "I'm having a good attitude". And, she did. When she's gotten in trouble at home, she's been known to reply, "I'm sorry I disappointed you, Mommy." (Sigh appropriate here!) When her younger siblings get in trouble, she takes it harder than them. She has the biggest, most expressive eyes that always make you want to hug her. And, she's quite the joke teller, even when the punch lines are understood only by her.

The two younger girls are a little harder to get

a fix on at their ages, three-and-a-half for Miriam and two-and-a-half for Carys. Miriam is a combination of iron will, thus the Contrarian moniker, and easy charm. When I get out the camera (I got some 400 photos during Camp Mema), she becomes quite the little model, posing with body movements, hand gestures and facial expressions. When she concentrates on a task, her tongue reflexively slips out over her lip, making for another cute photo, of course.

Carys, by contrast, is a coy little one. She may be quieter because she seems to be the most analytical of the four. She sees a problem or a want and puts her mind to solving it, like the time at her home when she wanted in the bathroom sink and stacked two stools to climb up on the counter. She's adventuresome and fearless when it comes to heights, climbing on furniture and jumping between them when she thinks no one's looking. When it gets too quiet, you best find her because she's exploring something.

They are quite the little crew, and I am most proud to be their grandfather.

# CHAPTER THREE

*"And behold, a voice from heaven said, 'This is my beloved Son, with whom I am well pleased.'"*
—*Matthew 3:17 (English Standard Version)*

The first step toward grandchildren is having a family of your own, of course. I wanted a family and during my courting looked for a young lady that shared my desire, but grandchildren were the farthest things from my mind at that time. I sought in a wife a woman committed to her family and her children, placing them above everything else, including a job, though not a career.

While that attitude grew less fashionable during those years of the women's liberation movement, I found such a woman in Harriet Kocher, a Pennsylvania native and coed at Baylor University where we attended college. She had the cutest little knobby knees I'd ever seen on a young lady, and long, elegant fingers that seemed such a contrast to my stubby, ugly fingers. It's odd how little things like that attract you to the one you love, but those features lingered in my mind about Harriet. Though we shared an English class together the fall of our sophomore year, I didn't meet her until the next semester when a joint friend, the appropriately named Shirley Love, introduced us.

Shortly after that, I started courting Harriet, though I still maintained an off-and-on-again relationship with another coed, who lived in the same dorm as Harriet. While I didn't care if my other girlfriend saw me with Harriet, it petrified me that Miss Kocher might find out about my ongoing dates with her residence hall neighbor. At that point in my college dating career, I began to have various stomach and digestive issues, so much so I feared dying young of some horrible malady. I secured an appointment at the university clinic, and the medical staff ran multiple tests before the physician called me in for what I assumed would be the bad news. The doctor informed me that from a medical standpoint nothing was wrong with me. He said the only explanation might be what was known as "stress diarrhea". I nodded and realized the fear of Harriet finding about my previous girlfriend caused my problems. I also understood that once I got married, I could never carry on an affair outside our matrimonial bonds without making a physical and emotional wreck of myself.

Following my medical diagnosis, I went on my final date with Harriet's predecessor. We had a heated exchange that ended our relationship that Saturday night. Sad and depressed, I returned to my dorm by nine o'clock and called Harriet, uncertain if she would even be in her room on a weekend night. When she answered the phone, she seemed so excited to hear my voice that I instantly felt better. I never dated another young lady after that evening. Years later, we compared notes about that night, and it turned out Harriet had been two-timing me as well. She and her other boyfriend had also gone out that Saturday night and had also broken up. She was as despondent as me and welcomed my

West Texas drawl as much as I did her Pennsylvania accent. It's funny how God's timing worked out for us both, and how he kept our "cheating" from each other until years after the fact.

Our courtship blossomed in the late sixties and early seventies when sexual mores started evolving across the nation. We became conscientious objectors in the sexual revolution. Sure, intimacy intrigued us, but we knew our parents, who raised us in the church with traditional values, would kill us if we strayed before marriage. Overflowing with unfulfilled desires, I accepted but didn't appreciate the wisdom of pre-marital abstinence. Now after almost a half century of marriage together, I value our commitment to each other and that we have shared our intimacies only with one another.

On November 22, 1970, I first told Harriet I loved her and wanted to make her my wife. We got married 394 days later between the fall and spring semesters of our senior year, though I believe our parents would've preferred we waited until we graduated. But after counseling with our pastor, Peter McLeod of First Baptist Church in Waco, we accepted his recommendation that if we were truly in love we should marry sooner rather than later to eliminate the physical temptations natural to all young adults. So, we wed on the day of the winter solstice, the longest night of the year. We took a lot of ribbing from my parents especially over that date and the long evening of honeymoon festivities that would follow our marriage vows.

Almost immediately after the teasing stopped about our wedding date, our parents began to pepper us with questions about when they might call themselves grandparents. We didn't know. We had just gotten married and had to adapt ourselves to one another. Too, we were only starting out and the thought of having the parental and fiscal responsibility of a child intimidated me because we remained financially insecure, and I knew not where my career would take me. I had obtained a degree in journalism and had begun newspaper work, confident that I could always find a job as there would always be newspapers. What I didn't realize then was that U.S. newsroom jobs peaked about the time that I graduated. What I didn't foresee was the Internet and its implications for print journalism.

Harriet, by contrast, had taken a degree in physical therapy because she had always been interested in helping people. That was a characteristic I thought would make her a good mother. Yes, she would have a satisfying career, but not at the expense of a family. I often joked that Harriet went into physical therapy to save lives while I went into journalism to ruin them. After I got out of grad school in Ohio and took a college teaching job in Michigan for a year, Harriet finally convinced me we had to trust in God to work out the uncertainties of family and finances.

When we moved up north after almost four years of marriage, the calls for grandchildren increased from our parents. Never a phone call or a letter came without some plea for their first grandchild, and it was not like we weren't trying by then. Michigan was the perfect place to conceive, as once the snow arrived, we didn't get out much. The problem was, Harriet had trouble conceiving. Every month, when her period came, she grew depressed. In a journal I kept at the time, I wrote "Each time that happens she becomes discouraged because she is not pregnant. I hope she can get pregnant soon and have a child." The incessant parental calls for grandkids just made matters worse, deepening her sense of failure each month when her cycle came. "The remarks by both sets of parents have hurt us," I wrote. "It is the same every month. I can't even talk about children now because I feel like it hurts her. She said she felt like such a failure." I began to wonder to myself if we ever would have children, and then feared it might turn out I was the one at fault. What would we do then?

Harriet saw a doctor in November, and he thought he found a cyst on an ovary. Though counterintuitive in my mind, he put her on birth control hormones for two months with the possibility of surgery if that didn't work. At that point she feared she would be barren and childless. The questions about grandchildren kept coming, even after we tried to explain the difficulties. We asked for prayers instead of requests from our parents. Shortly those prayers were answered. Two months later during her January follow-up with the doctor, Harriet got an all clear report. The cyst had disappeared and the doctor saw no reason she couldn't become a mother.

As the Michigan winter gradually melted away, I was hired by the Lubbock, Texas, newspaper once I finished my teaching contract. We grew excited to be heading back home in my mind, though Harriet still missed her native Pennsylvania. We took our spring break and drove to Pennsylvania to share our last extended visit with her parents before we returned to the Lone Star State. Though we enjoyed our time with her folks, the big news we shared with no one—she was late. On the long drive back to Michigan we discussed the possibility that she might be pregnant, though we had a hard time believing it could be true, even after we got home and Harriet started throwing up every other day.

Several days later on April 7, we went to see her doctor. I waited in the reception area during the exam until a nurse came and escorted me into her room. The moment I saw her demeanor I knew she was pregnant. Harriet had tears in her eyes and that goofy look she gets on her face when she's happy beyond words. She just nodded, and I realized we would become parents. After we had had a few moments alone, the physician returned and told us the expected due date was November 19. Our answered prayers had been confirmed by the doctor. That evening we called our folks with the news they would be grandparents by Thanksgiving. They were excited, of course, but the call became a bittersweet experience for me as their comments and expectations had pressured Harriet and contributed to her insecurities and my anger.

Eleven days after our visit to the doctor, I wrote, "She is probably the happiest she has been in her entire life. The approach of motherhood fulfills her childhood desires. She is a traditional woman who believes in children and motherhood in the traditional sense." Harriet remained happy despite the nausea and fatigue. She wrote an aunt and uncle of mine to tell them the good news. She started reading the letter to me, but broke down when she came to the part about her pregnancy as she was so joyful she couldn't speak of it without becoming emotional. I had to complete her missive myself, just as to this day I sometimes have to finish her sentences when she gets emotional about her children or grandchildren.

By nature, Harriet always remained the optimist, except when it came to getting pregnant. By contrast, I countered her outlook as the perpetual pessimist on nearly everything. I wrote to myself, "I just pray that the child will be born safely and healthy. I hope there are no complications with Harriet. I want the child to be okay because I feel I could not accept the adversity of a deformed or retarded child. All types of fears are running through my mind."

As our May move approached, my brother called to say he and Lee Ann were expecting their first child, too. My folks should really have been happy by then, with two grandchildren arriving within weeks of each other at year's end. When it came time to return to Texas we had help as Lee Ann and Harriet's mother flew up to assist. It turned out to be a challenging trip with two pregnant women and my mother-in-law, me driving the rental truck and them in our car. The journey evolved into a tedious and tense 1,400-mile drive, largely because I clashed with my mother-in-law, but we eventually made it and found a rental home, where we would welcome our firstborn in five months.

On June 19, Harriet started crying without cause, I thought until I asked her what was wrong. She said she felt the baby kick for the first time. The movement came more as a flutter than a jolt, but it provided confirmation that our first child was indeed taking shape within her. Nine days later I wrote in my journals, "Last night Harriet held my hand on her stomach, and I thought I felt the baby kick, but I couldn't be certain. She enjoys being pregnant and exudes a motherly glow. I hope everything goes well with the child." In the ensuing weeks, the kicks grew stronger as Harriet's stomach enlarged. She loved the movement because it confirmed her baby was growing. A major part of our entertainment in those months was watching her belly as the child moved and kicked. While I worked at the newspaper, Harriet found a job in the physical therapy department of a local hospital. In her free time, she read books on breastfeeding and motherhood, and on Sundays we visited various churches, in mid-September joining Second Baptist Church, where our children would be raised and baptized.

Four days after moving our letter to Second B, we started Lamaze classes so I could be in the labor and delivery room with her. That possibility worried me as I have always been squeamish with medical procedures, passing out when giving blood or growing faint when receiving shots. It would be embarrassing to faint on the delivery room floor. However, Harriet informed me that since I had been there for the conception, I would be there for the delivery. I replied, "Yes, ma'am!"

And, I was there for what turned out to be the greatest moment of my life. "It's a boy," the doctor pronounced as Scott Bracken Lewis made his world debut, immediately tee-teeing on the floor. "His plumbing works," announced the doctor. Scott emerged into the world wide-eyed and calm, only crying when they put him on the cold scale for weighing.

As the obstetrician finished tending Harriet, the nurse handed our swaddled son to me as Harriet cried tears of joy. As she remained restrained on the delivery table, I held him close to her so she could see him. "Talk to him," she told me. "I don't know what to say," I replied. Yes, we were rookie parents, even uncertain how to talk to this new life we had brought into the world. Shortly, the obstetrics staff completed with Harriet and removed the constraints. I handed her our son. Harriet never appeared more beautiful than with the look of total joy as she held our first child for the first time. At the nursery she handed Scott to the staff and then was wheeled into her room to rest after an exhausting evening. I saw her to her bed, kissed her good night and drove home to call family, even if it was well before dawn.

My journal entry for November 4 reads, "Today was the most beautiful day of my life. Twenty-four hours ago it was just Harriet and I. At 1:43 a.m. I witnessed the birth of a child, our child. A miracle of answered prayer, it was. The only thing that can compare was my marriage to Harriet, who made it all possible. She is even more beautiful now with our child in her arms. It seems that a lifetime has passed since this morning. When I think of all the fun Scott Bracken has already brought us, it seems impossible he isn't even twenty-four hours old yet."

I rested as best I could from all the excitement, then went shopping. Our children arrived in an era before ultrasound identified the sex of a child prior to birth. So, we didn't know whether to prepare for a boy or a girl. While we had a going-home outfit for Harriet after the delivery, we lacked one for our newborn because we weren't sure the baby would be male or female. So, I found a children's store and bought a little blue suit with cowboys and a stagecoach on the front along with a little cap. Then I stopped by the florist and bought Harriet a single yellow rose because I couldn't afford a dozen. The yellow rose became a family tradition.

That day marked our initial step toward grandparenting and Camp Mema/Gulag P-Pa. Decades after our son's birth, as I prepared for our second camp, I wanted to do something new and fun with The Grands. After considerable thought, I decided to write a script and tape a "movie". I had several objectives in mind. First, it would be a project everyone would be involved in. Second, it would take up some time both for The Grands and me, providing some variety to our activities. Third, we would demonstrate that you can't always believe what you see on television. And fourth, it would be fun, documenting each Grand's growth and development. Sure, The Grands wouldn't remember all their lines, but that was okay because their impromptu responses would add charm to the project. Thus was born the first of our camp movies, Escape from Gulag P-Pa.

# CHAPTER FOUR

## *YEAR TWO*

**Gulag P-Pa Diary/Pre-Camp:**

Preparations are underway for the second annual extravaganza starting Independence Day when we host The Grands, well four of them at least, little Jackson at 15 months still being a little too young for us to manage until he can speak a little more to make his needs plain. So, beginning July 4th it'll be the four girls – Hannah, nine; Cora, six; Miriam, four; and Carys, three – versus P-Pa in another battle of survival.

Preparations are taking two separate paths. For Camp Mema, it's wrapping birthday presents, baking cupcakes, arranging bedding, creating menus, determining each day's activities, selecting stories to read and sewing a summer outfit for each Grand.

At Gulag P-Pa, it's installing concertina wire, opening the watch tower, feeding the guard dogs, installing searchlights as well as metal detectors, fixing pots of gruel and filling the moat with alligators. So, P-Pa, as Hannah called the Commandant last year, has his hands full, assuming the alligators don't bite one of them off.

Details to follow in the Gulag P-Pa Diary, 2014 edition.

**Gulag P-Pa Diary/Day 1, Part 1:**

The preparations are complete, now it is just a matter of waiting. Mema has been involved in incidental tasks such as baking and icing forty-three birthday cupcakes (one mysteriously disappeared), fixing twenty-four muffins (blueberry and chocolate chip), cooking chicken for one meal, prepping for other meals, and cleaning the house.

By contrast, The Condamant has been involved in the important stuff, like putting bars on the windows, installing triple-locked doors with combination locks, putting new batteries in the escape alarms, and hiding all the guns, especially those with the large magazines as some in his arsenal hold up to a quart. You just can't take too many cautions around this crew.

The inmates are expected to arrive in two waves by suppertime. The first is the Kemp contingent, then the Lewis legation. The K Team is headed by Cordial Cora, who is as caring and considerate a six-year-old as you will ever see. She is proud she has never been banished to Gulag P-Pa, like all the others. Next is Charismatic Carys. She's got a sly, mischievous smile that reflects her adventurous three-year-old spirit. When she gets quiet, you better find her because she's into something. Then there's Action Jackson, aka "The Uh-Oh Kid". The 15-month old hasn't yet learned that the word goes best with accidental rather than intentional actions. Spilling his drink, for instance, is an "Uh-Oh" moment. Holding his corn popper over his head and body slamming it to the floor is also an "Uh-Oh" moment. Discernment is not one of his strengths at the moment.

The L Squad is headed by Handful Hannah. At nine years of age, she is the senior Grand and the most devious, always playing jokes on the poor innocent Condamant, even if he did start it. Yes, she's a handful for him to stay a step ahead of every minute of the day. Then there's Myriad Miriam, who's loaded with determination and the master of disguise. Whenever she realizes The Condamant is trying to take candid photos, she starts posing like a four-year-old starlet on the red carpet and displaying a myriad of faces and gestures for the camera.

The Condamant will have his hands full for sure this coming week.

**Gulag P-Pa Diary/Day, Part 2:**

Trouble has arrived, and the five inmates have been processed. Line of the night came from Cora, who was explaining her active little brother to her aunt and uncle. "He's a baby," she said. "He doesn't know he's causing trouble."

All the girls decided they want to go to the Freedom Fest for fireworks. So, they dressed up, got their American flags and convinced their parents to take them. Patriotic little girls? Hardly. The Condamant thinks they are doing recon on explosives for when they try to make their break next week. He'll have to keep an eye on them.

Action Jackson has been moved to solitary confinement in "The Slammer" as the playpen is affectionately called. Mema and The Condamant are standing guard. We understand "playpen" is no longer considered a politically correct term and that "pen" is viewed as demeaning to little egos. The correct terminology today is "play yard". It's not a yard, however. It is a pen. Wikipedia says the venerable term "playpen" has been around since at least 1902. If the term was good enough for our kids, it should be good enough for theirs.

## Gulag P-Pa Diary/Day 2:

The terror has begun. The Condamant got up at seven o'clock this morning. Cora was up shortly thereafter, doing recon. In the afternoon, The Condamant found himself alone in his bedroom, at least he thought he was alone. He heard the door shut and this sweet little voice say, "Now, you're trapped." It was Cora. He turned to see Hannah and Cora at the entry, their arms crossed. Miriam, Carys and Jackson were there as well, looking menacing. The gang of five cornered P-Pa on the bed and began to attack him unmercifully, ripping off his shoes and socks, then tickling him until he cried out desperately for help. Fortunately, Mema heard his cry, came to his rescue and saved the day. P-Pa will have to watch his back from now on.

The Condamant was shocked at his treatment since he had coordinated the summer birthday party this morning when the summer birthday kids (and adults) were recognized. The final gift each kid opened was a summer outfit made by Mema. The girls in their outfits sat for pictures in their new outfits. Jackson was indisposed at the moment and will need his picture taken later. He was delighted!

Hannah and Miriam's parents returned to Spring Saturday while Cora, Carys and Jackson's parents leave Sunday. P-Pa is getting nervous, especially after the bedroom attack. How will he make it until next Saturday when the parents return?

Hannah has informed P-Pa that he needs to report about Black Cloud, the American Paint Horse she got for her birthday to accompany her American Girl Doll Amy, or his future is in grave doubt. Gulp! P-Pa complied. Black Cloud is the most wonderful and beautiful horse in history.

(Note: Hannah is standing over P-Pa, patting a crowbar in her palm in case he doesn't obey). So, let me repeat what a spectacular and amazing and magnificent and awesome and pretty horse Black Cloud is. (Note: The crowbar is quite persuasive.)

The terror continues!

**Gulag P-Pa Diary/Day 3:**

The Menace of Camp Mema is young Jackson. He is so dangerous he has failed the admissions requirements for even Gulag P-Pa. He will be returning home with his parents today. Jackson's pretty much a jolly little fellow, except when you want to get a photo of him in Mema's new outfit or when you scratch his stubborn streak. Then he raises… well, you know, as reflected in the photo of the day. Except for his photographic shyness, he pretty much grins all the time. He's equally adept at running around the house with American flags (permissible) or scissors (not permissible).

Nothing is safe from his curiosity. Seems he gets into everything, but his heart is in the right place as he tries to clean things up by putting stuff in the trashcans, like LEGO Duplo pieces, clothes, his sisters, Mema and the piano. So, whenever The Condamant empties the trash, he has to check it for non-trash items, valuables and people.

Miss Miriam, our fair-haired Alaskan, remains the Contrarian. Got donuts this morning. "I don't like donuts," she said. Mema heated her a waffle. "It doesn't have chocolate chips." As that was a major contention last year, Mema was prepared this year and sprinkled chocolate chips on it, then melted them in the microwave. Problem solved, we think. Or, should I say we hope?

Despite her set ways, you have to admire her tact! Last night when Mema gave her a good night kiss, Miriam brushed her hand over her cheek.

Said Mema, "Did you just wipe my kiss off?" Responded Miriam, "I just like my mommy's kisses." Maybe honesty is the right term! Her honesty is only surpassed by her expressiveness. When she hears a song or hears one in her head, she will often dance very elegantly. She is a better dancer at four years of age than P-Pa is at six decades older. Too, she doesn't seem to have as many aches and pains as P-Pa.

**Gulag P-Pa Diary/Day 3, Part 2:**

Now Mema and P-Pa are alone, surrounded by a female army of four. The family room looks like a LEGO Duplo minefield. P-Pa thinks it's a trap. While they play, they keep watching him out of the corners of their eyes, just waiting for him to stumble. If he falls, he fears they will pounce on him. He's got to watch where he steps. If it's not LEGOs, it's My Little Ponies that he will trample. They are tiny pony/unicorn toys with rainbow hair and names like Pinkie Pie, Fluttershy, Twilight Sparkle, Rainbow, Beachberry and Peachy Pie. It's amazing the pop/kid culture Mema and P-Pa are having to learn to blend in with the young ones for their own safety.

After picking up the LEGOs, the girls got their first experience of movie making this evening when they started filming of the Camp Mema production Escape from Gulag P-Pa. This is a challenge for P-Pa's movie camera and editing skills so we will see what comes out of it. Hannah has helped with the dialog. Miriam came up with the most dramatic moment of the day with her line, "I'll take one for the team," before the spanking scene. Cora was most animated in the prison cafeteria riot scene, crying, "We want ice cream." Carys was a bit bewildered at first, but quickly got into the swing of things. Shooting continues tomorrow with the on-screen debut of the voluptuous Mema van Doren.

We ended the evening watching *The LEGO*

*Movie*. There was a sweet moment for P-Pa when Carys moved from the couch and walked over to The Condamant in his easy chair. She climbed up in his lap and watched the movie with him. It was a fun conclusion of the evening for P-Pa.

**Gulag P-Pa Diary/Day 4:**

Girl of the day was Hannah, who proclaimed Monday as Horse Day. Everybody got a horse name: Hannah was Willow; Cora, Goldie; Miriam, Majesty; Carys, Yellow; Mema, Buttermilk; and P-Pa, Trigger. The girls got to pick three plastic horses each for their remuda, use their artistry in a horse coloring book, match animals in a horse sticker book and enjoy an afternoon horse snack of oats, disguised as cookies baked with chocolate chips by Mema.

As girl of the day, Hannah got to pick the flag to raise on the flagpole. Her favorite color is blue so she chose the Bonnie Blue Flag of a single white star on a navy blue background. The girl of the day also gets to pick the movie for the night. So, following the horse theme, Hannah chose Spirit: Stallion of the Cimarron, a 2008 animated Dreamworks production about a mustang in the Old West.

Progress on the Gulag movie is slow but steady, the girls' acting skills stronger than P-Pa's editing skills. Nonetheless, the girls are enjoying seeing themselves on the screen.

The Condamant blew his nose this morning, and Carys announced, "P-Pa is a tuba!" For years P-Pa would try to distract the kids for a nefarious move, like stealing their cookies, by pointing over the child's shoulder and saying, "Look, an elephant!" Yesterday he tried that on little Miss Carys, who looked over her shoulder and said, "Yeah, a baby elephant." It's embarrassing to be out-conned by a three-year-old. One of The Condamant's moles quoted Miriam as saying, "In this house, there's too much P-Pa!" Miriam is on lockdown now.

Watching *The LEGO Movie* last night may have been a big mistake because the girls have spontaneously started singing the theme song, "Everything is Awesome," throughout the day. It goes like this, "Everything is awesome, everything is cool when you're a part of the team; everything is awesome when you're living the dream." Once, twice, even a dozen times is fine, but a thousand times by the cute little soprano quarter eventually grates on the nerves, at least for P-Pa, who is musically challenged.

The adventure continues.

**Gulag P-Pa Diary/Day 5:**

Whew! We are at the halfway point, and we have survived, but just barely. Perhaps it is summed up by one of Miriam's favorite questions: "Do you know what you are doing?" Well, P-Pa and Mema thought they did, but they are no longer sure! Having so many questions thrown at us does tend to diminish our confidence.

Cora was girl of the day so this was Dress Up Day. If it is true that clothes make the man, then it is even truer that shoes make the woman. They all seemed more interested in the shoes, especially the single red one, and the jewelry than the dresses. Photos of the three younger ones reflected their fashion sense.

If ever there was a girl destined for the red carpet, it is our blonde Alaskan Miriam. Ever since she was two, she would start posing whenever she saw me trying to take candid photos. Today she put on some dress-up jewelry and shoes and started doing her "moves", as she calls her posing. She wanted all the girls in a photo. As she said, "Let's take a picture with all of the girls doing their moves." Believe me, none of the other girls can match her moves.

Cora chose to fly the Texas flag today so she raised it up the flagpole. For her Bible story, she picked the story on the baby Moses. Then to end the night, she selected the movie of day, picking *The LEGO Movie* for our second viewing in three days. Everything isn't always awesome.

Movie time was more than P-Pa could take, so he retired to work on editing the movie. He's getting the hang of it and now has faith the movie might be in theaters in time for the Christmas rush. Today we shot two scenes. The first, covering The Grands plotting to escape, featured the debut of Mema van Doren, the girls' Fairy Gun Runner. The second involved the actual escape while The Condamant was dozing on the sofa after reading his favorite book, Gulags for Kids. Hannah had a dramatic scene when she opens the back door, sticks her head inside and yells, "Oh, Condamant, we're escaping. Bye bye!"

Tomorrow is the climactic gun battle, which is projected to deplete about seventeen percent of San Angelo's available water supply, but that's a small price to pay for cinematic art. The filming schedule works out well because on Wednesday Miriam is girl of the day and she wants to have Splash Day. We have also scheduled the pie-throwing contest. We will vote on who will be the target. P-Pa thinks Mema will be the winner—or should he say loser?—after the votes are in. Hannah is responsible for the contest after making a Christmas card that said: "Winter Fun: Making Pies with Mema, Throwing Pies at P-Pa!" So, how could we not have a pie-throwing contest?

The Gulag saga continues tomorrow.

### Gulag P-Pa Diary/Day 5/Investor Edition:

P-Pa's never been a sophisticated investor, generally getting in on a good thing right before the bubble bursts and taking centuries to recover. Ooops! However, P-Pa thinks he has stumbled onto some surefire investments for next year.

First, paper goods. Mema keeps a dispenser of tiny paper cups in the guest bathroom for the convenience of visitors. In an average year, she uses a package or less. When The Grands visit, however, the cups go quickly. If The Grands wash their hands, they need a cup and a drink. If they brush their teeth, ditto. If they walk by the bathroom, the siren call of the paper cup beckons. The Grands are using the cups by the boxcar load as documented in one of our photos.

Second, LEGOs. Apparently everything IS awesome with the little plastic blocks, according to The Grands. In fact, the Kemp Grands were shopping with their mom at Target a while back. When they turned down the LEGO aisle recently, Cora turned to Carys and said, according to their Mom, "This is just like Mema's and P-Pa's house." As of last year, LEGO corporate offices estimated some 560 billion Lego blocks and pieces have been produced over the years. The Condamant figures about a million of those are now scattered around the family room floor.

Saturday when we got the LEGO blocks out, Carys sidled up to P-Pa with one of the little catalogs. She pointed to one of the Duplo sets and in her shy little voice said, "It's sad we don't have the Cindewelly castle." Then Sunday, Miriam strode up to P-Pa and with her usual confidence said, "We want the castle for Cinderella!" Fearing for his own safety if a full-scale Cindewelly castle riot broke out, The Condamant ordered a set online. Thanks to Amazon and UPS, the potential Cindewelly confrontation should be averted by nightfall if UPS comes through

So, for investment advice, next year when the dates are announced for Camp Mema/Gulag P-Pa, The Condamant recommends moving heavily into paper goods and plastic toy blocks.

**Gulag P-Pa Diary/Day 6:**

Well, Splash Day was a disaster—for The Condamant. Everybody else seemed to enjoy it, but of course they didn't get soaked from head to toe with a garden hose nor get a whipped cream pie in the face, thank you Miss Hannah. The hero of the day was Miss Carys, who opted not to throw a pie at P-Pa. Thank you, Carys!

Miriam was girl of the day and started out by raising the Alaska flag in honor of her birthplace. UPS came through Tuesday night with the delivery and all the girls put the Cindewelly (as Carys calls her) castle together. The girl of the day pointed out that Cinderella couldn't get to the ball without a carriage, specifically LEGO Duplo Set 6153. So, if UPS comes through again, Cindewelly will be able to go to the ball Friday morning. Mema says P-Pa should have "sucker" tattooed on his forehead, but it's hard to refuse the girl of the day.

Mema was working with Carys on the alphabet and asked if she had a name that started with an A. "Isn't your name Carys Anne?" Responded the little one, "That's my name when I'm in trouble." Well, Miss Carys wasn't in trouble today, not after sparing P-Pa from another pie to the face. By contrast, the other three girls spent much of the day on the Gulag Chain Gang.

After Cindewelly castling the morning and a lunch that included for dessert cookie pizza, a real hit with the inmates and one reason they always seem to prefer Mema to The Condamant, it was an afternoon of Splash Day activities starting with the filming of four of the last five scenes of Escape from Gulag P-Pa. Scenes included the climactic water gun fight. All that's left to shoot is the dénouement, which will be filmed tomorrow. The film's starlets got their first view of the rough cut before supper.

They were excited.

Then it was the pie-throwing contest, which has already received enough attention. Then after P-Pa was hosed off, it was splashing in the two wading pools and more water gun fights, followed by snacks on the patio.

After supper, it was the movie of the day. Miriam chose wisely, picking Brave and answering P-Pa's prayers that she pick anything except the *The LEGO Movie*. It was a brave choice, especially since Miriam was terrified when the malevolent Mordu, a giant bear, attacked Merida, the heroine. Miriam bolted from the sofa to Mema's arms for protection. Though The Condamant thought he would have been a better protector, Miriam must still have been smarting from the Chain Gang assignment.

So much for today. Tomorrow's girl of the day is Carys. It will be textile arts day with weaving projects and lessons on the mill girls of the New England textile industry.

**Gulag P-Pa Diary/Day 7:**

After a week of incarceration, the inmates finally made their break. Escaping mid-morning, they slipped to the nearby park. They got distracted by the playground equipment long enough for The Condamant and Mema to catch up and recapture them.

Carys, the girl of the day, appears to have been the mastermind of the daring break. The Condamant keeps a bolt in the back gate latch when The Grands visit so they can't get out and others can't get in. The senior Grand couldn't figure how to open the gate, then gave up and walked away. The littlest Grand walked over, removed the bolt, pushed on the latch, and opened the gate. She then pushed the gate shut, replaced the bolt and walked confidently away. She enhanced her reputation as our little problem-solver, junior engineer and escape mastermind.

As girl of the day, Carys chose to raise the Stars and Stripes up the flagpole after a breakfast of homemade pancakes. The park escape was an hour-long adventure and little Miss Carys seemed to be the most adventurous of the four, though she did have a close call dismounting from her swing and running in front of Cora's swing! It was a near miss, but no harm done.

After a lunch of tacos (Miss Carys ate three), it was rest time for the quartet. The Condamant has learned that rest time is not for The Grands, but for the Camp/Gulag staff to get a break. Then it was filming the final scene of Escape from Gulag P-Pa. It took three takes, but we finally got it. Final edits tonight and then it's on to theater bookings and the advertising campaign after checking the Oscar rules for live action short film entries. The project has been blessed by the directorial talents of Cecil B. DeeP-Pa.

Then it was textile arts time with a lesson on the mill girls who worked in the textile factories in New England in the 1840s. The "girls" were between the ages of 13-30 and were some of the first women to fully enter the work force in America. The epicenter of the mill girl movement was Lowell, Mass., where Mema and P-Pa visited on their New England vacation a couple years ago. It was an interesting look into America's industrial revolution and the often overlooked role women played. For their textile arts activity, each girl made a potholder on an Easy Steps Weaving Loom as a gift for her mother (but don't let their mothers know).

Mema made another cookie pizza for dessert after supper. Then it was Miss Carys's movie choice. She chose Cindewelly, as she calls it, while she played with the Cindewelly castle and carriage she and Miss Miriam conned out of P-Pa.

The Grands voted unanimously that Mema should be girl of the day for Friday. P-Pa suspects she swayed their votes with all the cookie pizzas. He can't compete with that.

**Gulag P-Pa Diary/Day 8:**

Since they had unanimously voted to make Mema the girl of the day for Friday, The Grands decided she deserved breakfast in bed. So, they sent P-Pa to get donuts at 7 a.m. After breakfast in bed, Mema raised the Pennsylvania flag in honor of her home state.

Miriam requested magic so P-Pa got out his magic hanky and made it disappear in his hand for each of them. Then he pulled the hanky through the ears of each of the three youngest. The hanky was so magical that they didn't feel it go in or out, but their ears were clean when it reappeared. Miss Hannah figured out the secret but didn't reveal it to the young ones so The Condamant is still magical in their eyes. Hannah knows in reality he's just another con man.

The breakout yesterday was nothing compared to the Cindewelly Wars today. It seems the four inmates could not share the castle and carriage sets. After threats and beatings (of us, not them), The Condamant brokered the San Angelo Peace Accords (SAPA). Under the agreements, Hannah and Cora will play together with Hannah getting Prince Eric and the carriage horse as well as delivering Cindy anywhere requested by Cora, who will get both Cindewellys plus Prince Charming. In the second section, Miriam and Carys will each get a Cindewelly; when one has the horse and carriage, the other will use the castle and vice versa. Each signed the document with the understanding that if she broke the deal, she would be banned from

Cindewelly play.

Miss Miriam informed The Condamant that the preferred solution to the Cindewelly Wars was to buy another carriage set with a horse, the source of much of the conflict. The Condamant informed her he had been conned the last time into buying more Duplos. In light of his negotiating success, The Condamant plans to have the sucker tattoo removed from his forehead and expects to receive a Nobel Peace Prize next year. Scoff if you must, but his peace-making accomplishment is more than that of some recent Nobel Prize recipients as the SAPA maintained the tranquility for the rest of the evening.

For the Bible story of the day, Mema chose the story of Esther. It was so good, Hannah had P-Pa keep reading more on Esther. Then The Grands put on a puppet show they wrote and directed about two competing kingdoms—the animal kingdom and the Elsa-Dita-Snoopy kingdom. Though they fought at first, Elsa won the animals over after she started petting them and they lived happily ever after in a unified kingdom.

For the movie of the night, Mema picked Lady and the Tramp, the first movie she and P-Pa saw as man and wife, decades before they ever realized they would be hosting Camp Mema and Gulag P-Pa. Then for good behavior in the wake of SAPA, they got to watch Bambi as a bonus. P-Pa, feeling overwhelmed, wrote a letter from the Duplo Alamo he built:

To the People of Texas and All Americans around the World:

*Fellow citizens and compatriots: We are besieged by four or more cousins under the leadership of Hannah the Terrible, Cora the Cordial, Miriam the Militant and Carys the Bashful. We have sustained a continual bombardment and cannonade of questions and excuses for eight days and have yet to provide a satisfactory response to our attackers. The enemy has demanded we surrender to their every whim and want. Otherwise, the garrison is to be put to the test, if the house is taken. We have answered the demand with food, treats, baths and beds, and our flags still wave proudly from the flagpole. We shall never surrender to their juvenile demands or retreat from our principled stand that they eat everything on their plate, that they play nice and that they pick up their toys.*

*Now in our time of need, we call on you in the name of liberty, patriotism and everything dear to the American character, to come to our aid, with all dispatch. The enemy is growing daily and will increase no doubt their questions and demands to three or four thousand per hour. If this call is neglected, we are determined to sustain our sanity as long as possible like soldiers who never forget what is due their family, their state and their country. Victory or Insanity.*
*The Condamant*
*of The Duplo Alamo*

### Gulag P-Pa Diary/Day 9:

The Grands were faced with a major political problem this morning: They had run out of girls to honor as girl of the day. They voted unanimously against designating a boy of the day, but by a 3-1 vote (Hannah being against the motion) they decided to name P-Pa the non-girl of the day. P-Pa was excited when they informed him they wanted him to feel just like Cindewelly. The excitement died, however, when he realized they planned for him to wash dishes, scrub floors, launder clothes and clean toilets. He did so without the benefit of helpful songbirds and little mice as in the Disney movie. P-Pa did not realize the honor of non-girl of the day came with such awesome responsibilities or he might have declined the recognition!

Feeling besieged, the non-girl of the day opted to raise the Alamo flag over the Duplo Alamo for the last full day of Camp Mema/Gulag P-Pa. The San Angelo Peace Accord held and all was tranquil on the home front until P-Pa found the little duo hiding under a desk trying to dig an escape tunnel.

The evening ended with the awards ceremony. The Gulag P-Pa awards went to Miss Carys for "Best Scene Stealer", Miss Miriam for "Best Team Player" and Miss Cora for "Most Enthusiastic Actress", all for their roles in Escape from Gulag P-Pa. Miss Hannah won the "Best Pie Thrower Award". The Camp Mema awards went to Miss Carys for "Best Eater", Miss Miriam for "Most Prolific Questioner", Miss Cora for "Best Behaved & Best Attitude", and Miss Hannah for "Best Equestrian".

Tomorrow, the quartet heads back to their homes. Mema and P-Pa found an adorable couple (Scott and Celeste) who just arrived in this country on Friday after a Haiti vacation and agreed to come to camp and return all four to their respective homes. Mema and P-Pa were so relieved to find this taxi service because they were sooooo tired.

**Gulag P-Pa Diary/Day 9, Whew Edition:**

Our plea and our prayers have been answered. Reinforcements arrived this afternoon, but just in the nick of time. The Condamant found the two littlest inmates under a desk, trying to tunnel out again. You can't turn your back on them for a minute before they have put together another plan to escape.

## Gulag P-Pa Diary/Day 10:

Ah, the tranquility since 8:15 a.m. when the inmates left by van for transfer back to their original facilities. The San Angelo incarceration was a great success, primarily because Mema and P-Pa survived. However, once the quartet left, Mema and P-Pa collapsed in bed and slept, her for three hours, him for two. No emergencies, no issues, no interruptions, just blessed sleep.

Though running a summer holding camp for The Grands requires a combination of talents, The Condamant has narrowed them to the essentials. At its basics, it's a mix of short-order cook, traffic cop, encyclopedia and disaster recovery, as exemplified by their cell, which looked like the site of a chicken-plucking contest when their cots were cleared. Once we removed their bedding, we found a bushel of feathers. It seems the Grands had discovered a rip in a corner of a pillow and had been pulling some feathers out every night and playing with them.

The award ceremony Saturday night was a great end to their incarceration. Each girl received a certificate for each award. It was great fun to watch their excitement as their names were called.

Miriam and Carys made sure we remembered to say our blessing before each meal. Our favorite prayer line was from Miriam, who asked God to "give us food we like." Our favorite prayer from Carys was when she ended her turn with squinted eyes, going around the table and saying "Bless Miriam and bless Hannah and bless Cora and bless P-Pa and bless Mema." The two young ones played together quite well for their ages.

Hannah and Cora also played well together. Hannah was patient in helping Cora read some books above her reading level. Overall, they made good examples for their younger sisters and are both quite proud of their younger siblings.

As to their favorite activities, Hannah like creaming P-Pa in the face with a pie (figures!), Cora liked going to the park, Miriam liked Splash Day and anything with chocolate chips in it, and Carys liked soaking P-Pa with the water hose for the climactic water gun fight in Escape from Gulag P-Pa.

Mema enjoyed those little special times with each granddaughter, just being able to cuddle or talk or play hide-and-seek. P-Pa enjoyed how well they took to the movie-making and then how much they wanted to see the final production once it was done. They must have seen it thirty times between when it was finished and when they left.

For all the fun we had, there was a poignant moment when our daughter Melissa reminded us that Hannah at nine years old was half grown. We had enjoyed them so much in the present we hadn't looked to the future. That makes us all the more glad to share these fun times while such things are still magical for them and for us.

**Gulag P-Pa Diary/Epilogue:**

Just got the 2014 class photos processed for both Camp Mema and Gulag P-Pa. It's apparent from the results that The Condamant has more work to do for next year on attitude adjustment. Planning is already underway. Next year will be different, if for no other reason Jackson Josiah will join the mix. As a result, The Condamant has notified his insurance company, which has informed him that his liability rates will quadruple at a minimum. That will be a small price to pay to get an army of one to help counter the Cindewelly complex.

# CHAPTER FIVE

*"When a woman is giving birth, she has sorrow because her hour has come, but when she has delivered the baby, she no longer remembers the anguish, for joy that a human being has been born into the world."*
—John 16:21 (English Standard Version)


Harriet had worked at her physical therapy job until the Thursday of Scott's birth. With his arrival expected for November 19, she had given notice for the Friday that turned out to be the day after his early appearance. Her coworkers had even scheduled a shower for her the day that Scott was born. That would not be the last time our children disrupted our plans.

When we talked about having kids, we decided on two as a manageable number to support and put through college debt free. I wanted a boy. Harriet desired a girl. I came from a family of two boys. She grew up in a family of two girls. I figured that was the natural order of things and whatever the first child's gender, so too would be the second. Ever the pessimist, I believed one of us was destined for disappointment. I had my boy, and I felt sorry that Harriet would never have her girl.

As we adjusted to parenthood, I tried to ease the letdown sure to come by highlighting the fun of a family of boys. It started that first Christmas with our son. We had our modest little tree and a few gifts for each other, but we saved most of our skimpy discretionary funds on getting Scott little rattles, teddy bears and other age-appropriate toys, though it's hard to get any toy that can intrigue a little fellow barely fifty days old. We excitedly sat our son up in his tiny seat and helped him unwrap the many presents we showered on him. He could not have cared less, never once grabbing a toy to play with. Instead, he picked up pieces of colorful wrapping paper, shaking the trash and cooing in contentment while his mom and I were disappointed with his disinterest in his first Christmas.

Two months after Scott arrived, we took a big step and bought our first house, signing papers on a $26,000 mortgage. We never knew how we would re-pay such a mortgage, but we needed our own place to raise a family. I pointed out which bedroom would belong to the boys after our second son arrived and which would be the guest room. Harriet held out that the guest room would be her daughter's, but I tried to ease her down from that unrealistic expectation, suggesting that it double as a sewing room since she was an excellent seamstress.

Even without a daughter, Harriet was never more contented, breastfeeding our son, tending to his needs and even changing his diaper. When she would wash dishes, she would put him in a little sling and he would often fall to sleep resting on her bosom. She could sit for hours breastfeeding him, letting him slumber on her shoulder or cooing at him. Me, I didn't have the patience for extended activities like that. Those first six months were a time of bonding for mother and son. I became an afterthought, the odd man out in the family until one Saturday morning when Harriet showered and I went to check on our three-month-old son.

As I bent over to pick him up from the crib, I bumped my head against one arm of the "Old MacDonald Had a Farm" mobile that had a plastic horse, pig, cow and sheep that would revolve in a circle when we wound the toy. At the clatter of the farm animals, Scott laughed for the first time. I banged my forehead against the mobile again and got a big belly laugh. Then I hit my head against the crib toy a third time, and Scott cackled even more exuberantly. Ecstatic at Scott's joy, I ran to the bathroom and shouted for Harriet to get out of the shower, put on a robe and come see Scott.

Fearing something wrong, Harriet raced after me. As I reached our wide-eyed son, I bent over the crib and smashed my forehead against the mobile. Silence! I did it again. Nothing! Scott just lay there staring solemnly at us. I banged the toy again. Not even a grin from you-know-who. By then, Harriet was glaring at me as if I was crazy and wondering why I had gotten her out of the shower for this display of paternal stupidity. I tried to explain how he had laughed, then swatted the mobile in frustration. Bless his little heart, Scott erupted with a belly laugh that proved to his mom, at least for the moment, that I wasn't insane. Then she slapped the mobile and extracted a huge laugh as well from our son.

After three months, Scott became more attentive and active, able to roll around and then crawl. Those were the times I enjoyed, playing on the floor with him, letting him climb over me, tickling him, blowing on his belly and making him chuckle. I loved the sound of his laughter. I tried new things with him like rolling a ball at him and having him push it back to me. One time, I imitated a lion and roared at him. Big mistake! His little face crumpled into a frown, and he started wailing. Talk about feeling bad! Me and him!

After only a few months with Scott, I began to understand that morning newspaper work schedules undermined a good family life or an exceptional salary so I looked for a job with more family friendly hours, using my contacts from the paper and working first for a non-profit organization and then in higher education communications and marketing. While I had not found college teaching that satisfying, I loved college administration and would finish my career in the field. Harriet, meanwhile, dedicated herself to being a good mother, but wanted to keep her hand in physical therapy. So, she worked Saturdays at the same hospital that had employed her before Scott's birth. We needed the extra money, and it was an eye opener for me about the challenges of parenting, at least from a mother's perspective. It was a work to manage Scott, keep him changed, fed and happy. I remember one morning he started crying and wailing and carrying on unlike anything I'd ever seen. At first I grew concerned, then frustrated and finally angry. When I had the impulse to slap him, I knew he was breaking me. I took him to his crib, put him down and walked out closing the door behind me. I fell on my knees and prayed to God, never to let me strike my son like I had been tempted to do. It was a horrible moment etched in my mind for the rest of my life, and I saw how a parent might so overflow with frustration or helplessness as to unintentionally abuse a child.

Harriet's earnings from her part-time job became her pen money, set aside for what she wanted. The first thing she sought was a washing machine. I had promised her I would handle the laundry at the laundromat until we could afford such a luxury as a washer, and I kept that promise except for a few times she wanted to handle the washing or just get out of the house. Even so, it remained a great inconvenience to us both. Though she saved enough to buy the appliance, we lacked the additional funds for a dryer. So, I installed a clothesline. Unfortunately, the washing machine discharged water so fast that our plumbing couldn't handle it, and rinse water backed up into the utility room. Evidently, there was a blockage somewhere in the pipes. Unable to afford a plumber for such a job, I put on my handyman clothes and spent my Christmas break digging an 88-foot ditch and installing a separate drain pipe from the washer to the main sewer line in the back yard. But for all the economic hardships of a young family, we had each other, and we bonded as father, mother and son, some of our greatest memories coming from those days with the three of us.

As Scott's first birthday neared, we decided the time had come to consider adding the final member to our family. We thought three or four years difference in age would be optimum, but we had had such trouble conceiving the first time, we decided we should start trying again after Scott turned one so we would have plenty of opportunities to hit our schedule. Well, we didn't need that time as we connected right off. By February, it became obvious Harriet was pregnant, and we'd be dealing with two boys under two years old for a while.

I kept preparing Harriet for her second boy, assuring her that everything would turn out okay and that the guest room would double as her sewing space so she could make outfits for the boys, though deep down I knew she wanted to sew frilly dresses for a special little girl, her daughter. I feared she would want to go for a third child after we had our second son, but I doubted we could afford three children over the long term. And, what if it was a third boy? Would we need to try for a fourth child?

I prayed for another healthy baby and for Harriet to find peace in her daughterless world.

As with Scott's pregnancy she thrilled when she sensed the first flutter of a new life within in her. Later both Scott and I got to touch her stomach and feel the baby kicking, though I doubted our son understood the implications. To prepare him for the arrival of his new sibling, Harriet read to him about babies entering a family so he could adapt to the impending appearance of his little brother. Finally, the day came in late July when Harriet went into labor. We left Scott with our neighbors and rushed to the hospital to await his junior mischief-maker.

Hospital staff put Harriet in a labor room and prepped her for delivery. They attached a fetal monitor and we could hear the baby's heartbeat. One nurse checking the little heart rate said it was faster than average, which generally meant we would have a baby boy. I took Harriet's hand and told her it would be okay as she grimaced through the labor pains. The nurse left, then returned a few minutes later, saying, "Oh, my!" Harriet had dilated sooner than expected, and we needed to get her to a delivery room. Immediately! Calling for assistance, she started pushing the bed out of the room, as other staff helped wheel Harriet into delivery.

As they rolled Harriet into the birthing facility, I scurried after them, glimpsing the black hair of our newborn's head emerging from Harriet's womb. For an instant, I feared I would have to deliver our next son. Harriet's ob/gyn doctor was off that week so the on-staff obstetrician rushed in, just in time to deliver our second child. That instant became the second greatest moment of my life, exceeded only by watching Scott's delivery simply because he was the first. This beautiful moment, however, provided the greatest SHOCK of my life. Scott's little brother was a girl!

"It's a girl," the obstetrician announced, as our second child took a breath and began to wail.

I grasped Harriet's hand, squeezing it gently, and said, "You got your girl. I guess life is fair after all."

"No it's not," interjected the obstetrician. "I have four girls!"

After delivery room staff weighed, cleaned and swaddled our daughter, a nurse brought her over and offered her to me. I declined the honor, saying her mother deserved to hold our daughter first. Harriet took little Melissa Irene, kissed her softly on the cheek and looked up at me with that goofy look of loving contentment I always found so endearing. Now our family was complete, father, mother, son and daughter. The perfect family!

Once Melissa went to the nursery and Harriet settled in her room to recover, I returned home and made the obligatory calls to grandparents, informing they had their new granddaughter and Harriet were doing fine. I collapsed in bed and got what sleep I could before retrieving Scott from the neighbors and telling him he had a baby sister, not that he understood the implications, the biggest of which was he would have a room of his own until he left home. Together Scott and I went to a baby store and bought his new sister a coming-home outfit, a yellow gingham dress with a frilly matching bonnet. Then we stopped at a florist where I again purchased another single yellow rose for Harriet.

Scott and I then visited the hospital, where I pointed out his sister through the nursery window, then took him to see his mother. Harriet was proud to see her son and satisfied to know she had delivered a baby sister for a playmate. We were blessed that both our children entered the world healthy and whole. Twenty-six years later we would learn that wasn't always the case, but for the moment we had unknowingly taken the second step toward the joys of grandparenting.

A day later I brought Melissa and Harriet home, where my parents awaited with Scott. Our daughter was tiny and the little yellow dress engulfed her, but Harriet clothed her in it and the bonnet that enveloped Melissa Irene's head. When we reached the house, Harriet made certain that Scott held his little sister first. We sat him in the same rocking chair that Harriet had breastfed Scott, placed a pillow in his lap and put Melissa before him. He offered us a shy grin, uncertain what to make of this latest addition to the family. Harriet made sure to attend to Scott's needs, even when she first breastfed Melissa in his presence. Scott crawled up beside his mother, seemingly jealous. Though it was uncomfortable, she freed one arm to hold Scott close beside her as she nursed Melissa. Mother, daughter and son seemed content.

Breastfeeding gave Harriet the first lesson that our children had different temperaments. She was accustomed to Scott, who suckled leisurely, always taking his time, never in a rush, always patient when his mother moved him to the other breast. By contrast Melissa was a fast, impatient diner, suckling so hard it left her mom sore, and eating so fast her mom didn't always have time to switch her to the other spout before Melissa was full. Besides the soreness, Melissa's eating habits left things unbalanced in Harriet's life. But uncomfortable as it might have been, Harriet minimized the discomfort. After all, she had the daughter she had always wanted.

Melissa's first laugh came at the instigation of her brother, who did something that tickled her and we rushed in to see. Melissa giggled at Scott's antics, and her laughter—like her brother's—was music to our ears. To this day, I think no sound is sweeter than the sound of children laughing, especially if they are your son or daughter and even more so if they are your grandchildren. Their laughter is the joyous soundtrack of our family's life.

More than a quarter of a century later, the opportunity for laugher increased by 25 percent at the third Camp Mema/Gulag P-Pa as grandson Jackson joined the festivities for the entire week. I was ecstatic. Finally, I had some male company to help me counter Princess Fatigue Syndrome, which had plagued me throughout the preceding two camps. Though I was delighted, Jackson's female cousins were befuddled. Hannah and Miriam had never been around a two-year-old boy for an extended period and his antics bewildered them at first, creating more memorable moments at camp.

# CHAPTER SIX

## *YEAR THREE*

**Gulag P-Pa Diary/Pre-Camp No. 1:**

Next month is the big event, yes, the third annual Camp Mema/Gulag P-Pa! Things are progressing nicely as we work down our preparation checklist. Partial Mema List: Birthday gifts, wrapped. Patterns and fabric, bought. Bible stories, selected. Summer outfits, in progress. Prayer, constantly!

Partial P-Pa List: Stun gun, check. Insurance coverage, quadrupled. Karate training, in progress. Movie script, story boarded. Disney Princess Overload Syndrome, vaccinated.

Pre-camp updates to follow.

**Gulag P-Pa Diary/Pre-Camp No. 2:**

Things are shaping up nicely for Camp Mema/Gulag P-Pa, in spite of the long checklist only partially completed! The working script is now complete for the Camp Mema/Gulag P-Pa production of the western epic, The Good, the Bad and the Cutely.

Now the title roles haven't yet been assigned, but it's obvious that "the Cutely" would have to be P-Pa in his role as Kid Condamant. Mema van Doren makes another acclaimed appearance, this time as

The Fairy School Marm, after her stunning portrayal last year of The Fairy Gun Runner.

Method actor Jackson has been cast as Silly the Kid. And Hannah, Cora, Miriam and Carys will have dual roles as the damsels in distress as well as members of Silly the Kid's gang! In fact, they will actually rescue themselves before the climactic water gun fight.

The dialogue ranges from the sentimental: CARYS (to Kid Condamant): You're no kid. You're a bad man. KID CONDAMANT: My hat is white so I'm a good guy! CARYS: Your hat may be white, but your heart is black!!!

To the poetic: CORA: Kid Condamant is a meany. MIRIAM: More like a wienie!

To the reverent: KID CONDAMANT: You do the girly work. I do the man's work. HANNAH: Like what? Sitting on your big behind and giving us orders?

Yes, we haven't even started shooting and already there's Oscar buzz because of crisp, insightful dialogue like that!

Further, we're in merchandising negotiations for Kid Condamant and Silly the Kid Action Figures as well as Hannah, Cora, Miriam, Carys and Mema van Doren the Fairy School Marm Dolls. So, just seventeen days out from Camp Mema's opening ceremonies and things are shaping up nicely.

**Gulag P-Pa Diary/Pre-Camp No. 3:**

Like every well-managed and precisely run camp, Camp Mema/Gulag P-Pa compile to-do lists, to-bring lists and even camp mottoes to provide the full camp experience for our precious little inmates. The to-do list is longer than the inmates' to-bring list, but that's the sacrifices we as wardens make to provide the complete experience for the little ones. The Condamant thinks the spirit of all that work is best exemplified in the camp mottoes.

Camp Mema Motto: Making Memories for a Lifetime!

Gulag P-Pa Motto: Amnesia Is Our Friend!

Then, of course, we want to make sure all their needs are met, so we provide a list of to-bring essentials for each little camper:

Camp Mema: suitable clothing; swimsuits; favorite toy; stick horses; curiosity; and, most of all, appetites.

Gulag P-Pa: suitable clothing, girls, orange jump suits; suitable clothing, boy, black-and-white striped jump suits; pest repellant (good for bugs and The Condamant); liability insurance, girls, $100; liability insurance, boy, $10 million; least favorite toy for company in solitary confinement (princesses and weird Monster High dolls prohibited); craving for gruel; and, most of all, the willingness to follow orders.

The Condamant has had a little problem the last two years getting the inmates to do the last item, but he's got greater confidence this year because of his new assistant, Mr. Belt, who was an extra in last year's hit movie Escape from Gulag P-Pa. He was most intimidating until the Grands kidnapped him, but he has just finished his psychiatric therapy, and we think will be okay unless he has a relapse when he sees the Grands again for the first time since the trauma of his kidnapping. By the time the Grands finished working him over last year, his tongue was literally hanging out. It was either hire him or put him on Worker's Comp, so we'll see how he does this year.

Next on the to-do list is build the set for The Good, The Bad and The Cutely. Updates to follow.

**Gulag P-Pa Diary/Pre-Camp No. 4:**

We always know it's getting close to Camp Mema/ Gulag P-Pa when we have to visit our local banker for a loan to cover the cost of provisions. It's quite an undertaking feeding the ravenous five, especially when their food preferences are so varied. Here's just a partial accounting of what's on the grocery list for tomorrow.

**For The Grands:**
- Apples—One sack
- Bananas—One bunch
- Broccoli—One floret
- Chicken Nuggets (preferably dinosaur shaped) —Enough to avoid extinction.
- Chips—Six cubic yards
- Chocolate Chips—One metric ton
- Cookie Dough—One refrigerator car full
- Corn Dogs—Eight per Grand
- Crackers—Six cases
- Grape Jelly—One barrel
- Green Beans—Three
- Ice Cream (Vanilla, Chocolate) —Forty gallons each
- Juice (Varied) —Twelve Gallons
- Lettuce—One leaf
- Napkins—One package (10,000 quantity)
- Peanut Butter—One 55-gallon drum
- Paper Cups for Bathroom—One boxcar load
- Pizza (Pepperoni, large)—Six dozen
- Pizza (Vegetable, small)—Zero
- Waffles—One gross

**For the Wardens:**
- Sedatives—One case
- Panic Pills—Just in case
- Depends—Four cases (so P-Pa can bond with Jackson doing boy things without having to take those annoying bathroom breaks)

Not only is the grocery list completed, but so is the moat. Now, all P-Pa is waiting on is the alligators. There'll be no tunneling out this year! Not everything has gone well, however. The rental lion P-Pa had ordered from Zimbabwe to stand watch apparently had dental problems and will not be able to make the trip to Texas.

Updates to follow.

**Gulag P-Pa Diary/Pre-Camp No. 4:**

Making cinematic masterpieces is expensive. Just ask P-Pa, who paid a fortune for the set—a Playmobil western town—that will be featured in the opening and closing scenes of The Good, The Bad and The Cutely. After appropriating the dining room table, P-Pa spent two days putting together the town, fort and Indian village. It all went well, save for building the windmill, as he doesn't care for heights or, more precisely, edges and had to take one of the Panic Pills purchased by Mema this morning so his hands and knees would quit shaking enough for him to put the mill on the tower!

On top of building the set, he had to hire all the extras, including 25 town folk, 19 Indians and 16 soldiers, not to mention secure one stage coach, one wagon, 11 horses, one pony, three buffalo, four longhorns, one bear, one wolf, one coyote, one bald eagle, two fish and, P-Pa's favorite, a skunk!

On top of that, P-Pa has to acquaint himself with his new movie camera, which is smarter than him and has more bells and whistles than a circus ride, all necessary; however, to implement his vision of the greatest western ever filmed, assuming his lead actor takes instructions well.

Mema thinks P-Pa went overboard with the western set, but P-Pa responds that the western outfit is the antidote to years of Disney Princess Overload Syndrome. Further, with the arrival of Action Jackson it provides some boy things for the guys to do, rather than simply dress Cindewelly for the ball. Mema was not convinced by that line of reasoning, saying she thinks P-Pa just wants to play with the western toys. It's not as if she hasn't had little princesses to play with and princess movies to watch over the last few years!

So, while P-Pa was working hard, Mema had it easy, unloading six truckloads of groceries, baking four dozen muffins and nine dozen cupcakes, grilling 200 hamburger patties, making seven gallons of taco meat, roasting six chickens, juicing two bushels of apples and then washing all the dishes—both of them—that got dirtied during the cooking.

The inmates start arriving tomorrow with the Kemps, then the Lewises on Saturday. So, P-Pa is busy rehearsing his Kid Condamant movie lines, such classic dialogue as "Ouch," "Please don't hit me again," and "That really hurts!"

Tomorrow morning will be a blur as we finish chores for the afternoon arrival of the Kemps. It's getting close!

**Gulag P-Pa Diary/Day 1:**

Well, 60 percent of the inmates but 99 percent of the trouble arrived at Camp Mema/Gulag P-Pa at 6:30 p.m. That's right, Mr. Jackson showed up for his first camp experience. He breached the moat with a Duplo bridge (amazing isn't it what you can build with LEGOs?) and grinned at the alligators. They were so scared, they scrambled out of the moat and turned themselves in to an animal control officer.

Multiple times Jackson charged at P-Pa, yelling Pie-Pie and grabbing him around the legs. P-Pa, though, stood firm and wasn't about to be tackled by such a small force. Mema said Jackson was just trying to give P-Pa a hug, but The Condamant was a little more skeptical, wondering if Pie-Pie was actually a coded signal, a plea for dessert or a subtle reference to P-Pa's waist size.

Next came the artillery, Cora and Carys, firing off a barrage of laughs and squeals. The noise was deafening, while their mother made numerous trips to and from the car to unload their luggage. There was one suitcase for Cora, two for Jackson and seventy-three for Carys, who has been known to change her outfits eight or nine times a day. Carys comes prepared for any type of sartorial situation.

Almost immediately, Carys wanted to know where the Cindewelly Castle was so P-Pa got it out, and she and Cora began to put it back together as it had been in disrepair since camp last year. As Jackson is a big fan of trains, P-Pa got him three little wooden ones. He spent much of the time calling "Choo choo" as he drove the train around the floor.

It was cute, but a distraction as he drove the train into his assigned bedroom. When no one was looking, he got the desk phone and started punching out a number. We think he was calling his Lewis cousins with instructions on what tools to smuggle in for the planned breakout. Since Jackson is a night wanderer he can't be trusted to stay in his night cell, so P-Pa is assigned to be his cellmate. P-Pa sleeps on the bed and Jackson in the playpen, or "The Slammer" as it is affectionately called at our house. Every time P-Pa saw a little head rise up from The Slammer, he would look that direction. Mr. Jackson would smile and then lie back down, like a turtle disappearing in his shell. P-Pa had the distinct feeling the little one was casing the joint for his escape or worse, an attack on The Condamant.

P-Pa felt lucky to survive the night! The adventure continues on Day 2!

**Gulag P-Pa Diary/Day 2, Part 1:**

Disaster has struck the western town! We can't decide whether it's an earthquake or the plague. Yesterday, all was well. All sixty characters and all twenty-three animals were standing and happy. Further, all the buildings and the fort were standing. Now the fort guard tower looks like the Leaning Tower of Pisa and all but four characters are face-down in the street. Problem is, there's no doctor among the folks to help them recover. Of course that's the way it was back in the old days.

P-Pa survived the night and Mr. Jackson awoke all happy and angelic. That was all an act! About mid-morning, he slipped from the watchful eyes of the guards. No one thought much of it, until his mother heard the sound of ripping paper. Melissa knew right where to run, the cache of birthday gifts Mema and P-Pa had wrapped for our unified birthday party. Yep, Mr. Jackson had picked out one of his birthday gifts and had it 90 percent unwrapped before his momma busted him (metaphorically, not physically). There were more than twenty wrapped gifts in the cache so he may be smarter than we think and able to read, since he picked out one of his own gifts. That means P-Pa and Mema may not be able to spell out words without him understanding.

Next the inmates were sent to the field to do farm labor. No need for illegal immigrants to do our work when we have child labor. The Kemp crew picked tomatoes. As Cora said, "I like to pick tomatoes. I don't like to eat tomatoes." That can be said of all the Kemp kids.

Since Jackson is such a train fanatic, we took him and his sisters to the railroad museum downtown so he could get on some train cars and engines. Each of them got an engineer's cap as a souvenir.

Then at 3:30 the remaining two inmates arrived for processing. It went well with Misses Hannah and Miriam as they straightened up when they realized Mr. Jackson was in solitary confinement in The Slammer during nap time. The Condamant fears they smuggled in tunneling tools in their luggage as there was too much to go through item by item. To minimize the tunneling possibilities,

The Condamant assigned the five inmates to a chain gang to reconstruct the western town. Miss Hannah is the foreman and things are progressing nicely.

Filming on The Good, the Bad and the Cutely begins tonight after supper, so the western town has to be in filming shape. P-Pa's holding the birthday gifts hostage until the filming is done to his satisfaction.

More to come!

**Gulag P-Pa Diary/Day 2, Part 2:**

After the first day of filming, P-Pa knows how David O. Selznick must have felt when he started Gone With The Wind: Ecstatic, as The Good, The Bad and The Cutely is definitely a cinematic masterpiece in the making. The crew shot both the opening and closing scenes and the actresses were phenomenal. Here's the opening from the script:

*FADE IN:*
*INT. Western Town Set Up on Dining table;*
*four girls in contemporary outfits*
*playing with western toys*
*HANNAH: I wish I lived back in the Wild West.*
*CORA: Me, too!*
*MIRIAM: Me, three!*
*CARYS: Me, four!*
*CORA: I can just hear the cattle at the start of a new day!*
*(Sound Effects: Mooing Cows)*
*HANNAH: Me, I hear the sound of mustangs galloping across the prairie!*
*(Sound Effects: Running Horses)*
*CARYS: I hear the coyotes howling.*
*(Sound Effects: Coyotes Howling)*
*MIRIAM: I hear the sound of bad guys getting shot.*
*(Sound Effects: Bubble Wrap Popping)*

Wow! Great writing such as that falls flat without actresses of great skill and patience to bring it to life. Each did, especially Miriam, who brought great emotion to her lines. Of course the filming wasn't without controversy. When Director Cecil B. DeeP-Pa explained the title, Miss Cora said Jackson must be "The Cutely". P-Pa said no, he was thinking of himself as more of "The Cutely" to which Miriam replied, "No, you're 'The Chubby'." It seems Miriam is an Honor Graduate from the Trump School of Sensitivity!

After the successful taping, we had the unified birthday party. We have Grands with birthdays in April, May and June and ones with birthdays right before and right after Christmas in late December and early January. So Mema and P-Pa decided to start holding a common birthday during Camp so it was like a mini-Christmas in August.

Unfortunately, we had an emotional meltdown by Miss Carys, whose favorite color is purple. When Mema passed out birthday cards, Hannah got the one in the purple envelope. Ooops! What was Mema thinking? Even the cute non-purple card, the $20 bill inside from her Lewis great grandparents and all the sympathy the rest of us could offer failed to stop her tears. P-Pa had to mop the floor to keep everyone else from drowning. On the positive side, Mema and P-Pa now know what book and video to get Miss Carys for Christmas— The Color Purple, of course.

Eventually, everyone was happy once they opened up the outfits Mema had sewn for them. We will have a fashion show later in the week when The Grands wear their Mema outfits as well as one of their own making. On Sunday, The Grands will dress up in their cowboy outfits for two of the outdoor scenes for The Good, The Bad and The Cutely once The Chubby rounds up their stick horses. Giddyup!

## Gulag P-Pa Diary/Day 3, Part 1:

We went from Gone With The Wind to Ishtar in less than 24 hours. Yes, the movie's simplest scenes—riding to the rescue and riding into the sunset—were a disaster. First of all, Silly the Kid wouldn't ride his stick horse, but rather dragged it by the ears, crying all the way. Second of all, the fearsome foursome that was his band of good gals had no scripted lines, but improvised with such classics as "I'm hot," "I'm tired," "I'm bored," and "I'm thirsty." Talk about temperamental performers. Never in the annals of movie history have so few complained about so much to so few who cared. Those ruined movie comments aside, the "Silly the Kid Gang" did look cute when they got dressed up before the filming for the publicity stills.

There comes a moment at every Camp Mema/Gulag P-Pa when the last parent leaves and reality sets in. That moment came about 1:30 p.m. today when the Kemp vehicle rode off into the sunset, its occupants never uttering a single complaint about being hot, tired, bored or thirsty, we might add. Then, it was just us against them, two over-the-hill wranglers with aching joints trying to manage a skittish herd that is liable to stampede at any moment on any excuse, ranging from menu selection to bedtime chores to clothing choices.

Miss Carys was in a down mood after the filming because she forgot to wear socks in her boots and rubbed a blister on her heel. After Mema amputated the foot—it's great to have medical expertise among the Camp Mema staff—Carys was a little down. Seeing that her cousin seemed despondent, Miss Miriam decided to cheer her up. So, Miriam made up a game where she hid the ascending-size donut rings from a stacker toy and let Carys find them. By the time she found them all and stacked them back up in the correct order, Carys was happy as a lark, missing foot or not.

Then the three youngest girls played a game they made up called "Protector Mermaids", where they defended themselves from "the big whale". Guess who was the big whale? That's right, P-Pa. "Why am I always the bad guy?" he asked the Mermaid trio. "Because we don't like you as much," answered, you guessed it, Miss Miriam. There's just no filter on that girl's speech!

Mr. Jackson is learning to fend off the four girls. After his mom left, P-Pa found him on the living room sofa with a nerf sword, defending himself against the sword attack of the four girls. He did quite well, even if the ladies were proclaiming themselves the Four Musketeers. P-Pa thinks it's more like the Five Fussketeers.

Jackson's still having trouble pronouncing the name P-Pa. He says Pie-Pie and will walk into a room and say, "Hi, Pie!" The girls think that's funny and have taken to calling him Pie, too. Now it's time for Pie to say goodbye!

**Gulag P-Pa Diary/Day 3, Part 2:**

Let us set the stage for a class of statements or commentaries we have come to call "Miriamisms". From his easy chair, P-Pa sees the back of a little blonde girl jumping on the couch. This conversation ensues:

> *P-PA: Who's jumping on the couch?*
> *(Unidentified girl jumps off the couch and onto the floor, out of P-Pa's sight.)*
> *Who was jumping on the couch? Was that you, Miriam?*
> *MIRIAM: No, it was a mystery girl.*
> *P-PA: Who's a mystery girl?*
> *MIRIAM: Some girl we don't know.*
> *P-PA: Are you sure?*

*MIRIAM: It could've been Jackson. His hair's the same color as mine.*
*(P-Pa's no Sherlock Holmes, but he believes Miss Miriam just incriminated herself.)*
*CORA: Miriam, just tell the truth. You'll feel better afterward.*
*MIRIAM (reluctantly): It was me!*
*P-PA: How should we punish you?*
*MIRIAM: Really, it's not a big deal.*
*P-PA: Okay.*
*(End of Discussion)*

We also drew names for the Girl of the Day and Non-Girl of the Day honors. The breakdown was: Monday, Cora; Tuesday, Hannah; Wednesday, Miriam; Thursday, Carys; and Friday, Jackson. The little one of the day gets to pick the flag we raise, the Bible story we read and the Disney Movie we watch. Mema tried to pick a movie everyone would enjoy for the evening, but all four girls could not agree on a single one, so we had competing features, 101 Dalmatians (the original) in the family room and Aladdin in the bedroom.

Prior to bedtime, Mema read the second chapter of the Beverly Cleary book, Socks. Then we watched the scenes we've shot for The Good, the Bad and the Cutely. All five Grands loved it, then insisted on seeing last year's masterpiece, Escape from Gulag P-Pa. Laughs abounded as the four girls relived last year's adventure.

The day ended at bedtime with the next Miriamism. We've split up the girls this year with the two older ones sharing a bed in the guest room and the two younger ones sleeping in the living room, where all have slept in the past. So, it is past bedtime and Carys and Miriam are still talking. Enter Mema with an admonition to quit talking and go to sleep. Responds Miriam, "But we are talking about night things." Mema had to squelch a laugh.

Miss Miriam can spin anything!
Monday is Safety Day and more filming.

**Gulag P-Pa Diary/Day 4, Part 1:**

P-Pa got up and left about 6:45 a.m. today to run to the store to get some milk and a few other things for Camp Mema. When he got home about 35 minutes later, the house was still dark and everyone was still asleep, or so he thought until he heard a familiar voice: "Hi, Pie." Yep, Mr. Jackson was up and about, so glad to see his male counterpart that he ran and hugged P-Pa's legs. Of course, he had pulled one corner of the sheets off of P-Pa's bed, though that may have been just a distraction as P-Pa thinks he's working on a secret escape tunnel.

Breakfast was a challenge with all the varied juvenile preferences, though ultimately everyone settled on waffles with a chocolate chip in each square. When P-Pa took credit for the delicious breakfast all the girls cried, "No, Mema did it." Responded P-Pa, "Why does Mema get credit for all the good things?" Answering shyly, Cora said, "Because you're the bad guy in all the movies." Talk about typecasting!

After breakfast, Mema and P-Pa gave lessons in safety with strangers, especially those who might want to entice The Grands into a car. "No, no, stay away. You're not my father," they were taught to yell. If the stranger got out of the car, they were taught to run and scream. Then they had practice runs with each of the girls, P-Pa drove the car around the block while Mema and The Grands waited on the driveway. P-Pa wore a wig and moustache and was so creepy, little Carys was too scared to take a turn. But the girls passed with flying colors not being enticed by candy, a puppy or a request for directions. Even when P-Pa jumped out of the car and gave chase, they ran and screamed like they were supposed to. It's a shame to have to be so mindful of these types of hazards in this day and age. P-Pa, however, was just glad none of the neighbors—or the Police—saw him during this instruction time.

Quote of the Day So Far (Miriam, of course): While watching a monkey video, she said, "Monkeys are cute, but they're not as cute as Jackson!" Some might argue they are one and the same.

After lunch, Mema began teaching Hannah how to sew, starting with cutting out the pattern and the material. The sewing lesson begins tomorrow on a Featherweight Singer Sewing Machine like Mema learned to sew on as a little girl.

The rest of the Grands went to rest time. Mr. Jackson is learning that Mema and P-Pa are serious when they tell him to stay in his bed.

**Gulag P-Pa Diary/Day 4, Part 2:**

After naps, Mr. Jackson quickly established himself as the Picasso of refrigerator magnets. While the girls have made some interesting patterns, the boy is the first to have stacked the magnets on top of one another for a three-dimensional design. The winning smile and impish look at the icebox easel is pretty much how he walks around the house. It's hard to determine if he's cute or just mischievous, like at bedtime when he got up for the second time. When he was caught, he said, "Poddy," and marched into the bathroom, lifted the potty lid and sat down in his jammies and diaper for about five seconds. "Done" he said, then got up and marched back to bed. No way P-Pa could discipline him without setting back his potty training for decades.

Filming resumed on The Good, The Bad and The Cutely with excellent results, though P-Pa will have some extensive editing to do. Certain dramatic scenes, however, will have a certain two-year-old interloper wandering through them as he certainly likes screen time—at least on his terms. Miriam is the most dramatic, some might say melodramatic, actress, while Carys is soft spoken and shy. Hannah is good at improvising lines while Cora is good at remembering everyone's lines and helping others with theirs. P-Pa as Kid Condamant was the ultimate villain, his treachery only undermined by his mustache, which kept falling off to everyone's delight.

Cora was the Girl of the Day and decided to raise the Texas Flag. She chose a Bible story on Baby Jesus and then was excellent in the filming. Day 4 ended with everyone joining P-Pa to watch the rushes of the day's taping. Then Carys wanted to watch the "ice cream move", what she calls last year's classic Escape from Gulag P-Pa. As Escape is about to end, Miss Carys turns to P-Pa and says, "Your big scene is about to come up." She loves the scene where The Condamant is tied up in a chair with a sock stuffed in his mouth while The Grands eat ice cream in front of him. P-Pa did not consider it his best scene, but Carys thinks otherwise, apparently because of the sock!

**Gulag P-Pa Diary/Day 5, Part 1:**

P-Pa's worst fears came to pass today with confirmation that tunneling is under way. His discovery came about quite by accident. He had to do some yardwork in the morning cool and he got up early. Then Mema heard noise and got up to find Jackson wandering around in search of Pie. So, she set him in his high chair at the back door so he could watch P-Pa.

When P-Pa finished work he came in to a pancake breakfast Mema had prepared for the entire crew. Then when Mema went to take a shower, P-Pa realized Jackson's diaper was a little (actually a lot) full. Expecting to earn his third Poople Heart as a grandparent, he went to change Jackson and received the shock of his life. The heavy load was soil and caliche. Jackson had been smuggling out the tunneling debris in his diaper. Technically, Mema and P-Pa were smuggling the detritus out to the dumpster, but it was Jackson's cunning scheme. So, Jackson was sent to the box for punishment, while P-Pa searched unsuccessfully for the tunnel.

Hannah was Tuesday's girl of the day, but was a little puny most of the time, so she spent a lot of time resting. When she felt like it, she and P-Pa talked about reading and horse books and writing and imaginary friends. By supper Hannah felt up to eating and telling P-Pa about this cool TV show *Lab Rats* about some bionic kids in the basement of Tasha Davenport, who was a former news reporter. When P-Pa asked Hannah if news reporters were cool, she answered yes, absolutely. Then when P-Pa told her he started out as a news reporter, Hannah decided to reassess the coolness of news reporters. Next she read a Bible story about Hannah, what a surprise, and picked the movie of the day, Spirit: Stallion of the Cimarron, another surprise.

Before the movie, the girls were all singing a song with words like "we're rotten to the core." When P-Pa asked about the song's name, the four girls responded in unison, *Rotten to the Core*. Miriam put her hands on her hips and shook her head. "It's from Descendants! Don't you know?" Well, no, P-Pa didn't. Apparently, Descendants is a live-action Disney movie depicting the teenage offspring of Disney villains and characters, such as the daughter of Maleficent, son of Cruella de Vil, son of Cinderella and Prince Charming, and son of Dopey, among others. Frankly, P-Pa was surprised at the last one as he didn't know Dopey had it in him. In reality, the movie is just another Disney scheme to pick the pockets of grandparents too far removed from juvenile popular culture to know what they are buying their grandkids.

No filming today due to puny Hannah. Hope to pick it up on Wednesday, when Miriam is Girl of the Day, assuming P-Pa can take time out from the tunnel search.

**Gulag P-Pa Diary/Day 6, Part 1:**

Disaster struck overnight. P-Pa woke up this morning and found an inch of water in his room. Apparently, Jackson reached the moat with his tunneling and the backwash flooded Jackson's and P-Pa's room. Jackson had a smile on his face and mud on his hands. As if that wasn't incriminating evidence enough, P-Pa did a surprise inspection of The Slammer and found Jackson's orange and green shovels. Jackson was sent to the box for punishment while P-Pa ordered three cubic yards of cement to plug up the tunnel.

Today is Princess Day, thanks to Miss Miriam, who is girl of the day. In her honor, we raised the Alaska flag in recognition of the state of her birth. She insisted in only doing princess things all day. So, Mema got out princess posters for them to color, and all the girls obliged. After that was done, Miriam wanted to play princess cards but no one else wanted to play. In desperation, she invited P-Pa to play and he reacted so enthusiastically that he deserved an Oscar for his performance. In fact, he was so convincing that Miss Carys reconsidered and decided she wanted to play after all. Miss Miriam responded she only wanted two to play, and Miss Carys was crestfallen until Miriam said she wanted to play with Carys instead of P-Pa. Poor P-Pa, always the prince, never the princess.

Always a finicky eater, Miriam was not impressed with Mema's wholesome lunch and the aroma of baked chicken, green beans and baked squash so she sat through most of lunch squeezing her nostrils shut with her fingers. It's hard to eat a peanut butter sandwich with one hand attending to nasal duties, but Miss Miriam managed to eat a third of hers, before retiring to watch a princess movie, Snow White.

Mr. Jackson was sent to The Slammer for nap time, but about thirty minutes later, Miss Cora reported the little scamp had escaped and was watching Snow White with the girls. He either slipped by P-Pa and Mema unseen, or he's using another tunnel. Keeping Mr. Jackson in bed is akin to stopping the ocean's waves.

While the other girls were watching Snow White, Mema helped Hannah start sewing a coat for Hannah's American Girl Doll. Hannah is learning there is a lot more work to sewing than she previously realized.

Movie filming is way off schedule and P-Pa is going to have to cut the script to complete the movie as there are too many prima donnas who can't all agree when they want to film. He's not sure the editing will be done before they leave, so he may save it for a Christmas gift and debut the movie at the end of the year.

The adventure continues!

**Gulag P-Pa Diary/Day 6, Part 2:**

The movie's back on track. P-Pa learned the most critical factor in contemporary movie-making: Shoot while Mr. Jackson is napping. Today's filming had beauty with the voluptuous Mema van Doren as the blonde-wigged Fairy School Marm. Then there was the chase scene so essential to any western. The girls excel in action scenes, not needing as much practice as dialogue.

Line of the day went to Miss Carys, though unfortunately it wasn't on tape. P-Pa was putting on his Kid Condamant outfit, including his six-gun from when he was a kid, back in the good old days when toy guns were made of metal instead of plastic, looked real and didn't have orange tips on the end of the barrels. As he was putting on his gun belt, he pulled out the gun and the following exchange occurred:

*CARYS: Is that a real gun?*
*P-PA: No, it's a toy gun.*
*CARYS: Wheeewww!!!!*

Then it was supper time and Mema fixed five plates, each with a different main course on it to satisfy discriminating appetites. When she sat down as the seventh and last person at the dinner table, she sighed. P-Pa asked if she was okay. "Just tired," she replied. Responded Cora, "Why?" Mema answered, "Because I've been on my feet all today." Her response would've been more accurate in P-Pa's mind, at least, if she had said, "I'm tired because I've been waiting hand and foot on four girls and two infant boys all day."

It didn't stop after supper as she bathed the three little girls while P-Pa showered Mr. Jackson. Then, while Hannah read, Cora, Miriam and Carys ran around the house being chased by the "Baby Monster", as they called Jackson. The three girls tried to teach Jackson the game of "Red Light, Green Light". Jackson understands the concept of the green light, but red light is beyond his comprehension as nothing can stop him. Jackson also created a new superhero named "Snailman" when he couldn't disconnect from a booster seat he belted himself in.

Apparently, P-Pa doesn't understand the concept of tea parties. Earlier in week, Miriam and Carys invited him to their special tea party using dishes Carys's mother had used when she was a young girl. Miriam filled a cup from her teapot and offered it to P-Pa with a big smile on her face. P-Pa gulped down the cup of tea and bragged it was the best tea he had ever had. Then Miriam smiled even bigger. "It was poison," she said. P-Pa began to feel weak and the room began to spin around until Carys offered him the antidote or "unpoison" as P-Pa thinks she said, though he wasn't thinking straight at the moment.

P-Pa doubts he will survive until Saturday, but to be on the safe side he's not drinking anything else Miriam offers him. Wheeewww!!!!

**Gulag P-Pa Diary/Day 7, Part 1:**

It was an uneventful night until P-Pa's alarm accidentally went off at 6:30 a.m. Jackson bolted up. "Hi, Pie!" P-Pa negotiated him back to sleep by telling him if he stayed in The Slammer P-Pa would go get donuts. It actually worked, and Jackson slept until 8 a.m., his latest rising time to date.

Then things went downhill from there. Though P-Pa took donut orders the night before, he didn't get them right. In his defense, a supercomputer couldn't have kept up with all the details. Some wanted chocolate, others wanted chocolate with sprinkles or strawberry or strawberry with sprinkles. Though he didn't get Miriam's order right, she was the most accommodating of them all on this occasion, debunking her finicky eating reputation, probably thinking she could get even by inviting P-Pa to another tea party.

Carys is Girl of the Day, and she wanted another Princess Day, so we had a Princess Fashion Show, featuring Mema's summer line of outfits and the freelance outfits of the Grands themselves. P-Pa filmed the fashion show and the young girls did fine, though the rookie Jackson ran screaming from the runway. In the freelance fashion show, Mr. Jackson did a good imitation of Mr. T from the A Team. Hannah was a little too big for the fashion show, but did agree to a sitting with Mema for a group photo of her models and outfits.

For her flag, Carys chose the Alamo flag, since the Alamo is in downtown San Antonio and she was born in a downtown San Antonio hospital. Very appropriate! Since Hannah was a little puny and didn't feel up to picking and raising a flag when she was Girl of the Day, she asked if she could pick the flag for Jackson on Friday. P-Pa said yes, but was secretly disappointed because he had the perfect flag for Jackson. Hannah had fifteen flags to choose from and, miracle of miracles, she picked the one P-Pa wanted, the Come and Take It Flag from the 1835 Texas Battle of Gonzales. It was appropriate because Jackson is without a doubt a loose cannon!

Then we shot the shootout scene between Kid Condamant and Silly the Kid. Silly was as temperamental as we expected, but Hannah came through with a stuffed puppy incentive. It's amazing the influence a beautiful starlet with a puppy can have on a young, aspiring but finicky actor.

Carys was off her game for lunch, eating two beef tacos. Last year, she ate three so Mema thought it appropriate to serve tacos when Carys was Girl of the Day this year. After lunch the four younger ones watched Cindewelly as part of Princess Day, The Sequel, while Mema and Hannah continued their sewing.

This afternoon about 4:30, the movie shooting concludes with the chase scene where Kid Condamant is roped, tied and taught a lesson by Silly the Kid and his gang! It should be interesting, assuming P-Pa survives.

**Gulag P-Pa Diary/Day 7, Part 2:**

Against all odds, P-Pa survived the filming of the final shots of The Good, the Bad and the Cutely, though he has moved it back for a Christmas release instead of a summer debut. He was attacked with water guns, water balloons and a water hose. There was a certain theme to the final shot, which the girls seemed to enjoy best of all, and P-Pa did not have to shower after it was all said and done.

By this time in Camp Mema/Gulag P-Pa, The Condamant begins to feel the wear and tear of days without rest, peace or quiet, having been a target, a pillow, a sounding board, a punching bag, a counselor, a horsey, a dart board, an airplane, a ringmaster, an errand boy, and a physical and emotional wreck! Realizing he had only one more full day of camp, he broke out in his best baritone voice "Some enchanted evening, things will become normal." Before he could finish his impromptu celebratory song, Miss Miriam interrupted. "You're not that good," she said.

His spirits were lifted, momentarily at least, when Cora walked by and said, "Hi, Cutie Pie!" P-P answered, "Thank you, Cora." She shook her head and continued on, "I was talking to Carys! You are too old."

After supper Hannah and Cora wanted to watch Ratatouille while Miriam and Carys wanted to put together a dinosaur floor puzzle. Once the movie started, Miriam looks up and shakes her head. "I can't finish the puzzle. The movie's distracting." With a little help from Mema, Carys and Jackson, she finally completed the task. Then all five watched the movie, Jackson calling the rat "Remy Rabbit".

Mema's been the real trooper, cooking some 300 meals, providing more than 7,000 drinks of water, refereeing seven minor disputes, chasing Jackson back to bed some 83,000 times, making specialty surprises like a cookie pizza, reading them a chapter a night from a children's book and even doing loads of laundry so the kids would return home with a minimum of dirty clothes for their mothers to wash.

Just one more day to go. Mema is a certainty to survive. P-Pa is questionable and will likely need a lot of soothing music and soft lighting to calm him down, if not a year's worth of psychiatric counseling.

**Gulag P-Pa Diary/Day 8, Part 1:**

The Longest Day has arrived, the last before Mema and P-Pa are relieved of the awesome responsibility of maintaining their sanity against five of the shrewdest little rapscallions ever to set foot in Texas. P-Pa arose early to handle hand-watering of the yard and soon was informed by Mema that Mr. Jackson wanted to watch. So, he came outside and helped, prior to breakfast.

Then everyone took the short walk to the park, though it must have seemed like 500 miles the way a certain young boy squawked on the way back when Mema couldn't carry him any longer. The park was fun, the younger the age, the more the fun! Miriam was sweet and pushed Carys in the swing. Carys was a bit of a daredevil with some of her antics. Cora climbed on everything. Hannah was a little more subdued, as playgrounds don't hold as great appeal as when she was younger. Jackson was as happy as if he had escaped Gulag P-Pa, until the death march back home.

Then it was pool time, Hannah choosing to read while the four younger ones played in the Olympic and standard size pools in the back yard. When Cora and Carys were ready to come in and shower off, Miriam looked at her pool partner and said, "Don't let Carys leave, or I'll be alone with Jackson." Despite her trepidation, she and Jackson handled things very well and actually enjoyed playing together.

After lunch, Jackson called a Kids Meeting. He and the Girls then summoned Pie and sent him on a secret mission under the guise of getting a paper and a loaf of bread. Mema never caught on. When he returned from the grocery store, Miriam loaned P-Pa her blanket, informing him that since he had successfully completed his secret mission, he could snuggle with the blanket as long as he didn't rip or tear it. Her final admonition had P-Pa scratching his head: "Don't trick me into making you keep it!"

As Jackson was the Non-Girl of the Day, everyone agreed this was Disaster Recovery Day, when the massive cleanup began. It was a month-long job squeezed into an afternoon. Everyone was so busy, we forgot to raise the loose cannon flag until mid-afternoon and then only after everyone heard the rumble of approaching thunder (no rain, unfortunately). While P-Pa went outside to raise the flag, The Grands watched from the front windows. As P-Pa dodged lightning bolts, The Grands laid odds whether P-Pa was too old, too big or too slow to avoid the lightning strikes. P-Pa covered all the odds, much to the surprise of The Grands!

Then it was suspense time, waiting to find out what P-Pa's secret mission was and what awards each little camper would receive this year.

### Gulag P-Pa Diary/Day 8, Part 2:

The stress and tension is palpable as time winds down on the third annual Camp Mema/Gulag P-Pa. The inmates have turned surly, calling The Condamant "Poopy Pants," then just laughing their little heads off. It's tough on P-Pa to keep from cracking.

At movie time, Jackson chose to watch Disney's Robin Hood movie. Poopy Pants felt pressured when the menu came up on the TV and everyone was yelling for him to press play, even though play was hard to find on the remote. When he finally punched the right button, he looked at the unappreciative crowd and said he thought he deserved a round of applause. Everyone clapped. Poopy Pants felt appreciated until Miriam said, "I'm just doing this so you won't feel bad. I don't really want to."

Mr. Jackson called a second Kids Meeting, inviting P-Pa this time to help them complete the secret mission. While Mema wasn't looking, they all signed a thank you card that read, "From All of Us, Thank You. You're simply the Best of the Best!" Then they gave her a floral arrangement of roses, carnations and sunflowers. Mema was touched. Poopy Pants was jealous!

Then it was time for the awards ceremony, which P-Pa videoed. The recipients were as big a bunch of hams as you've ever seen, but their comments were about ten times more articulate than the best you will see at the Oscars or Emmys. The Gulag P-Pa recipients were Hannah, "Best Watergun Shooter Award"; Cora, "Never Never Award" for exceptional behavior in never being sent to Gulag P-Pa; Miriam, "Drama Queen Award" (self-explanatory); Carys, "Best Line Award" for her "Wheeewww!" when she learned the western gun was not real, but a toy; and Jackson, "The A.W.O.L Award" for vacating his post in The Slammer 83,000 times.

The Camp Mema honorees were Hannah, "Best Seamstress Award"; Cora, "Best Script Director Award" for helping everyone with the movie lines; Miriam, "Best Game Inventor Award" for creating the "find the donut game" to help cheer Carys up; Carys, "Best Princess Fashion Model" for her exquisite creation; and Jackson, "Picasso of Refrigerator Art Award".

After the award ceremony, everyone gathered around Pie's computer and watched the video, then it was off to bed. Some might think running a camp like this is time consuming, but believe it or not Poopy Pants has had time to read three books from cover to cover each night since the inmates arrived. Now he no longer has to read them as he can recite Toot Toot Beep Beep, Tip Tip Dig Dig and Chugga Chugga Choo Choo, Jackson's favorite.

By now Mema thinks Poopy Pants should clean up his act!

### Gulag P-Pa Diary/Day 9, Part 1:

"Free at last, free at last, thank God almighty we are free at last" were the words on the lips of each inmate, not to mention Mema and Poopy Pants as the third annual Camp Mema/Gulag P-Pa staggered to a conclusion. Mema and The Condamant decided to adopt a new joint camp song, Happy Days Are Here Again.

On the final day, P-Pa got up at 6 a.m. to get to Jack & Jill Donuts, praying he would get the order right this time. He succeeded, though the level of praise did not meet his expectations as the decibel level never surpassed zero.

Jackson chose his outfit for the return trip home and selected camo shorts and red tee-shirt with the words "Mom's Lil' Romeo." If truth in advertising applied to kids' tee-shirts, Mr. Jackson's shirt should have read "Mom's Lil' Roam-eo." Then Jackson ran around the house chasing P-Pa, yelling, "My Turn," or at least that's what Poopy Pants thought until Cora interpreted. "He's saying 'Monster'," she informed P-Pa. So much for P-Pa bonding with his bedroom buddy!

Then all the inmates gathered for the annual Camp Mema/Gulag P-Pa group photos. For some reason, the inmates started a tradition that the Camp Mema photo was a happy face while the Gulag P-Pa photo was crazy face.

Scott and Celeste arrived about 9:15 to take all five inmates back to their homes. It took an hour, three forklifts and the Longshoremen's Union to get the van loaded and car seats secured. Once everyone was buckled in with their earphones and iPads (Jackson doesn't have an iPad, though he carries around an iMad whenever he needs it), the Scott Lewis Express headed south. The wardens were told by both sets of parents to limit iPad usage or they would do nothing else. So, usage was restricted to afternoon rest time and it kept them quieter. What transistor radios were to Baby Boomers, iPads apparently are to Generation Z or Boomlets, those born after 2000.

From P-Pa's perspective this latest generation is misnamed. Rather than Boomlets, it should be "Sonic Boomlets". After the Lewis van disappeared around the corner and Mema and Poopy Pants walked back into the house where zero decibels never sounded better.

Then came unconstruction and cleanup time. Put away the potty seat, high chair, playpen, bathroom stool, diaper pail, booster seats, wipes, and that's just for P-Pa. Then it's wash sheets, pick up stray toys, vacuum, get things back in order, then start a lost and found. Actually, the five grands only lost one sock, while P-Pa alone matched that and is still looking for his camera's lens cap.

Rather than take a Rip van Winkle nap this morning, they toughed it out, but will be in bed by 8 p.m. to try to get their lives back to normal. P-Pa'll have at least one last post, once he wakes up.

**Gulag P-Pa Diary/Epilogue:**

Once P-Pa woke up from his hibernation, he was no longer suffering from the delusions and bouts of fantasy that plagued him and his posts during the nine-day ordeal of Camp Mema/Gulag P-Pa. So, it's time to wrap it up for 2015. Another year and another success, thanks largely to the endurance of The Grands. Each is special in her or his own way.

As leader of the pack, as Mema described her, Hannah is the intellectual, the one who loves to read and is intellectually precocious. At ten, she's straddling the line between childhood and adolescence.

Cora is the caregiver. At seven, she is the most compassionate and obedient child P-Pa has ever been around. She's proud that she's never broken the rules and been sentenced to Gulag P-Pa. She is becoming a good reader, which is opening up new worlds to her.

Without a doubt, Miriam, age five, is the most quotable, a trait that Poopy Pants—a name she gave P-Pa—loves. She also displayed a sensitivity not always present in her comments. She invented a game to cheer Carys up and tried to mediate disputes among others.

Carys is the impish little daredevil, virtually fearless, pleading for P-Pa to help her to the highest point on the playground equipment at the park. At four, she's become quite the competitor, not liking to lose at anything. She has the cutest smile, except when in a contest.

As the camp rookie, two-year-old Jackson is a bundle of curious energy. He communicates well for his age, though enunciation is still a challenge. He has a stubborn streak as well as a conscience, especially noticeable when he would leave his bed and get caught. The wardens never had to say anything as he'd just hang his head and crawl back in The Slammer.

Thanks to everyone for the generous comments on the Facebook posts. The question that seemed to come up frequently about the posts was if folks could send their kids to Camp Mema/Gulag P-Pa. Unfortunately, space is limited and the wardens cannot take on new inmates without jeopardizing the full service incarceration they provide.

However, P-Pa has decided to start offering Camp Mema/Gulag P-Pa franchises for the nominal fee of $5,000. As a franchise owner, you will be get exclusive use of the CM/GPP name in your residence; a list of daily activities; simple menu ideas (fix them whatever will shut them up); templates for regular Facebook Posts that will make you seem the intellectual equal of your charges; a $100 coupon for follow-up psychiatric service; and the ultimate satisfaction of knowing you survived the experience. Order soon as franchises are limited to one per household.

**Gulag P-Pa Diary/Epilogue, Part 2:**

We had an opportunity for a quick trip to Round Rock to spend some time with the Kemp Grands and actually got to accompany them to their Classical Conversations Classes, P-Pa sitting in on Cora's class and Mema joining Carys's class while Jackson was on his own in the Nursery.

Cora's instructions to P-Pa: "Don't embarrass me in front of my friends." P-Pa thinks he succeeded.

Carys is not so direct. In fact, her instructions can be downright perplexing. When begging P-Pa to chase her, she yelled, "Catch me if you can't!" P-Pa is still pondering those instructions, not quite sure what the appropriate course of action is.

As for Jackson, he's in his own little world. At naptime, he signaled P-Pa he wanted his radio on. So, P-Pa obliged and left the radio on the country station it was tuned to. When P-Pa returned to check on him, the radio had been changed to a Spanish language station! That boy just won't stay on his bed. When he's busted, though, he just offers the cutest little smile and goes about his business.

# CHAPTER SEVEN

*"And the two shall become one flesh. So they are no longer two but one flesh. What therefore God has joined together, let not man separate."*
—Mark 10:8-12 (English Standard Version)

We loved watching our children grow, each age coming with its particular advantages and drawbacks. From birth to three months, the babies were too little to do much but eat and sleep, so I didn't care for that period as much as others in their lives because they belonged to their mother. But after they started laughing and moving around, then I could enjoy their development. We were old school in their rearing, believing in discipline. Early on when the babies would reach up and yank her hair, Harriet would say no emphatically and move their fingers away. If that didn't work after a few times, she'd say no and swat their hands. Those were little things, but we believed children needed restraint if for no other reason than their own safety.

Though we didn't always agree on the extent of that discipline, we adjusted. Many times I had told Harriet that our kids would never throw a hissy fit in a store like I had seen so often over the years.

I was wrong. Each threw one wailing tantrum in public over a toy or some other nonsense. On each occasion, I lifted them up by the arm and gave them a couple swats on the bottom. Both times our son and daughter squealed even louder, embarrassing us even more. But they got the message that if they embarrassed us in public, they would be disciplined and embarrassed as well. After the first time, it never happened again with either child. Today, sadly, some busybody would've reported me to Child Protective Services for such public discipline, and I'd be doing prison time for abuse. When child abuse became common in the vernacular, my father once told me the worst child abuse is letting a child grow up without discipline, a trait necessary to face the challenges of life. I agreed, and I told Harriet people would notice, if we disciplined our children properly and with love. Sure enough, we received many compliments in church about how well our children behaved. Of course, we let them draw or read in the pew, and we bribed them with LifeSavers, but they learned there were times and places where they needed to be on their best behavior.

Since we couldn't always predict our children's emotions or moods in public, we saw few theatrical movies during their early years, tickets and babysitting costs being a strain on our budget. We made the conscientious decision that Harriet would stay home with the children and help raise them until they started first grade. Harriet still worked Saturday mornings and as the kids matured, she'd leave them at mother's day out at the church twice a week where she would work six hours a day. I remember money was so tight that one February, we needed to have our trees pruned, though we desperately wanted a video cassette recorder. I opted for the pruning, in retrospect a poor choice. When we bought our first VCR a couple months later, we realized they were the greatest inventions in our lifetime, or at least our lifetime as young parents. Now we could see many of the movies we had missed in the theaters. Movies in the comfort of your own home! We doubted civilization would ever get any better than that, even if you had to make multiple trips to the video store each week.

Even from a young age, we began to notice differences in our children, part of it in their personalities, some of it in their preferences and the rest of it in their gifts. Though it grew fashionable among elites and feminists during this time to say that no differences existed between the genders, we found it quite the opposite. Scott enjoyed building things and, like most boys, knocking those same things down. He was precocious, teaching himself to read before kindergarten age and being exceptionally talented with numbers, winning his elementary school math bee in the third grade, defeating all the fifth and sixth-graders. That year he went on to win the city-wide math contest as a third-grader. Scott would become a mechanical engineer.

Melissa preferred dolls and possessed wonderful nurturing talents, wanting from her earliest memories to be a school teacher. When she got to know her numbers and ABCs, she would set up a chalk board in her room and teach them to her dolls. Later, she'd take her chalkboard to the front yard and teach the younger neighbors their letters and numbers. Years later as we are driving her to Baylor for her first semester of college, she informed us at one point she needed to get something off of her chest. Harriet and I prepared for the worst about some parental failing. What Melissa said was even more shocking. "All my life when I've told people I wanted to be a school teacher, they told me I would change my mind by the time I grew up. Well, here I am headed for college, and I haven't changed my mind." She graduated as the top elementary education major in her class at Baylor and taught nine years of kindergarten and grade school before giving it up, frustrated at how insensitive school district administrations were to the real needs of their students. Because of that frustration and the amoral if not immoral direction she saw public education heading, she and her husband opted to home school their three children.

Throughout Scott and Melissa's childhoods we stressed on them the value of learning. While we had a strict bedtime that meant they had to put up their toys and end their play, we allowed them to keep their lights on as long as they wanted, providing they were reading books or Bible stories. Harriet read them lots of books as did I. One of my favorite was a picture book of a thousand different objects or animals. I'd go through the pages first with Scott and later with Melissa, identifying the illustrations and asking them to repeat it. After a while, I would point to the pictures, and they would shout out what it was. Though we were stingy with toys until birthdays and Christmas, we bought them all the books they wanted, and Harriet even purchased a set of Sesame Street books a volume at a time at the grocery store.

Scott loved that set of books. One night when he was four or so, I heard him laughing his little head off. That could only mean one thing: Melissa had escaped from her crib and was playing in his room with him. However, when I walked by her room, Melissa was sitting up in her crib wide-eyed and innocent. When I entered Scott's room, he was propped up on his pillow still laughing. "What's so funny?" I asked. He pointed to a page in one of Sesame Street volumes and cackled, "Bert called Ernie 'cuckoo bananas!'" That's when we knew Scott had taught himself to read.

By elementary school both of our kids had been designated as gifted. Thanks to the help of the director of our church mother's day out and day care program, we were able to guide them toward schools that maintained their enthusiasm in learning. They were blessed to have exceptional teachers in elementary, junior high and high school. And, they were equally blessed with good Sunday School teachers and mentors at our church. By junior high, both had accepted Jesus Christ as their Lord and Savior and were baptized in the Baptist faith. As proud parents, we felt we had satisfied our most important responsibility to our offspring.

Each age offered joys and challenges as we watched our son and daughter grow. In the early years, we relished their unrelenting love and being the center of their universe. They had so much to learn, and we had so much to teach them that it bonded us as parents and children. Then with formal school, they took their first steps into the real world and faced outside influences that sometimes challenged our teachings. In the early years of elementary school, they didn't mind being seen by our sides at the mall on Friday nights when we opted for cheap entertainment. By their later years in elementary school, they preferred to walk a few steps behind us in case they ran into any of their friends.

Next came junior high where parents were best unseen and unheard. Junior high was the most challenging time in our experience, as Scott and Melissa weren't children any more, but they weren't adults either. Junior high or middle school as it is now called is like the Twilight Zone of adolescence. On top of that their activities were so many that in addition to our day jobs, we worked afternoon and evenings as their chauffeurs. Then came high school and their flights of independence once they got their driver's licenses. Though we once thought we'd never be comfortable with them driving, by the time they ended junior high we were relieved not to have to chauffeur them everywhere.

As they neared high school graduation, their hard work had put Scott and Melissa among the sharpest kids in the school district. After taking the Preliminary Scholastic Aptitude Test in the fall of his senior year, Scott was named a National Merit Scholar, which meant he would get a significant financial aid wherever he decided to attend college. By the time he settled on a university, he had received scholarship offers totaling near a half million dollars from some of the nation's most prestigious universities.

Though they were twenty months apart in age, Melissa entered school only a year behind Scott and often fell under his shadow because of his precociousness. She was equally as smart, though in different areas, but always had to work harder than Scott to achieve the same end. She too took the PSAT, and we prayed hard for a comparable outcome as she had worked so diligently for everything she achieved. Then one day when I was at home during lunch, the phone rang, and I picked up the receiver. It was Melissa. She announced that she, too, had been designated a National Merit Scholar. I cried. Never had a young lady deserved it more than Melissa for all the hard work she devoted to her studies. She also got hundreds of thousands of dollars in scholarship offers and chose to accept one from her mother's and father's alma mater.

A few weeks after that, I was in my study and had just watched a television news report about breastfeeding helping children's intellectual development. Harriet had seen the same report in another room and came marching in, both index fingers pointing at her bosom. "National Merit Scholars," she announced. I couldn't argue against that.

By that fall, Harriet and I had become empty-nesters. The greatest thrill of our lives had been becoming parents, and now except for a few remaining summers when the kids returned home, it was only the two of us, just like in the beginning, though a little wiser and a little heavier. Just as my father had told me, I informed our kids that we would pay for their stay in college no more than four years, though we would help them buy dependable transportation with whatever their savings wouldn't cover. We provided for their room and board and everything else their scholarships did not cover, though they would need to work for their spending and entertainment money.

Their discipline and their work ethic saw them through four years of college, both graduating on schedule and beginning their careers, our son with a multinational corporation in Houston and our daughter with a mid-sized Texas school district. We had much to be proud of about with their college careers, but we were disappointed that neither of them found a spouse during those years. Toward the end of his college career, I expressed to Scott my concerns that he hadn't dated more because he would never find a greater pool of eligible women. "Dad," he said, "I just haven't found that many that share my values." At that point I knew that Harriet and I had raised our son right, and that God would handle the arrangements as necessary.

After graduation, Melissa moved back to our town and taught a few years before deciding to move to a larger city with a greater population of eligible bachelors because she was interested in matrimony and, like her mother, committed to raising a family. In the end, both of our children found their spouses in the church. That pleased Harriet and me that the values we had tried to instill in both our son and daughter had taken.

We met our future daughter-in-law Celeste in Galveston one winter evening. Harriet and I had returned there to celebrate our anniversary in the town where we shared our honeymoon. We rented a condo, and Scott drove Celeste down from Houston to meet us. We were waiting in the parking lot when they arrived. As soon as Celeste stepped out of Scott's vehicle in a black-and-white outfit, Harriet nudged me in the ribs. "She's the one," she announced. "How do you know?" I responded. "Because she's wearing an outfit like mine." That sartorial prediction confused me. Later Harriet explained that the night I first introduced her to my parents, she was wearing a lime-green outfit the same color as my mother's dress. None of it made any sense to me, but I couldn't remember what I wore the day before, much less thirty or more years previous when I first met her parents. But, her woman's intuition was right. Scott and Celeste would soon marry.

Celeste reminded me of Harriet. She was of northern birth, like my wife, and had that maternal look about her that enhanced her natural beauty. After graduating from college in Iowa, she attended a local job fair and accepted a teaching position in Texas. She moved to Houston without knowing virtually anyone and settled into her career and her church where she met Scott, who was working in the nursery. That impressed her.

Like Celeste, Melissa took her second teaching job in Austin without knowing anyone and settled into a large church as well. After a spell we began to hear the name of John come up in her conversations more and more. Once when she came to visit us, she spent most of her time in our guest room talking on the phone to John. Even with the door shut, we always heard her laughing and giggling at the conversation. Harriet informed me this was the one for Melissa. "How do you know?" I asked. "Because he makes her laugh just like you've always made me laugh." Once again Harriet was right.

As things grew serious between Melissa and

John, she wanted to introduce us to him, but our schedules were tight. We finally agreed to drive the three-and-a-half hours to Austin for lunch and then turn around and come back home that Saturday afternoon so we could meet our church commitments the next day. We arrived at Melissa's apartment and peeked out the window, waiting for him to arrive. He drove up and as he got out of his vehicle, Harriet gasped, "He's handsome!" We scurried to the couch so we would be innocently sitting there when Melissa answered the door.

John was a good-looking young man with a firm handshake, a gentle smile and a wonderful sense of humor as I quickly learned. As we were on a tight schedule, we soon marched outside to our sedan. I was so nervous that instead of punching unlock on the key fob, I hit the trunk button. The trunk flew open, much to my embarrassment. "Is that where you want me to ride?" John asked. We all laughed as I shut the trunk and John opened the door for Melissa. Harriet just gave me that "you dummy" look as we got into the car. The steakhouse lunch went well, and we returned the three-and-a-half hours home impressed with John.

As both of our adult children grew serious about the young Christians they were dating, we became more and more excited about us welcoming a daughter-in-law and a son-in-law into the family. Things were shaping up nicely for us to become grandparents.

# CHAPTER EIGHT

## *YEAR FOUR*

**Gulag P-Pa Diary/Pre-Camp No. 1:**

It's the decision Hollywood has been awaiting—the casting for the Gulag P-Pa production of The Amazing Adventures of the Amazing Five. Though previously titled The Amazing Variable Man for the villain, financing was not forthcoming without a name change to reflect the real stars of the movie, The Grands. P-Pa bowed to fiscal realities and agreed to the change, even if it meant bottom billing.

As you may recall this year's Camp Mema movie is a superhero movie, where the Amazing Five save the world or at least the mini-world that is Mema's and P-Pa's place. Here's the cast:

Jackson as Arachnid Boy, whose superpower is casting a web of entrapment.

Carys as Princess Girl, whose superpower is making everyone's dreams come true.

Miriam as Super Sparkle, whose superpower is blinding people with her dazzle.

Cora as Super Good Girl, whose superpower is killing people with kindness.

Hannah as Everest, whose superpower is being so cool she can turn things into ice.

Mema as The Incredible MULK (Mema [Yo] u'd Like to Know), whose superpower is running camp.

P-Pa as Variable Man, whose superpower is becoming his enemies' biggest nightmare.

It's guaranteed to be a great movie once P-Pa writes the script and The Grands provide their ad-libs. Mema's not worried about the ad-libs, but rather the script as camp starts Saturday with the arrival of The Amazing Five.

**Gulag P-Pa Diary/Pre-Camp No. 2:**

It's D-3 before Camp Mema/Gulag P-Pa and trouble has already begun, a dispute between Mema and P-Pa over the activities for each day. Mema wants fun days while P-Pa wants educational days. Mema's thinking Splash/Park Day; Creative Arts Day; Horse/Animal Day; Reading Adventure Day and Birthday Party Day (which is redundant in P-Pa's mind). Overall, BORING!

P-Pa's thinking more educational, useful days, such as Automotive Day; Farm Labor Day; Haircut/Hair Styling Day; Power Tools Day; and First Aid/Call 911 Day. Overall, EXCITING!

Take Automotive Day, for instance. The Grands will get experience changing the oil and rotating the tires on P-Pa's car, experiences that will come in handy in the future when they want their own car. In the interim, it will save P-Pa money on car repairs. Then there's Farm Labor Day when The Grands can pick produce, chop weeds and learn that groceries don't grow on the shelves at the local retailer. A bonus here for The Grands is they'll be able to tell their own children how rough that had it as kids, having to work under a broiling sun, pick tomatoes and chop weeds.

Haircut/Hair Styling Day goes back to the days when Mema was known as Mom and she had to go to church early for choir, leaving P-Pa, then known as Dad, to get the kids ready for Sunday School. Even at three years old, Melissa knew Dad was not a good stylist and refused to let him do her hair. But P-Pa's had a lot of experience combing his own thinning hair since then and wants to make amends for his previous deficiencies by giving all The Grands a contemporary haircut and style.

Power Tools Day comes next with training on the usage and care of chainsaws, lawn mowers, circular saws, band saws, table saws, electric drills, routers, air compressors and jack hammers. After all, power and tools are our friends. First Aid/Call 911 Day will provide training in what to do in an emergency or an accident, though P-Pa is debating whether this should come before or after Power Tools Day. Or maybe it should come before Mema finishes reading this post!

Regardless of what Mema thinks, The Grands are certain to love his ideas.

**Gulag P-Pa Diary/Pre-Camp No. 3:**

After a night of tense negotiations, P-Pa is pleased to report that Camp Mema/Gulag P-Pa is saved and back on track with a unified vision of activities. Negotiations began after Mema read the previous post and concluded only after P-Pa finished up a lengthy visit to the emergency room. Yes, Camp Mema will follow Mema's schedule of activities (except when she's in the shower or not looking, but don't let her know! Please, I beg you!) So fun wins out over educational, boring over exciting, Mema over P-Pa, but P-Pa will accept that decision for his own safety.

As D-2 got started, P-Pa was doing yardwork, though it was difficult mowing and trimming the lawn with a cast on his foot and with all the stitches aching and itching. But he's a trooper and did it for three reasons. First, everyone knows the first things grandchildren check when they arrive at their grandparents' house is how well the yard is manicured. Second, he needed to cut the weeds down to knee level so The Grands would have fewer places to hide in case they try to ambush him during one of their expected escape attempts. Third, and most importantly, working with dangerous power tools is safer than "negotiating" with Mema.

Now Mema is working on the grocery list. It's so complicated she had to computerize it with a spread sheet that lists each Grand and his/her food likes, dislikes, allergies, preferences, including chocolate or vanilla icing over chocolate or vanilla cake. Her grocery list prints out a quarter of a mile long and we are going to have to rent a refrigerated trailer to store everything.

Sure, you say, just cook pizza or hamburgers every meal and be done with it, but it's not that simple. We have one who doesn't like pizza. We have another one who used to think Mema's sizzle burgers were the best hamburger in the world. Now, she can't stand them. We have some that don't like vegetables, and some that don't care for meat. All like chips and donuts (if they are the right color, of course), but their parents don't always approve so it gets complex. Mema is not as successful negotiating menus with The Grands as she is determining camp activities with P-Pa. On the positive side, the hospital bills aren't as big either.

P-Pa's started the movie script with "FADE IN" but that's as far as he's gotten. He's never believed in writer's block until this script so he's not sure whether it's that or the splints on his fingers that is making it difficult to write. On the positive side, Gulag P-Pa Productions has just released the first promotional still of Arachnid Boy.

More later, assuming P-Pa isn't in any more "negotiations" with Mema!

## Gulag P-Pa Diary/Pre-Camp No. 4:

D-1 was a disaster, no time for a post as P-Pa was wandering around aimlessly and mumbling incoherently after he saw the bill for Mema's grocery shopping. The total was the equivalent of some undeveloped nation's gross national product. Having work to do, Mema took him to his computer to get him out of the way and encourage him to work on the script. All he got after a day staring blankly at the computer screen was the first line of dialogue, "Why? Why? Why?" Not only that, the stress got to him, and he took to the bottle again, having himself a Mountain Dew after swearing off the vile concoction as part of the sixty-eight-step program with Soft Drinkers Anonymous. He was doomed to fail SDA's program from the beginning as he can barely count that high, words—not numbers—being his strength.

As for Mema, she started cooking by digging a pit in the back yard, building a fire and when the wood was burned down to coals, threw a side of beef on so she would have genuine barbecue for The Grands Saturday night. Then after she got the beef going, she did an analysis of her dietary spread sheet and found that the only other food item that The Grands can all agree on other than chips and donuts is ice cream. And then, only if it is vanilla and lactose free! Next she started fixing twelve dozen chocolate chip muffins, which was simple compared to the cupcakes, which had about a million permutations—white icing on white cake, white icing on chocolate cake, chocolate icing on chocolate cake and chocolate icing on white cake. That's why we have to have cupcakes rather than a single cake.

Still delirious, P-Pa suggested it might be a lot simpler if she just made one type of cupcake, then blindfolded The Grands before serving them. Mema was not amused!

Since we celebrate all of The Grands' birthdays during camp with one massive party, Mema was finally able to bring P-Pa back to his senses enough to wrap all the birthday presents. They don't look that good, but pitiful though his wrapping is, it is a lot better than his cooking or his permutation skills.

About midnight, it was bedtime, Mema's sleep coming fitfully as P-Pa's snores alternated with the screams from his nightmares. Drinking Mountain Dew will do that to a fellow!

**Gulag P-Pa Diary/Day 1:**

D-Day is here and so are The Grands. It's a long way from Houston for Scott and Celeste, especially since they had to double their load in Round Rock. P-Pa, though, needed the extra time to recover from his nervous breakdown yesterday.

He's refrained from drinking MD today, and Mema provided some incentive to get the script and other chores done. Mema explained to P-Pa that they were going back into "negotiations" if he didn't get cracking on the movie script. Since the last set of negotiations ended in the emergency room with a cast on his foot, several stitches above the neck and his fingers in splints, P-Pa decided he would get over his writing block and start work on the script. Mema has an effective way of inspiring P-Pa—or else!—which is why she's the Incredible MULK in The Amazing Adventures of the Amazing Five. Here's a sample of the dialogue:

*CARYS: What's your superpower?*
*MEMA: I've lived with P-Pa for forty-five years?*
*GRANDS: (in awe) Whooooo, you do have superpowers then!*

Besides that sterling prose, P-Pa got the western town set up and the railroad laid out for our little trainiac, Mr. Jackson, in the living room. On top of that, after wrapping the birthday gifts, P-Pa stacked them in the living room, which is where all The Grands headed, once they got their suitcases unloaded.

As his final task, P-Pa raised the hurricane warning flag on the pole out front. Based on the first few minutes, it's a Category 5 hurricane! Once the Amazing Five got playing good with the western town, P-Pa asked if he could participate. "Sure," said Hannah, "you can be the donkey." Then we had our first Camp Mema spat over who owned one of the western town dogs. When P-Pa informed them that all the play figures belonged to P-Pa, Carys shook her head and said, "You're forgetting Mema." P-Pa stood corrected.

Then at supper, Jackson decided he needed to go to the bathroom, confirming previous reports he was well potty trained. When he was done, he ran back to the dining table and took a bow, holding in his hand both his drawers and his short pants. We have to admit he's got the pre-commode protocols down, but he's still a little vague on post-potty procedures!

After supper, it was disaster recovery (toy pick-up). Then Hannah read the script of The Amazing Adventures of the Amazing Five and gave her approval with several smiles. Next, Cora read it and thought it was so good she called it "the movie scriptures." It's good, though P-Pa's not sure it's in the divine realm. Then everyone took in a Disney movie, Zootopia, a new one for Mema and P-Pa!

The Adventure begins!

**Gulag P-Pa Diary/Day 2:**

D+1 started great with Scott and Celeste providing reinforcements. Then they left. No sooner had the door closed, than sweet little Cora said, "Now we can do what we want, like smack P-Pa in the face!" Whooo! Ever the diplomat, P-Pa countered, "Nobody'll open birthday presents if you do." "Just joking," Cora replied.

P-Pa's plan was to delay opening presents until the day The Grands left, but Mema told The Grands they could open presents once everyone was dressed and showered. P-Pa decided he would take a five-day shower until he heard a banging on the bathroom door. When he peeked out and saw the pitchforks and torches, he decided to expedite his shower. Now he has no leverage and fears for his safety.

Gift opening was chaos, but everyone seemed happy, none more so than Jackson, who got an excavator truck with an electric drill (a sneaky way P-Pa slipped Power Tool Day past Mema). When the mess was all clean, Jackson sidled up to Mema and asked. "Mema, did you get any presents?" Mema said no. "I'm sorry," Jackson answered.

We did the traditional photo of Mema with The Grands in the outfits she made for them. This is the first time Mr. Jackson wasn't crying in the photo, so either Jackson's getting more mature or Mema's outfits are getting more satisfactory to the young man. Even so, not everyone was happy.

At naptime, all the kids went to bed with their iPads or cell phones. Jackson's phone is the only thing that kept him glued to the bed, but unfortunately his battery ran down and then he was up bouncing around like a slow-motion pin ball. Carys and Miriam had some technical issues with their iPads and came to P-Pa for assistance thinking they weren't connected to P-Pa's Wi-Fi. He showed them that they were. "Good," said Miriam. "We can't live without electronics." They went from high tech to low tech after supper, going outside and mounding the crushed granite in P-Pa's back yard. P-Pa went out to check on them and make sure they weren't destroying his landscaping. Carys accosted him with her hands on her hips. "You're standing on my rocks!" P-Pa stepped aside.

P-Pa's dream of an Oscar for best original screenplay died hard today as two of the five actors weren't really interested in filming and child labor laws prevented him from handling the situation in his own inimitable way. The other three are panicked that their superhero costumes will go to waste. P-Pa may have to adjust the "movie scriptures" on the fly as his Oscar hopes fly away.

At supper, Jackson made the mistake of telling Miriam what to do. It did not go over well. "I'm used to adults telling me what to do, but not little kids," Miriam explained to Mema. "I should be telling them what to do."

And so it goes!

### Gulag P-Pa Diary/Day 3:

Today was D+2, D as in Disaster. It started off great for P-Pa as he had the option of going to the dentist or staying home. So, P-Pa took the fun option and went for his dental checkup. It was the only time he ever begged his dentist to drill or grind or excavate, anything to delay completion of his checkup, but the dentist wasn't cooperative and sent him back home, much to Harriet's relief. She got even with P-Pa, though, by saying she had some business to attend at church. P-Pa thinks Mema just wanted a little peace and quiet plus an opportunity to pray for deliverance.

When we were all together again the movie

came up, and Miriam wanted to know why P-Pa was always the bad guy, saying a change was due. P-Pa agreed as he knows what it's like to be typecast. He suggested Mema as the villain to a chorus of "No's!" from the little ones. Then he suggested every grand from Hannah to Jackson and the response was even more emphatic, always no with an exclamation point. Then it became obvious to everyone that P-Pa was not only a natural bad guy, but also the only real option. Miriam, who started the conversation, ended it by saying, "Well, you're the goodest bad guy!"

P-Pa supposes that's better than being the baddest good guy, but it turned out to be a moot point as the movie is on the skids. Hannah is on the verge of her teen years and not so interested in little girl things anymore, deciding she'd rather read than act. Cora didn't think it would be as much fun without Hannah so she was less enthusiastic. Miriam and Carys were bewildered by the fickleness of the senior leads. On top of that Jackson didn't care to take any directions, except his own. P-Pa even offered to quintuple everyone's salaries, but it was a matter of principle rather than money so P-Pa's acting and directing careers seem over. Mema did help them get in their costumes so P-Pa could take pictures of what might have been.

Poor Mema, though. Menus are driving her nuts, best represented by today's taco luncheon. Last year, Miss Carys ate three so Mema added tacos to this year's menu as she knew at least one would like it. Wrong! The 2015 Carys may have cared for tacos, but not the 2016 Carys. Five guests, five little unpredictable appetites.

So, it was a disaster all around, sort of a combination Great Chicago Fire/Galveston Hurricane/San Francisco Earthquake! On the positive side, the house is still standing, even if the western town isn't.

After today's experience, Mema and P-Pa agreed with the quotable Miss Miriam that we can't live without electronics. After lunch Mema and P-Pa sent the formerly Amazing Five to rest time with their electronics so the Exhausted Two could get some Amazing Peace and Quiet! The electronics worked. Mema and P-Pa can't rest during camp without electronics.

**Gulag P-Pa Diary/Day 4:**

D+3, D as in Delightful. P-Pa thinks it's because everyone got a good night's sleep. Mr. Jackson was asleep by about 6:30 and slept to 7:30 and all the girls were asleep by 9:30 and slept until around 8 a.m. P-Pa got up at 6:30 a.m. and had about an hour of tranquility before Jackson awoke and came in grinning. So much for serenity.

Then P-Pa fixed breakfast for The Grands (actually, he just gave them muffins Mema had already baked) so Mema could sleep late. She joined the gang about 9 a.m. just in time to save P-Pa, who was bound, gagged and being lowered into a vat of boiling water by The Grands. Apparently, he doesn't do breakfast as well as Mema! On the positive side, he was steam-cleaned and didn't have to shower later in the day.

As P-Pa surveyed the damage from the previous twenty-four hours, he realized the western town was a wreck, the town folks, the Indians and all but one of the lawmen all knocked over. Only a half-dozen soldiers remained standing. P-Pa's not sure the cause of the disaster, though he's still analyzing photos to determine the culprit. If anyone sees any clues, please advise P-Pa. In the interim, two construction angels—Hannah and Cora—rebuilt the town and made it perfect in spite of you know who! Enter Mr. Jackson after rest time. "Here comes trouble," P-Pa said. Responded Jackson, "No, you're trouble."

P-Pa was looking for something in his office and Carys joined him, then started rearranging the chairs and office implements on the desks. "I'm trying to make it look like a real office," she explained. P-Pa thought the clutter gave it the authentic office look.

Hannah showed the other girls how she plays Minecraft and they spent much of the afternoon enthralled with more electronics, giving Mema and P-Pa a break.

Come evening, they all watched Old Yeller. The movie was not as exciting as the conversation, Miriam asking more questions than there were answers, like why do cows have horns? That being a science question, P-Pa deferred to Mema. "Just because they do," Mema responded, proving once again the value of her biology degree from Baylor.

Miriam, our only non-Texan grandchild, couldn't wait for the outcome and asked older sister Hannah how it ends. "Old Yeller gets rabies," Hannah said. "What," interjected Carys, "Old Yeller gets babies?" One of the neat things about Old Yeller is the kids all pass through Mason, home of Old Yeller author Fred Gipson, on the way to and from San Angelo. That allows P-Pa to give them a little frontier Texas history. Hannah loves the movie so P-Pa is always glad to share it with her, though it loses some of its charm when our little Alaskan keeps asking questions galore.

"Are there still rabies?" she asked at the end of the movie.

"Yes," answered P-Pa.

"I don't ever want to go outside ever again," she concluded.

**Gulag P-Pa Diary/Day 5:**

D+4 and P-Pa is terrified. It all started innocently enough when he heard his daughter's voice in the front room. Only problem was, Melissa was in Round Rock. The Kemp Kids were apparently

FaceTiming with their mother. When they saw P-Pa peeking in on them, they kept talking to their momma. They didn't say anything to P-Pa when they ended their talk with Momma, but P-Pa could read their eyes, and he knew they had put him on notice. If he didn't do what they wanted, they could tell their momma. Worse yet, they could record him at one of his worser, less patient moments and make a viral buffoon of him on YouTube or Facebook! Now, P-Pa's on his best behavior, even saying excuse me every time he burps for fear he could wind up a social media laughing stock.

In fact, P-Pa didn't complain too much when all the girls gathered around him in his easy chair and began pounding on his legs. "You're going to kill me," P-Pa said. "We don't want to kill you," Miss Carys replied. "We just want to hurt you," clarified Miss Miriam.

Then at supper, P-Pa was having a conversation with Miriam and said, "You're crazy!" Miriam thought for a moment, then replied, "That's fair."

Supper also resulted in a world's first. Jackson informed Mema and P-Pa that his piece of pizza "was broken." Perplexed, Mema exchanged the defective piece for a whole piece. He took a bite out of it, and then informed everyone it was broken, too. P-Pa finally realized that when he took a bite of the pizza, he pulled some of the topping off of the dough, thus breaking it. P-Pa amputated the broken piece of pizza with his fork, and Jackson was satisfied that his pizza was fixed.

The day started off with a trip to the park, the younger three making the hike to the end of the block with Mema while the older two weren't interested. Neither Hannah nor Cora wanted to play in the wading pools for the annual Splash Day. It seems some of our babies are growing up!

For the evening movie, Mema picked Lady and the Tramp, a sentimental favorite of hers and P-Pa's as Lady was the first movie we saw after we got married. Little did we realize when we saw it in a Houston theater that no longer exists, that forty-five years later we would be watching it in San Angelo, Texas, with five grandchildren that resulted from our union, not only that but that we would be watching it on a DVD player in our home whenever we wanted to. It's amazing how much things have changed in that almost half a century.

In fact, a lot has changed in the last half day now that P-Pa has to scour social media to see if The Grands have posted any embarrassing videos of him! It's not Big Brother but Big Grandchildren that now scare P-Pa!

**Gulag P-Pa Diary/Day 6&7:**

Wheewww! P-Pa survived, barely. Yesterday he didn't Facebook as he was all tied up. To a tree in the backyard. It seems The Grands wanted quality time with Mema. Apparently, quality time means no P-Pa so the girls sent him outside where Jackson roped and hogtied him to a tree. Melissa arrived about supper time and saved P-Pa. He was so grateful for her rescuing him that he offered to load her SUV right then so they could return home immediately. Melissa said she needed a good night's sleep before heading home so P-Pa spent the night in the corner whimpering.

Consequently, P-Pa wasn't able to schedule the annual awards ceremony. He promised to mail the certificates to The Grands. By his reasoning, The Grands would have a surprise in the mail in a few days and P-Pa would be safer if he was out of range should they not like their awards.

Other than that, everything was perfect. After a week with a little boy, the Lewis girls were a little perplexed by the vigor of his activities. Speaking on behalf of the Kemp girls, Miss Cora explained little brothers this way: "Sometimes they're annoying; sometimes they're cute; sometimes they're crazy; and sometimes they're just nuts."

Another moment of wisdom came from Miss Miriam. She was helping Miss Carys get over her fears of the dark at bedtime. P-Pa came to assist Carys, who explained darkness frightened her, in spite of the night light. "I'm scared of the dark, too," Miriam explained, "but I just think happy thoughts and work through it."

Well, P-Pa's still trying to work through the aftermath of Camp Mema/Gulag P-Pa. He's sweeping up broken glass, shoring up load-bearing walls, calling insurance adjustors, looking for booby traps and smiling at all the fun memories of Camp Mema IV.

The Grands are growing, Hannah nearing her teen years and more cynical about P-Pa's shtick, a sign of her great intellect. Cora remains perhaps the most loving and caring young lady P-Pa's ever known. Miriam has grown into a courteous and respectful young girl who keeps P-Pa in stitches with her stated outlook on life and issues. Carys is an imaginative and inventive young girl with a thousand charming smiles. As for Jackson, he's annoying, cute, crazy and sometimes nuts, but he's as charming as they come, especially when he hangs his head on the way to timeout, and when he returns two minutes later to apologize!

As always, the real star and hero of Camp Mema is its namesake. Mema's even more amazing than the Amazing Five. Jackson made her final day by selecting the outfit she had sewn for his birthday as the outfit of choice for his return home. Instead of a bouquet of flowers this year, The Grands decided to videotape a "bouquet of thanks" for P-Pa to give to Mema. She deserved their kind impromptu words and thanks for a great time!

## Gulag P-Pa Diary/Epilogue:

Later in the fall, Mema and P-Pa got to keep the Kemp Grands. We had two days with them and had the opportunity to tape a movie to make up for the shelving of The Amazing Adventures of the Amazing Five during Camp Mema/Gulag P-Pa. The Grands named the movie The Super Disappearance of P-Pa, an action-hero, special-effects production. Guess who was the villain? Yep, P-Pa. Talk about typecasting! But, the Terrific Trio did actually make P-Pa disappear on screen.

At one point all three of the Grands wanted Mema and P-Pa to watch them ride their bicycles/tricycles. P-Pa asked Cora if he could ride her bicycle. "No," she responded instantly, "because I've already taken the training wheels off." Touché!

Pretty cocky for an eight-year-old that learned to ride her bicycle in ten minutes without training wheels when it took P-Pa ten weeks to accomplish the same thing at her age. Some would say that P-Pa is unbalanced, but in his defense, he learned to ride a bicycle in an era without polycarbonate shell princess helmets, knee pads, elbow protectors, gloves, knuckle pads, chest protectors, shin guards, mouth pieces and umbrella insurance policies.

Yep, kids back in his era were tough, especially when they learned, like P-Pa did, to ride bikes on hard-packed caliche roads or, when lucky, on asphalt instead of namby-pamby concrete sidewalks. Sure concrete is as inflexible as hard-packed caliche or asphalt, but with concrete you aren't picking debris such as rocks, gravel, tree limbs and insects out of ensuing cuts, scrapes, gashes, lacerations, etc.

In those days, young, aspiring bicyclists got their protective pads (Band-Aids, Ace Bandages, splints and casts) after the fall, not before. Learning to bicycle in the old days brought great bonding with Momma and even quality squealing time when she put iodine or tourniquets on wounds. Yep, the Good Ol' Days were grand, even for the unbalanced.

# CHAPTER NINE

*"But Jesus said, 'Let the little children come to me and do not hinder them, for to such belongs the kingdom of heaven.'"*
—Matthew 19:14 (English Standard Version)

Because of the heartache our parents had caused us with their perpetual hints and comments seeking grandchildren, Harriet and I vowed not to ask or pressure our kids about grandchildren once they married. I think we kept that promise, though we were eager to welcome the next generation into our family.

Scott and Celeste wed during the summer of 2001 in a beautiful ceremony in Houston. As parents of the groom, we hosted their rehearsal dinner at one of their favorite restaurants. For a wedding gift we gave them an intricate framed sampler that Harriet had cross-stitched that said "Welcome to the Lewis Home". That artwork began a tradition for Harriet, cross-stitching pieces for weddings and the births to follow. The rehearsal dinner, wedding and reception spawned such happy memories with family and friends.

Then our silent wait for grandchildren began.

Though tempted to offer subtle hints or suggestions, we held our tongues about our desires for a new generation of Lewises. Two and a half years passed and then the call came. Celeste was pregnant, and we would have our first grandchild by the next summer. We shared the news with our parents, all four of whom still lived, and they were delighted that they would see a great-grandchild.

Beyond that, Melissa and John were planning to wed in the summer after our first Grand's scheduled debut. Harriet was so excited she could hardly speak of the many blessings coming our way the next year. And, she got busy. She had a complex birth announcement to cross-stitch as well as a new sampler for the future Kemp household. When she would go shopping for groceries each week, she would buy something for the baby. It might be a rattle or baby wipes or a teething ring, but she would bring home something different each week and place in a basket to present to Celeste. Those were wonderful and innocent times of anticipation for a grandchild and another wedding.

Christmas of 2003 became one of the most joyful times in our lives as we looked forward to the New Year and the blessings it would bring. Our children joined us for Christmas, Scott with Celeste and Melissa with her fiancé John. My favorite photo of that celebration pictured Scott standing behind Celeste, patting the bulge in her stomach where the baby grew. Shortly after Christmas we learned that the ultrasound results had revealed a baby boy. Technology had erased the surprise in childbirth since our parenting days. I was excited to have a boy as our first grandchild and realized that Scott and Celeste were on the way to having what I now considered the perfect family, a son and a daughter. Now we no longer called our grandchild the baby, but we identified him as "Benjamin Scott," the name his parents selected. We shared the news and the name with everyone as we burst with pride and excitement awaiting the joys ahead us.

One Sunday morning after we learned our grandchild would be named Benjamin, I sat in a pew while Harriet visited with church friends. As I took my seat an elderly woman in front of me turned around and started visiting, just chatting as you do with strangers in church. As she spoke of things I have long since forgotten, she pointed to a church father entering the sanctuary with his Down's syndrome son. She said she so admired that single dad and how he cared for his challenged son despite the difficulties. Instantly, I grew uncomfortable. Why was she telling me this? Why now, just after we learned we would have a grandson? I didn't mention it when Harriet sat beside me, but it bothered me throughout the sermon and lingered with me in the following days. I couldn't shake that conversation. Was God trying to tell me something? That question bothered me for weeks.

In mid-February we received a sweet Valentine note from Celeste, looking forward to a planned visit from Harriet. She said in her card, "The Baby is growing and moving around a lot! We love you both and know Ben will love his grandparents! Love, Celeste and Scott." Inspired by the Valentine card, Harriet found and purchased a little six-inch tan teddy bear wearing a red sweater with a pink heart on the front. She added the Valentine bear to Benjamin's basket. She glowed with each new acquisition for our grandson, always eager to show me her latest gift. I still worried about the impromptu church conversation, though I didn't share my fears with Harriet. We enjoyed a wonderful Valentine, excited that our love and marriage was leading to a grandson in a few short months.

Then two days after Valentine's Day, another phone call came.

Early that Monday afternoon our receptionist buzzed my phone and told me my son was on the line. I bit my lip. This was unusual. Scott never called me at work. I got up and shut the door, then took the call. Panic permeated Scott's voice. "Dad," he said in words I would never forget, "we are going to lose Benjamin." My spirits deflated in an instant. How do you lessen your son's pain in such a moment when your heart is also broken? I had dealt with his scrapes, bruises and disappointments as a child, but how could I lessen the anguish of such devastating news in my adult son? I think I said, "I'm so sorry, Son," but I don't know for sure as my mind raced with so many unanswered questions.

As Scott caught his breath, he explained that Celeste had gone in for her regular checkup. After examining the latest ultrasound, the physician told her to call Scott and get him there at once. When he joined her, the doctor explained that the baby's brain had not developed, and he would not live outside the womb for long, if at all. Scott's voice held strong, either from shock or the courage he knew he must show for his devastated wife. I asked Scott what he needed me to do, and he said first to inform his mother and sister and then to notify his grandparents. He asked that we not call him or Celeste for a while until they dealt with the shock and decided how to move forward. I told him we would honor his request, and we would intensify our prayers for him and Celeste. And, for little Benjamin!

After he hung up, I took a deep breath and called Harriet's receptionist, telling her that a family emergency had arisen but for her not to tell Harriet as I would be coming over to take her home. I fought tears, grabbed my coat, opened my office door and told my staff I was leaving on a personal matter. Though Harriet's building was only two blocks away, it seemed to take forever to drive that distance, everything moving in slow motion. I reached her workplace and walked in. Surprised to see me, Harriet knew by the look on my face something was wrong. "What's the matter?" she asked. "Just get your things and let's go home," I told her. She gathered her belongings, imploring me not to wait until we got to the house, but to inform her once she notified her receptionist she was going for the day. I advised her I had informed the secretary and would tell her the news outside. "It's bad, isn't it?" she asked. I could only nod as she locked her door, and we started for the parking lot.

Outdoors I grabbed her hand and looked in her concerned eyes as we walked away from the building. "We're losing Benjamin," I announced. Sadness and tears replaced the worry in those eyes. I had never seen such sorrow upon her beautiful face. I helped her in her car, then followed her home. Inside we held each other, uncertain what to do. As powerful as our anguish was, we knew it paled to that faced by Scott and Celeste. As a parent nothing could be worse than burying a child, and now Scott and Celeste would have to bury a son they had yet to even hold. We felt helpless dealing with our own pain and powerless to ease the grief of our son and daughter-in-law.

After we composed ourselves and managed our emotions as best we could, we called our parents and informed them of the sad news. Then we phoned our daughter and told her she would not be have a nephew after all. The heartbreaking message devastated everyone. We ambled around the house stunned. In such a mood, we did inexplicable things. As our children moved toward marriage, Harriet began collecting Susan Lordi's Willow Tree sculptures depicting family scenes and members. I had even surprised her with a figurine called "Grandmother" after we learned of our daughter-in-law's pregnancy. We boxed up those figurines that night and put them away. It made little sense then or now, but the boxes and their contents remain on a shelf in the garage fifteen years after that terrible day. Later Harriet would buy two new Willow Tree collectibles and place them on the table at family gatherings. One represented an angel hugging a baby, and the other denoted an angel dancing with a child. It was her way of saying we had not forgotten Benjamin, and he remained a part of the family even if he was not here.

Later that sad day, Scott shared the horrible news by e-mail with his Sunday School class and those who had been so supportive during Celeste's pregnancy. He wrote, "Please distribute to the entire Sunday School class. Celeste and I both are in need of your prayers. Celeste and I both appreciate all of your prayers during our pregnancy. We just found out this afternoon that the Lord feels Benjamin is too precious to send into this world and will be calling him home early. Benjamin has a rare birth defect that prevented his brain from developing and he will be joining his savior as soon as he is born.

"As you can imagine, Celeste and I are both devastated by this decision and though we both understand that the Lord works all things for the good of those that believe in Him, we have some very painful decisions to make over the next several weeks.

"We are thankful that we have so many friends to help us through this difficult time and we ask that you keep us and our families in your prayers as we deal with this personal tragedy.

"Thank you for your prayers, Scott and Celeste."

Harriet and I bawled when we read the message he shared with us. We wanted to reach out and hug them, but that was impossible. We so wanted to call, but they had requested personal time to work through their emotions. Fortunately, Scott and Celeste phoned later in the evening. They were still in shock but composed, and we visited, trying to offer comfort, but feeling woefully inadequate in our efforts. It was hard enough to face this sorrow as a grandparent, much less as a parent, and our hearts ached for our son, his wife and their first son. We agreed that we would take a few days at the end of the week and visit them for a long weekend.

The six-and-a-half-hour drive to Houston seemed longer than usual. It was definitely sadder. How do you comfort a husband and wife, your son and daughter-in-law, that are losing their first child? We ate lunch at a fast-food hamburger place, and I remember watching a Down's syndrome employee cleaning tables. I thought back to that impromptu church conversation a few Sundays earlier and wondered whether this young man or Benjamin might have been better off and which circumstance I would have chosen if given the chance. But I didn't have that opportunity, and it was fruitless to ponder it. That was what was so frustrating as thoughts and prayers provided no answers, though we couldn't help offering them.

Under other circumstances on the drive to Houston, Harriet would've spent her passenger time working on the cross-stitch birth announcement, but that was now pointless. We talked about how to comfort our son and daughter-in-law, who carried the biggest burden, both physically and emotionally. We met them at their house where we had first seen them after their wedding. We hugged and wept, except for Scott, who stood so stoic during this period, and we shared our love for each other. And, for little Benjamin!

Our visit fell hardest on Celeste, who felt responsible for the loss, even though it was God's will, no matter how difficult it was for any of us to accept. We tried to reassure Celeste and Scott that better days were ahead, though we found it hard to believe that ourselves despite our own words. The most touching moments came when Celeste allowed us place our hands upon her stomach and feel our grandson kicking. He was alive in the womb, and we enjoyed his movement with tears in our eyes. That would be the closest we would ever come to holding our first grandson.

The saddest room in the house was little Benjamin's nursery. Celeste had decorated it so beautifully with an elegant white wooden crib and blue mattress cover with a trio of plush teddy bears, bunnies and lambs in two corners. On the shelves of a bookcase she had placed tiny baby books, a Mother Goose story book, a Humpty Dumpty, stuffed dolls, a yellow rubber duckie and a handful of other children's knickknacks. We were saddened that all of Celeste's love in decorating the room would never be showered on Benjamin as he would never sleep in the crib, play with the plush animals or sit in his mother's lap as she read him one of his books in the rocking chair.

In Houston Harriet bought a preemie bodysuit for Benjamin and began cross-stitching his name on the chest along with a blue teddy bear. Whether the color was intentional or not, I don't recall, but we all felt blue. Cross-stitching kept her occupied and focused while dealing with the inevitable. We visited, dined out and said our silent prayers, still living in disbelief at how sadly our lives had changed. Harriet and I had had a blessed time together, still having our parents in our fifties and never having an unanticipated loss of a family member. Until now! And it was so unexpected. And so devastating!

On Sunday we accompanied Scott and Celeste to their Sunday School class, then church. I don't know that I would have had the courage to attend church so soon after receiving such tragic news, but Scott stood stronger than the rest of us. We were encouraged by seeing how his church friends and family showered them with love and sympathy. Scott offered his thanks for everyone's support and said he couldn't explain divine will unless God had found Benjamin Scott Lewis too perfect for this world. With tears in her eyes, Harriet squeezed my hand as if to say we had raised a son better prepared than ourselves to address this tragedy. She was right. I tried to manage my emotions as well as Scott handled his. After church we said our goodbyes and Harriet presented Scott and Celeste with the onesie she had cross-stitched with Benjamin's name and the blue teddy bear on the front. I gave them the gift we planned to give Benjamin, the little teddy bear with the pink heart on his red sweater. Then we began the long journey home while Scott and Celeste dealt with the unpleasant options facing them in the coming days. They could carry the baby to full term, though the emotional toll on Celeste would be overwhelming. They could abort the baby, a decision none of us supported or wanted on our conscience. Or, obstetricians could induce labor after preparing Celeste's body for the early delivery.

Reaching home, we went to the store where Harriet had bought the little Valentine teddy bear and purchased the last remaining one, which we kept for ourselves as a reminder of our grandson. Then we waited for the birth and death of our first grandson. The following Wednesday Celeste and Scott went to the hospital to begin the process where the obstetrician could safely induce labor. Eleven days after we learned his time on earth would be short, Benjamin Scott Lewis was born at 12:48 p.m. Friday, February 27, 2004. As a preemie, he weighed one pound and fifteen ounces and measured twelve inches long. Though his brain was weak, his heart was strong and beating at birth. He fought for life long enough to be weighed and dressed in the onesie Harriet had cross-stitched for him. The nurse apologized to Benjamin's parents for getting smudges on the little outfit when she made the ink prints of his hands and feet. When Scott told us of the nurse's regrets, we just smiled that it was just like a little boy to dirty his new clothes. Wearing Harriet's onesie that she had stitched with so much love, little Benjamin died in his parents' arms after forty-two minutes of life.

Ever gracious even in a moment of great personal tragedy, Celeste later wrote a note to Harriet. "Thank you for the time and care you put into making Benjamin's cross-stitch for his hospital outfit. Benjamin looked precious in his light blue onesie with his Grandmamma's stitching. We love you, Scott and Celeste."

# CHAPTER TEN

## *YEAR FIVE*

**Gulag P-Pa Diary/Pre-Camp Post No. 1:**

Well, the dates have been set for the next edition of Camp Mema/Gulag P-Pa. The 2017 disaster is scheduled for Aug. 6-12 when The Grands begin their annual assault on our sanity and endurance. Yes, it's later this year because it takes longer for P-Pa to heal. His cracked ribs, broken femur (thigh bone), dislocated shoulder and all the bruises have almost healed after his tree-climbing lesson went awry last summer. On the positive side, he was able to follow up immediately with a science lesson on gravity, a health lesson on first aid and a math lesson on calling 9-1-1.

P-Pa is now able to walk, or at least limp, without the aid of crutches or without muttering to himself, "Why, why, why?" Fortunately, he married wisely as Mema's physical therapy skills have come in handy since camp last year, especially after he got out of traction, which rhymes with Jackson, which spells trouble and that's only the beginning of P-Pa's worries.

There's Hannah the Elder, who was outsmarting P-Pa long before she turned twelve. Next there's Cora the Cordial, who is sweet as sugar. Then there's Miriam the Miraculous, who comes up with hilarious answers to every question P-Pa poses. Next comes Carys the Impish, our little engineer who can solve nearly any practical problem. Finally, there's Jackson the Unpredictable, who is P-Pa's only ally, assuming the girls haven't won him over now that he can reason at age four.

After the flop of last year's superhero movie The Amazing Adventures of the Amazing Five, P-Pa is writing a mystery movie, The Cookie Thief, assuming the actors won't go on strike again this year. Hopefully, The Cookie Thief will be a success in the vein of Escape from Gulag P-Pa and The Good, The Bad and The Cutely, rather than the disaster that The Amazing Adventures of the Amazing Five turned into.

Concurrent with the start of this year's camp is the release of P-Pa's latest book *Gulags for Kids*, published by Phantom Press. The book is written under P-Pa's latest pseudonym of "The Condamant," Hannah's pronunciation of "Commandant" at the first Camp Mema/Gulag P-Pa. Though P-Pa was scheduled to go on a month-long book tour in August, Mema put an end to that, saying she didn't want him selling books and missing out on any of the fun at camp. Of course she didn't break any bones last year, either.

Details will follow in the coming weeks.

**Gulag P-Pa Diary/Pre-Camp Post No. 2:**

Life always seems to get more complicated when you try to do the right thing, such as put on Camp Mema/Gulag P-Pa for The Grands. You would think you could pull off the annual grandkid retreat without interference from the outside world. Wrong, wrong, wrong!

First, we got a certified letter from the Academy saying no future Gulag P-Pa movies would be considered for an Oscar unless he used an official Movie Clapper Board in the production. Consequently, P-Pa ordered one to make it official. He's sure The Grands will enjoy working the clapper and yelling "Action!"

Second, P-Pa received a cease-and-desist order from the World Court at The Hague, informing him that the Russian government had filed a complaint on his use of the term "Gulag" to describe the lesser half of summer camp. So, it appears the Russians have been doing more over the past few months than just costing Hillary her throne. Apparently, they have been spying on Camp Mema, or at least reading P-Pa's Facebook posts, even if he hasn't befriended any known Russians.

Fortunately, P-Pa and Mema had connections, of their own creation, so to speak. Since their son works for a little old company that our current Secretary of State ran before joining the federal government, they passed the word along about this predicament. Thanks to those connections, you might say Mema and P-Pa Trumped the Russians and created Fake News in the process.

While the media were reporting that the White House meeting of the President and the Secretary of State with Russian Foreign Minister Sergey Lavrov and Ambassador Sergey Kislyak was to discuss collaboration on various items of mutual interest, the real reason was to negotiate the preservation of Camp Mema/Gulag P-Pa, an American cultural institution. Barely had the Oval Office meeting ended, than the World Court informed P-Pa that the cease-and-desist order had been withdrawn with apologies.

Barely had the Camp Mema/Gulag P-Pa celebration ended than P-Pa noticed protesters marching down the street to their house. Apparently, the Society of Sanctimonious American Dogooders (SOSAD) had discovered Camp Mema/Gulag P-Pa.

They were protesting his use of "Gulag" as a cultural misappropriation. P-Pa was dumbfounded and asked for an explanation. They explained that since he had no Russian Facebook friends or any other known Russian connections, other than reading From Russia with Love as a teenager, he was not permitted to utilize the term.

P-Pa was even more perplexed trying to figure out if SOSAD was a Russian front group or a troop of well-intentioned but misguided college students or, for that matter, a gaggle of tenured liberal arts professors. He tried to negotiate with them, saying he would reverse the name and call it "Galug P-Pa," but they refused his compromise. SOSAD is all P-Pa could respond. Fortunately, The Grands are oblivious to the protests, and we hope to screen them from the weirdoes when camp arrives. So much for a tranquil 2017 Camp Mema/Gulag P-Pa!

To be continued

**Gulag P-Pa Diary/Pre-Camp Post No. 3:**

The travails continue for the 2017 edition of Camp Mema/Gulag P-Pa. P-Pa's defiance to the demands of the Society of Sanctimonious American Dogooders (SOSAD) that he quit using the word Gulag as a matter of crass cross-cultural insensitivity has infuriated them. Since P-Pa has not yet budged from his stand, SOSAD lawyers have initiated a campaign of legal intimidation against him, requesting an investigation by the Justice Department of possible Gulag P-Pa civil rights violations.

In their accusations, the Dogooders have claimed that Gulag P-Pa discriminates. P-Pa countered that the camp is open to all The Grands, both boy and girl, male and female. Wrong answer! By listing boy and male first, he was accused of being a cisgender male devoted to perpetuating the abuses of the patriarchy on all of society. P-Pa corrected his statement by reversing the order of the gender specific nouns as it didn't make any difference to him, but the Dogooders told him it was too late, his true colors and his discriminatory tendencies had already been shown.

So, he was perplexed, not only had he been accused of being discriminatory, but also of being a sissy as he was unfamiliar with the term of cisgender, which didn't appear in any of his dictionaries. True, he'd always been a book nerd but that's at least a rung or two above sissy on the male macho ladder. In search of a definition of cisgender, he turned to the Internet where all society's problems are not only identified but also magnified. He searched more than two hours for "sis" before discovering it was "cis."

A cisgender male, he discovered, is a male who identifies as a male. Well, duh! Complications grew as he continued to expose himself to gender science. Apparently, you can self-identify your gender, meaning it's not so much about what's below the waist but rather what's above the neck. Now it's less biologically determined than socially constructed. Cisgender, it seems, is the opposite of transgender.

Now, even P-Pa admits he's behind the times, not even owning an ATM card, for instance. When he needs cash, P-Pa acquires it the old-fashioned way—he holds up a convenience store. He is so far behind the times that he has long subscribed to the Hot Dog Theory of sexuality—you're either a bun or a wiener. Now, so it seems, there's a Not Dog Theory as well! Not only that, some in society expect children to make complex identity decisions that even some adults are ill-equipped to make for themselves.

The shame of it all is that the window of innocence for The Grands is so much smaller today than it was in P-Pa's youth and even in the childhood of his son and daughter. For today's little girls, playing princess is no longer an innocent game, but rather submission to the patriarchy. As for little boys today, they are less Prince Charming and more Prince Harming. SOSAD. Even so, Camp Mema/Gulag P-Pa will survive. Somehow!

**Gulag P-Pa Diary/Pre-Camp Post No. 4:**

In today's polarized society, sometimes it's just easier to give in than to fight organizations like the Society of Sanctimonious American Dogooders (SOSAD) as they try to shut down an American institution like Camp Mema/Gulag P-Pa. It has been an eye-opening experience for P-Pa, who has been studying the cis and trans issues and their implications for the future as a result of SOSAD's legal threats against Gulag P-Pa.

After careful consideration, P-Pa has come to consider the cis and trans philosophy as the answer to all personal problems. To be honest, P-Pa has been battling personal demons for years in the Battle of the Bulge, to use a WWII metaphor, or in a more indelicate WWI metaphor, the Battle of Gutland. Following his recent studies, he has realized he has been fighting the wrong enemy. It's not himself that's the problem, it's everybody else.

So, P-Pa has decided to come out of the pantry, so to speak, and identify himself as Trans-Skinny. Yep, he feels better already. From now on when he goes to the doctor and the scale reads 471, he's gonna see it as 174 and challenge the scale's calibration because it does not match his self-image. Next time he visits a clothier and is told his waist size measures sixty-three, he's gonna see it as a svelte thirty-six, which is more in line with his newfound Trans-Skinny self-identity.

Just to make sure that health professionals and clothing sales representatives respect his newfound skinny-idenny, he's taking his lawyer with him to sue their pants off if they disagree. Bottom line, the science doesn't matter, just P-Pa's self-image. This strategy has already paid benefits as P-Pa's lawyer informed SOSAD's legal team that he was filing a complaint on P-Pa's behalf with the Department of Justice, claiming SOSAD is discriminating against the nation's first openly Trans-Skinny male.

P-Pa is pleased to announce that SOSAD subsequently backed down from trying to shutter Gulag P-Pa and even offered to sponsor Camp Mema/ Gulag P-Pa since he is now an oppressed minority. He has rejected the sponsorship offer because he is against any organization that tries to take the fun out of traditional family life. In fact, he'd rather deal with the Russians, though it is ironic that by utilizing the SOSAD narrative P-Pa was able to defeat them as well as improve his own self-image.

Now that all of that is resolved, he's ready for Camp Mema/Gulag P-Pa to begin so he can help The Grands develop their own positive self-images. Besides that, he can't wait for the unified birthday party and the accompanying cake and ice cream as the calories no longer matter. So Glad!

**Gulag P-Pa Diary/Pre-Camp Post No. 5:**

For fans of the annual "Gulag P-Pa Diaries," it's just a month until Camp Mema/Gulag P-Pa returns. P-Pa is busily working on the script for The Cookie Thief, the latest Gulag P-Pa Production. To be honest, P-Pa needs a hit after the disastrous failure of last year's The Amazing Adventures of the Amazing Five due to temperamental actors and costly special effects.

Sure, Escape from Gulag P-Pa was a hit in 2014 and The Good, The Bad and The Cutely was a western blockbuster in 2015, but last year's superhero movie was a flop and you're only as good as your last production in LaLaLand. So, P-Pa needs a hit or he'll lack the Hollywood credibility he needs to finance a major production.

His failure, however, has not seemed to diminish The Grands' enthusiasm for camp as exhibited by the follow text exchange this afternoon between Miss Cora and Mema:

> *CORA: This is Cora do you see this?*
> *MEMA: Yes, are you looking forward to Camp Mema?*
> *CORA: Oh yah!*
> *MEMA: P-Pa and I are planning lots of fun things to do.*
> *CORA: Great!*
> *MEMA: What is your favorite thing about camp?*
> *CORA: The movies!*
> *MEMA: We are having fun planning the mystery movie for this year. Who do you think should be the cookie thief?*
> *CORA: P-Pa! P-Pa! P- Pa!*
> *MEMA: Why should he be the bad guy every time?*
> *CORA: Because he's good at it! You're not upset, are you?*
> *MEMA: No way. I think you are right!*
> *CORA: Great!*

Well, it may be great for everyone else, but not for P-Pa. He's tired of playing the heavy! It's obvious he's been typecast, which makes it more difficult for him to break out into leading man roles. But at least he's the scriptwriter, director and producer, so he will have a hand in the outcome.

To be continued.

### Gulag P-Pa Diary/Pre-Camp Post No. 6:

It's that time of the year when the roar of the sewing machine from the front room sounds like a Corliss steam engine, patented in 1849. Yep, Mema is sewing the summer outfits for The Grands. She bought the material in May, cut out the patterns in

June but didn't begin sewing until last week. It's times like these P-Pa is grateful for the Industrial Revolution. Without it she would have had to have started the spinning, weaving and sewing in 1999!

Mema sews The Grands a winter and summer outfit apiece, presenting them at Christmas and at Camp Mema/Gulag P-Pa when we celebrate our unified birthday party (UBP). There are several advantages to celebrating the birthdays at the same time, not the least of which is that P-Pa doesn't have to remember all the dates as he has never been real good with numbers. On top of that, there are economies of scale, one party, one cake (or batch of cupcakes), one mess to clean up (two if P-Pa gets a slice of cake) and no spirited discussions (euphemism for arguments) over who gets to play with what as everyone has a new toy or two of her/his own.

A UBP, however, can create unforeseen problems like the year when Miss Carys was devastated her birthday card did not come in the purple (her favorite color) envelope that went to one of her cousins. P-Pa's solution was to dispense with giving birthday cards forever, but Mema said it was easy to just get Miss Carys a purple card. Unfortunately, P-Pa's not too good with colors, either. Just ask Miss Hannah about that.

While Mema has been sewing to take her mind off the impending eight-day disaster, P-Pa has been trying to come up with a new way to prepare himself for approaching doom. In the past he's tried psychiatry, sedatives, hypnotism, electrotherapy, new age music and aroma therapy with unsatisfactory results. This year, however, he's taken up yoga. Well, to be more precise, it's half-yoga. He's got the mental part down, able to concentrate and take his mind off things. However, it's the physical part that's killing him when he tries to get into the proper meditative poses. The Easy Pose or Sukhasana (which is Sanskrit for "sucker") ain't that easy and the Seated Spinal Twist Pose or Bharadvajasana (which is Sanskrit for "pretzel") is a killer. In fact, there's more snap, crackle and pop when P-Pa attempts one of those poses than if a train car-load of Rice Krispies collided with a tanker truck load of milk. All the noise (not to mention the pain) sort of detracts from his mental concentration. On the positive side, he's mastered the Corpse Pose or Savansana (Sanskrit for "I can't get up), which for obvious reasons is saved as the last pose of a yoga routine.

Fortunately, P-Pa married a physical therapist to help him get up from the floor. Unfortunately, he's on his own until she finishes sewing.

### Gulag P-Pa Diary/Pre-Camp Post No. 7:

The noise has abated because the sewing is done for Camp Mema. Yep, Mema finished up the outfits this evening, and they look absolutely adorable, as always. Now all she has to do is wrap them, which will take a half hour, and clean up the sewing room, which may take forty days and forty nights. There's threads and fabric and pins and buttons and ribbon and seam-binding and elastic and tissue paper patterns and lace or pieces of those materials scattered everywhere. Mema leaves a messy battlefield, which is to be expected from great artisans.

As for P-Pa, he finished the script for The Cookie Thief but ended it so the kids won't know the actual identity of the culprit until they watch the movie, assuming they follow the script, which is about as likely as Democrats and Republicans agreeing on anything. As is traditional with screenplays or playscripts, writers give a brief description of each new character entering the scene. Here's how P-Pa makes his first appearance as cookies are being moved from the cookie sheet to the cooling rack: "As kids back out of scene, svelte, handsome, debonair, charming P-Pa walks up in a plaid shirt and reaches for a cookie. Mema slaps the top of his hand with the spatula." After reading that introduction, Mema said, "I thought this was supposed to be a mystery, not a comedy or science fiction." Ouch!

That wasn't the only complaint. After distributing the script to The Grands so they could begin to work on their lines, P-Pa received a phone call from one of the actresses. Miss Miriam complained that her lines were too mean to P-Pa and she wanted to be a nice girl! So out went her line "Sing Sing for the Cookie Thief" and in went the line "But what if he's innocent?" The line "I've seen babies eat and not make as big a mess as P-Pa" was superseded by "Babies make a bigger mess than P-Pa, a lot bigger." The grandfather in P-Pa was touched that Miriam was concerned how he would feel about those lines, but the writer in P-Pa was devastated that a seven-year-old was changing his words. Untouched were such classic lines as:

*CORA: Why, P-Pa, why? (Spoken plaintively)*
*JACKSON: We need more boys around here! (Spoken hopefully)*
*HANNAH: Together, we're smarter than any detective that ever lived, including*
*Sherlock Holmes. (Spoken intelligently)*
*CARYS: His (the cookie thief's) name begins with P and ends with awe! (Spoken cleverly)*

With lines like that, the film is certain to get an invitation to the Cannes Film Festival, though it is unlikely P-Pa will be able to attend next May because it conflicts with the date of Mema's fiftieth high school reunion. He assumes, however, he can accept in absentia the Palme d'Or du court métrage (Best Short Film); Prix de la mise en scène (Best Director); and Prix du scénario (Best Screenplay) awards.

**Gulag P-Pa Diary/Pre-Camp Post No. 8:**

The Grands have discerning tastes and therein lies the problem: Menus! Yep, today was grocery shopping day and Mema went to the bank to take out the annual loan to cover the food costs for Camp Mema while P-Pa rented a refrigerated eighteen-wheeler to bring all the groceries home and keep the investment fresh and eatable.

So, here's the culinary minefield Mema must cross: We have one grandchild who is lactose intolerant. Okay, we can deal with that. Another doesn't like any food that has the letter "B" in its name, peanut butter being the only exception. Anything colored green is off the table, so to speak, for another one. Then we have one that won't eat anything at all and must be fed intravenously. One doesn't like Pizza, can you believe that? Another won't eat a hamburger if it has sesame seeds on the bun. Several don't like crusts on bread. Vegetables present their own set of problems and grimaces from several! And to top it off, just because The Grands would eat a dish last year, doesn't mean they'll eat it this year. The list goes on.

One of the major expenses of grocery day is rental of a pricey supercomputer to program all the permutations and come up with menus that will please such a finicky clientele. But that's just like Mema, always trying to please the little ones. By contrast, P-Pa is more matter of fact about the issue, believing in gruel and unusual punishment: eat it or go to bed. Of course, that manner of parenting is out of style these days, so P-Pa has to be careful that if he resorts to such primitive methods of grandparenting, that none of The Grands are filming him with their iPads, iPhones or iCameras so he won't become a YouTube sensation and a Child Protective Services client. Yep, life was much simpler in the good old days when there was no video evidence to counter an alibi.

For all the fun of Camp Mema, there's also a dark side in that Mema has more leverage over P-Pa for the next dozen days. If she wants something done, she just tells him to handle it. If he resists, she threatens to make reservations at a day spa for a couple days during Camp. P-Pa gets right on it because he can't deal with fixing their meals, as the complaints are too many and too vociferous. Time to take out the trash. P-Pa's on it. The rooms need vacuuming. Done. One typical exchange:

*MEMA: The gutters need cleaning.*
*P-PA: We don't have gutters.*
*MEMA: (Silence!)*
*P-PA: Okay, I'll get them installed and cleaned by supper.*

Needless to say, the stress is overwhelming, not only in installing gutters but also in awaiting the invasion of The Grands. When P-Pa's not doing menial labors at Mema's instruction, he splits his time between doing half yoga for stress relief and trying to get up from the floor afterwards for exercise.

**Gulag P-Pa Diary/Pre-Camp Post No. 9:**

The statistics (and the kitchen counter) tell it all: four dozen cookies, 45 cupcakes, two dozen muffins, just a sampling of the rations to be dispensed over the coming days as Camp Mema begins tomorrow evening when the Fab Five arrive. The most important of the pastries are, of course, the cookies which are props in the Gulag P-Pa production of The Cookie Thief. The second unit begins shooting tomorrow. For those of you unfamiliar with movie production, the second unit films shots and sequences without the primary stars to expedite production. So, we'll have some shots in the can, so to speak, before the big stars arrive.

The movie production generally seems to be a hit, but it gets more challenging to keep the Lewis/Kemp Cabal occupied with interesting activities as they grow each year and their interests change. In the past, we've had Splash Day, Creative Arts Day, Dinosaur Day, Horse Day, Pummel P-Pa Day (not a pretty sight), Baking Day and Child Labor Day (P-Pa's favorite). This year, our Senior Inmate, Miss Hannah, has requested that she be allowed to organize and teach Harry Potter Day.

So in addition to helping Mema with the cooking (actually he just cleans up the messes and washes the dishes) and with setting up the western town (done), he's had to develop a primer on Harry Potter. Thus, P-Pa has learned that Hogwarts is not a porcine malady requiring veterinary care, but rather a University of Arkansas extension campus located in the British Isles to teach kids magic. UofA at Hogwarts has four fraternities: Gryffindor dedicated to courage and chivalry; Hufflepuff committed to boring hard work and patience; Slytherin specializing in cunning and sneakiness; and Delta Tau Chi, dedicated to partying and tormenting Hogwarts Dean Vernon Wormer. "Woooo! Pig Sooie!"

P-Pa has also learned that a Muggle is a person who lacks magical ability. Mema, for instance, is a Muggle, outside the kitchen at least. P-Pa is an Unmuggle as he has performed tricks for The Grands like making a dollar float in the air (though it lost some of its mystery when our Senior Inmate announced "I can see the string!"). P-Pa could also make a hankie disappear (until Miss Carys found the false fingertip he forgot to hide and figured out the trick). Fortunately, he still qualifies as an Unmuggle since The Grands have not been able to explain his Magic Coloring Book. This year he's also got a magic ball that he can make disappear to maintain his Unmuggle certification. But he's got a lot of work to do to increase his Harry Potter literacy before Miss Hannah arrives.

In honor of Harry Potter this year, we thought we would give each Grand a magical name. So they are: Bookworm (Hannah), Songbird (Cora), Wordstar (Miriam), Saucepot (Carys) and Trainwreck (you guessed it, Jackson). Mema still carries the magical name Love Apron, which Miss Miriam bestowed on her two years ago. P-Pa is now Cookie Monster.

**Gulag P-Pa Diary/Day 1:**

D-Day is here even though The Grands aren't. And, the day has already gotten off to a HORRIBLE start. P-Pa was minding his own business this morning when he got an unexpected e-mail from Bookworm, aka Miss Hannah, with the Subject Line: "The Cookie Thief." P-Pa gulped. Here came more script changes, which was true, but it was worse than that. Not only does Bookworm want some script changes, she's also demanding producer credit because of...well read for yourself what Bookworm wrote:

*"I found out who the cookie thief is. It's Mema right? Mema planted the evidence in P-Pa's pocket so it would look like P-Pa did it. But I won't tell anyone else; your secret is safe with me. By the way, instead of getting my Harry Potter book can I get my wand/Gryffindor robes? Also can I say Azkaban instead of prison (another Harry Potter reference) in 'You'll look good in prison behind bars.' And I'm still demanding producer credit. Tata! – Hannah"*

Yep, she figured it out that Mema did it. Reading between the lines, P-Pa believes he's being blackmailed. If Bookworm doesn't get producer credit, she can spill the beans to the other Grands and ruin the production. Boy is Hollywood a tough business. P-Pa thinks Bookworm is a little stinker, but a smart one at that!

And, it was ironic that Bookworm sent her e-mail, just minutes before P-Pa and Mema started the second unit filming. This afternoon he starts editing the movie, though the excitement has been diminished by his Senior Grand's brilliance. Apparently, Bookworm takes after Mema who likes not only to watch mysteries but also to solve them. However, Bookworm is the first in our family ever to solve a mystery before it was even filmed.

The adventure continues. Tata!

**Gulag P-Pa Diary/Day 2, Part 1:**

A Category 5 hurricane hit Mema and P-Pa last night when The Grands arrived. A quiet, peaceful night disrupted by the howling winds of vigorous young lungs as they first found the foam swords and began swashbuckling. When P-Pa volunteered to join the fray, Miss Carys or Saucepot said, "P-Pa needs two swords because he's not that good!"

A house that was immaculate, quickly became a wreck with debris strewn everywhere and little body parts scattered all over the dining room table as The Grands played with all the little western town Playmobil folks. Saucepot, stuffed nine bad guys in a jail cell meant for two. So much for jail standards!

P-Pa and Mr. Jackson share a room. As has become custom, P-Pa reads Jackson a story or, in this case, a chapter from a book as he's now old enough for long-form stories. When he finished the chapter, P-Pa asked Jackson if he liked Camp Mema. Trainwreck nodded and said "I like Camp Mema!" After a short pause, "And Camp P-Pa!" Another pause, "And Camp Yia Yia!" A final pause, "And Camp Dado." This boy knows how to cover all his grandparental bases. When P-Pa told him it was "time to lie down," he replied, "At our house we say lay down!" Apparently Trainwreck is also a grammarian!

It was midnight before everyone got to bed so Mema and P-Pa were expecting the little ones to sleep late this morning. No such luck. All were up by 7 a.m. in time to bid Scott and Celeste goodbye for a little vacation. P-Pa fell to his knees, grabbing them by the legs, begging "Please don't go, please stay for the sake of all humanity." When he couldn't convince them to stay, P-Pa took them to the local nursing home to visit his mother where she now lives. As P-Pa was leaving, Mema fell to her knees, grabbing him by the legs, crying "Please don't go, please stay for the sake of all humanity," and making P-Pa promise he would return. But he forgot his sunshades and stepped back in the house to fetch them. The Grands asked why he was back so soon. P-Pa replied, "I just couldn't leave my children." He departed, then Miriam said, "We're not his children." Cora answered, "Yes, we are. We are his grandchildren." Wordstar then replied, "But we're not his friends." Songbird answered, "We're definitely not his friends."

As a prerequisite for opening birthday presents that afternoon, all of The Grands had to take one bite of everything at lunch: ham, parmesan-baked zucchini and mac and cheese. Bookworm and Wordstar resisted. P-Pa shamed Bookworm that she could not be considered a member of the house of Gryffindor, as she claimed, because members of this Harry Potter fraternity were brave and courageous, willing to stand up against all odds.

Bookworm gave into the pressure and actually ate a half-bite. P-Pa had finally discovered something Harry Potter was good for.

**Gulag P-Pa Diary/Day 2, Part 2:**

After Bookworm survived a half-bite of zucchini, all the dietary pressure fell on the tiny shoulders of Miss Miriam. Everyone had to eat a bite of zucchini if anyone was to open birthday presents, so P-Pa ordained. The pressure was overwhelming, Wordstar's sister and cousins pleading with her to eat a little bite or pretend it was birthday cake/ice cream or think she was a cute monster eating the biggest and meanest monster of all—P-Pa.

Then came the negotiations, something Wordstar excels at, began. First, she had to know if she had to swallow it if she didn't like it. No! Second, did she have to chew it up? No. Third, did she even have to bite it once? No, just taste it. Fourth, if it touched her tongue, would that be considered tasting it. "Yes," responded a defeated P-Pa. Miss Miriam then picked up her sliver of zucchini, touched it to her tongue, grimaced at the taste, threw it back on her plate, saved the birthday party and made the other Grands eternally grateful. It was a win-win-win. P-Pa got her to crawl outside the narrow culinary cubicle of her life. The Grands got to have a birthday party with all the trimmings. And Wordstar was scarred for life after her tongue's millisecond brush with zucchini.

The birthday party was a hit with Miss Cora repeating, "This is overwhelming" several times. Mema's outfits were adored. Miss Carys and Miss Miriam were so excited that they got dresses of the same design and material. "We're twins," Miss Carys cried. "I'm gonna wear this every day," Miss Miriam informed everyone. Cora said, "I love it," of her new dress. Mema made Hannah a set of leggings, shirt and lace jacket, more attuned to Middle School Society than to the Elementary School Set. She liked it all, especially the kimono. Mema's heart swelled with pride at the reactions, even from Jackson.

Trainwreck, who's not as into clothes as much as The Girl Grands, was excited about his outfit, especially with whales and boats on the pattern. Jackson had the line of the day for the regular birthday gifts when he opened his "Mickey Mouse Clubhouse Choo Choo Train" LEGO set. When he saw what it was, the four-year-old shouted, "I've wanted this all my life!" That and a Holstein cow costume (He requested it!) were his favorite gifts.

After the birthday party, though, things though fell apart. Two unknown, long-legged monsters attacked the western town and then after demolishing it, sat down and rested against the wall of the bank! Worst and most embarrassing of all, Jackson just up and disappeared. P-Pa and Mema searched for hours and couldn't find him, though they did discover a Holstein calf wandering about the house in a new birthday gift. Trainwreck was a little too frisky to be considered for a Chick-fil-A ad. However, when he put the outfit on, he said, "I want to wear this forever!" so he may grow into the role.

**Gulag P-Pa Diary/Day 3:**

Production has begun on The Cookie Thief and the taping is going fairly well with Miss Cora helping everyone with their lines and coaching them on the acting. Songbird's the only one that knows all her lines and even coaches P-Pa on his. The Grands did thirty-two different takes during the afternoon and have about a fourth of the taping done. Pressure's on P-Pa.

Though the taping is going well, things are

touchy behind the scenes as Bookworm is threatening to identify the cookie thief to other cast members unless she gets producer credit. P-Pa has countered that if she spills the beans, she will get no credit. Bookworm, under the counsel of her father, is demanding ten percent of the gross for her fee. P-Pa is offering twenty percent of the net. At one point in the negotiations, Bookworm leaned over to her father and said, "I don't even know what those terms mean." That's why P-Pa postponed the final agreement until her father left. Legal teams for both P-Pa and Bookworm are negotiating.

Everyone started the day by visiting P-Pa's mom in the nursing home with each of The Grands wearing their new Made-by-Mema outfits. The kids enjoyed seeing Gamma and watching from her window the birds and squirrels at her bird feeder. The Grands were exuberant, however, so much so that a staff member knocked on the door to see if everything was okay. P-Pa drove Carys and Miriam to the nursing home while Mema took Hannah, Cora and Jackson in her car. Overheard conversation in the back seat of P-Pa's car:

*CARYS: Do you speak Spanish?*
*MIRIAM: Yeah, I know all the words, I just don't know their meaning.*

Mema last night had to tell Misses Miriam and Carys, who share the front bedroom, that it was 10 p.m. and everyone was supposed to be in bed and quiet. Responded Miriam, "Well, why aren't you in bed, then?" Mema had to modify her statement that all kids were supposed to be in bed.

Wordstar also put P-Pa in his place the next meal after the Zucchini incident when he told Mema that he wasn't fond of the new chips she served for supper. The zucchini which touched her tongue apparently left a tart taste because she said, "Don't be picky, P-Pa. That's my thing!" Touché!

To help Mema with her menu choices that will keep the inmates satisfied without leaving tart tongues that put him in his place, P-Pa has developed the FICKLE Scale, or Food Index of Children's Known Likeable Eats. The F Scale, as it is now known in child psychology circles, rates food based on likeability factors from 0 (the lowest) to 100 (the highest). Results so far: Chocolate Chip Muffins, 100; Sugar Cookies, 96; Macaroni and Cheese, 84; Ham, 81; Rolls, 80; Bread (crustless), 78; Bread (regular), 42; Carrots, 33; Roast, 30; Cod Liver Oil, 15; Mashed Potatoes, 14; Green Beans, 13; Zucchini, 11; and Cole Slaw, 0.

**Gulag P-Pa Diary/Day 4:**

Last night we drew dates for child of the day and Miss Miriam drew Monday so we celebrated Miriam's Magical Monday, playing a game of "Elements" about earth, fire and rainbows. It was beyond P-Pa's comprehension, though he did awe the four little ones by making a magic ball disappear. With a little help Miss Hannah figured out the trick and has volunteered to do it tomorrow. In our Little Eskimo's honor, we raised the Alaska flag on our flagpole in celebration of the state of her birth.

The magical miracle of the day was performed by the Girl of the Day when Wordstar held one of P-Pa's famous baked beans against her tongue for five seconds to determine if she liked it. She didn't! Big surprise! P-Pa's legumes only earned a 42 on the FICKLE Scale. He is fixated on finding another food that will score an F-Scale 100 and has asked Mema to look for some chocolate chip mashed potato recipes. He got mixed reactions when he suggested it to The Grands!

Unfortunately, we almost lost Bookworm at dinner tonight as she nearly choked on words.

Miss Cora said, "I like everything about P-Pa." She paused then, as Hannah was taking a drink, said, "That's called sarcasm!" Bookworm almost lost it, spewing her drink, but she said it was worth it for the line of the night.

When P-Pa labeled himself as cool, all the kids agreed, and then P-Pa knew something was amiss, especially when the girls started giggling. Apparently, cool has a different meaning these days among the younger set: Constipated, Overrated Old Lady.

Filming on The Cookie Thief has gone well and is about half done, though the editing is slow going. We finished the pivotal scene today when The Grands discover the cookies are missing. Their impromptu, unscripted reactions have definitely put The Cookie Thief in contention for Oscar consideration.

Best description to date of a Camp Mema inmate came from Bookworm's and Wordstar's Mom, who called Jackson "a minority in a sorority." But the little fellow's done quite well among the non-Cools of Camp Mema, including chasing the girls as the "Jackson Monster". Trainwreck is also a LEGO innovator, coming up with amazing inventions like the front-loader airplane and an actual flying boat. Two years ago, his innovations earned him the title of "the Picasso of Refrigerator Magnets" as documented in my favorite photo of him ever. We have added "LEGO Leonardo" to his artistic titles.

There was a lot of swashbuckling today and, surprisingly, the littlest girl, Carys, was the most frequent sword-fighting champion, out-fencing even her oldest cousin, but that's to be expected from Saucepot, who's got a huge spirit in a small frame behind an impish smile! On top of that, she's a food fiend, willing to try anything once, making her decision whether she likes it after she has tasted it rather than making her mind up in advance.

Tomorrow we celebrate Miss Cora, or Songbird!

**Gulag P-Pa Diary/Day 5:**

Today was an intense day of taping to finish up The Cookie Thief. Cora and Hannah both did camerawork and handled the awesome responsibility flawlessly, though it means P-Pa will have to give them credits. Though the final edits (and credits, the most controversial part of this movie) remain to be done, the stars learned the shocking identity of the cookie thief, who, as it turns out, was Mema! The Grands were stunned that sweet, loving, compassionate Mema was taking cookies from their mouths and trying to set up P-Pa. Of course it didn't help P-Pa one bit as Hannah had figured it out and insisted that P-Pa should go to prison instead. After all, he doesn't cook their meals, even if they don't eat them.

In fact, when we were taping the climax and The Grands realized it was Mema, the Cora-Miriam-Carys trio started chanting, "P-Pa did it anyway." Miriam told Mema, "How could you, but I love you anyway?" P-Pa never gets such a break, but he's no longer typecast, even if he is in cinema prison for a crime he didn't commit! One of the great impromptu moments in cinema history occurred when Jackson, rather than saying his line, squatted down and licked the leg of the kitchen table. P-Pa thought he was ahead of Jackson for the Prix D'Interprétation Masculine for best actor at the Cannes Film Festival, but has now conceded he no longer stands a chance after that scene. How can you compete with such genius? Of course, when the scene was over, we took him to get a tetanus shot.

Cora was Girl of the Day so we celebrated with three of her favorite meals: biscuits for breakfast; Javanese Dinner (rice, boiled chicken and chow mein noodles) for lunch; and cheese pizza for supper. F-Scale Ratings: biscuits, 92; rice, 76; boiled chicken, 80; CM noodles, 72; and green beans, 13. She decided she wanted her treat to be a trip to the park. We had a great walk of a quarter mile, then tried out all the playground equipment. The Kemp Kids are like mountain goats, climbing on everything as high as they can go. Trainwreck gave us some scares, but Songbird and Saucepot are sure-footed little climbers.

Then when everyone returned we barely averted a major disaster at bath time. When the two youngest girls got out of the tub, the water didn't drain and the commode backed up. P-Pa called three plumbers and the Environmental Protection Agency for assistance. The plumbers arrived within an hour and snaked out the drain, clearing it of four years of accumulation from Camp Mema/Gulag P-Pa. When all was said and done, they extracted from the drain two alphabet blocks, five marbles, a Nerf football, a Raggedy Ann, a beach ball, 47 Princess LEGO pieces, P-Pa's missing lens cap, four tunneling tools, three floor puzzle pieces, a teapot and a plastic donut. The drain works great now.

Tomorrow is Jackson's Day. We have alerted Civil Defense.

### Gulag P-Pa Diary/Day 6:

Jackson was Boy of the Day and opted to raise the flag with all the stars on it on the flagpole and to choose Splash Day as the special event for his special moment. P-Pa filled up the two wading pools and furnished them with water toys and water guns. Miriam and Carys joined Mr. Jackson in the water while Bookworm and Songbird did more mature things, like read or iPad.

Miriam and Carys blasted P-Pa with water guns and water balloons, then got some beach buckets and began to douse him with water. Jackson joined them until P-Pa put a sprayer on the water hose to fight back. Jackson yelled, "Now I'm on your team, P-Pa," and raced over to turn the faucet on for P-Pa. For his movie of the day, he chose *The LEGO Movie* after spending a large part of the day building LEGO monstrosities right in the middle of the family room.

Hannah has found her a niche in the living room where she can read without being in the middle of the race track that goes from the living room then down the entryway and across the family room and through the kitchen before entering the dining alcove and the living room again. That impromptu race track remains one of the most dangerous places in Texas for the barefooted. LEGO pieces, plastic horses, blocks and assorted books are just some of the hazards, P-Pa and Mema must traverse just to get around.

Mema made a chocolate chip cookie pizza, which scored a perfect 100 on the F-Scale. Tacos had a 66 rating while lettuce came in at 19 and tomatoes crashed at an imperfect 0.

P-Pa spent most of the day editing *The Cookie Thief,* overcoming a few technical issues and pulling his hair out at others. The movie comes in at 16 minutes with 100 different shots or edits. Credits run three hours and seven minutes and, yes, Hannah, got producer credit and the biggest name on the screen, except for the voluptuous Mema van Doren, who got featured billing for her performance in the title role.

Hannah did a great job of keeping the thief's identity secret. After P-Pa edited in the second unit footage, the four younger ones watched the security camera footage of a torso wearing P-Pa's shirt and a pair of gloves, which Mema planted on him. As the camera pulls away from the arms and torso, it reveals Mema's face. Before the big reveal, though, Miriam, was pretty sharp in watching the security video and observing that P-Pa was really skinny in the replay. Cora and Carys assured her that sometimes cameras distort things. Throughout the filming Cora was the best prepared of all the young actors, pretty much knowing all the lines of all the characters and being able to help everyone.

Tomorrow is the day P-Pa has been dreading as Hannah is Girl of the Day, and he expects a forced feeding of Harry Potter lore.

**Gulag P-Pa Diary/Day 7:**

What a day, starting with Girl of the Day Hannah indoctrinating the inmates and guards with a primer on Harry Potterdork, including a dramatic reading of the so-called "ferret scene". It seems the wizarding world of Mr. Potterdork is a parallel universe accessible only to wizards and magical beings, certainly not Muggles or even Unmuggles!

As P-Pa understands it, the major characters are Harry Potterdork, the bespectacled hero with a lightning bolt scar; Ginny Weasleydork, Potterdork's love interest; Dumbledork, Hogwarts' headmaster; Lord Voldedork, evil wizard; Fangdork, dog; and Fluffydork, three-headed dog. Hogwarts is divided into four fraternities: Gryffindorks with a lion mascot and scarlet and gold colors; Huffledorks with a badger mascot and yellow and black colors; Ravendorks with an eagle mascot and blue and bronze colors; and Slytherdorks with a serpent mascot and green and silver colors. According to Bookworm, she and Carys are Gryffindork. Huffledorks are Cora, Miriam and Mema. Jackson is a Ravendork. P-Pa is a Slytherdork. As you can see, P-Pa has identified a consistent dork theme in Harry Potterdorkdom and thinks he may have found a surefire cure for insomnia, at least for Boomers!

Mema started off the day informing P-Pa she needed to go to the grocery store to buy more syrup, frozen waffles and chocolate chips. It seems a boxcar full of chocolate chips was insufficient for The Grands' appetites, while the truckload of vegetables is slowly rotting away in the driveway. P-Pa offered to go for her, but she insisted on handling the assignment herself, saying she needed to talk to an adult, even a cashier, for intellectual stimulus. Seems P-Pa doesn't fulfill her intellectual needs.

Then this afternoon in his office, P-Pa debuted The Cookie Thief and everyone enjoyed their time on the big screen. This was the most complex movie P-Pa has done to date and except for a few spots with pixilation it was good enough to bring smiles to their faces.

Unfortunately, we had our first race track accident this evening when a chair ran into Jackson headfirst. Apparently, the chair was jealous of Jackson's previous affection for the kitchen table leg. To ease Jackson's pain, Mema spanked the chair for recklessness. Come evening, everyone settled in to watch Hannah's movie choice, Mom's Night Out. It was the first Camp Mema movie that wasn't about princesses or LEGOs. P-Pa approved.

Tomorrow is fashion and creative arts day with Miss Carys, or Saucepot, as the honoree! Then reinforcements arrive just in time to rescue Mema and P-Pa!

**Gulag P-Pa Diary/Day 8:**

One of the fascinating things about rooming with Jackson, P-Pa has discovered, is the boy talk, especially when conversations turn to science. Last night the discussion explored the scientific topic of utmost fascination to all boys—breaking wind! Yes, P-Pa and Mr. Jackson discussed ill winds, bad breezes, cheese whiz and pungent fun without ever using the art-word. Toot was as close as

Trainwreck came to explaining the scientific phenomena. As Jackson explained it, "Everbody toots, except chickens and zombies." P-Pa learns something new every day he rooms with Trainwreck, but leave it to a big sister to dispute the science and the fun. As Carys said about toots, "It's unpolite, like uuuuuuuuhhhhhhh!"

Carys, or Saucepot, was the Girl of the Day and the first Grand to rise. As she put it, "I got up first because I have problems with waking up last!" While it was just her and P-Pa, he got out his magic ball and was able to make it disappear and reappear without Carys figuring out the trick! After a breakfast of Jack & Jill Donuts that P-Pa got up at the crack of dawn so he would be able to get each Grand's preferences, the Grand Girls played dress-up and the three youngest ones put on a fashion show they wanted P-Pa to tape, which he did. In this era of gender confusion, P-Pa was especially pleased that Trainwreck opted not to participate in dress-up day.

To thank Mema for all the work she's done, The Grands conspired with P-Pa to get something for Mema. The choices were (a) a box of chocolates that The Grands all liked; (b) an all-expenses-paid-by-P-Pa vacation to the Round Rock Kemp Resort and the Lewis Resort in Spring; or (c) flowers and a card. The Grands opted for the last option since it was convenient for P-Pa to pick up the gifts when he was getting their donuts. The card caption read: "It's like you took a scoop of Chocolate ice cream and poured some caramel on it, then some fudge, sprinkled on some candy pieces, another layer of fudge, a dollop of cream and topped it off with a cherry. What you did was THAT sweet! Thank you." It was the perfect card for Mema, once all The Grands signed it. Too, Mema loved her bouquet.

Miriam came up with the most innovative use of the western town with her "Longhorn Chef," a cow that holds a pot on its horn over the fire.

Thank goodness for iPads and cell phones, the sedative for both the young generation and their grandparents, desperate for some peace and quiet. Reinforcements arrive within the hour. Psychiatric help begins tomorrow for P-Pa and maybe even Mema!

**Gulag P-Pa Diary/Day 9:**

D-Day plus Yeah! Mema and P-Pa finally survived the Category 5 hurricane that blew in Friday night a week ago with sustained howling hilarity at 150 mph. The storm died out before noon today, leaving the house a complete wreck. The western town was demolished; LEGOs scattered everywhere; tiny clothes strewn in every room; Mema's orderly home in disarray; and P-Pa's disorderly mind empty of any coherent thought other than when will this all end?

Melissa rode to the rescue mid-afternoon Friday and her three Kemp Kids and her two Lewis nieces were not nearly as glad to see her as P-Pa was! But she had only been here a few minutes when P-Pa had to ride to her rescue. It seems she had to use the facilities and came to P-Pa, saying "We have a major problem!" As she had just come from the bathroom with the previous plumbing issue, P-Pa feared a backup of major proportions. When he reached the bathroom, he realized the problem was even worse than he feared: a cricket. Yep, Melissa was still his little girl! As afraid of bugs as ever.

With an opportunity to be a hero again, P-Pa loaded his elephant gun and stalked the intruder, winging him with his first shot. The critter charged, and P-Pa put him down with a shot square between the eyes. Then P-Pa had to rent a bulldozer to drag the carcass out in the pasture and bury it. Though he had to rent the bulldozer for twenty-four hours, it came in handy later in the afternoon when he and Mema had to clear up the debris.

After disposing of the creature from the back bathroom, P-Pa joined everyone for a supper of barbecued chicken, coleslaw, pea salad and corn on the cob. Nothing scored over a 66 on the F-Scale, except for—you guessed it—the chocolate chip cookies Mema had fixed for dessert. While Mema took Melissa to the Baptist Retirement Center to visit her grandmother after supper, P-Pa was sentenced to watch after the kids. He distracted them by putting Zootopia in the DVD player, but by the time Mema and Melissa had returned The Grands had cornered him, threatening him with little-fists-of-fury moves they had learned from the movie.

After riding to the rescue again, Melissa informed P-Pa that they were even for the cricket kill, then it was time for the award show. Camp Mema awards went to Hannah for "Best Harry Potter Authority", Cora for "Best Western Town Builder", Miriam for "Best Dancer", Carys for "Best Fashion Model" and Jackson for "Best LEGO Builder". Gulag P-Pa awards went to Bookworm for "Best Detective", Songbird for "Best Camera Operator", Wordstar for "Best Skinny Detective"; Saucepot for "Best Cartwheeler" and Trainwreck for "Best Tooting Scientist".

Then after an encore showing of Mom's Night Out in honor of Melissa, it was bedtime until this morning when the hurricane passed through and the sun once again shone on Mema's and P-Pa's house!

**Gulag P-Pa Diary/Epilogue:**

With a couple day's rest, it's time to reflect on Camp Mema/Gulag P-Pa. The Grands are growing, and you can see it each year in the changes. This year, for instance, we only had two potty accidents and, bless their little hearts, both times all The Grands forgave P-Pa. Seems they are growing up faster than him.

It's hard to believe Miss Hannah will be a teenager next year. You could see it in her reaction to the movie. While she had a blast, she asked P-Pa if he was going to post it on Facebook. It was obvious that she didn't want her friends to see it. However, she did want to write the script for the next one. So that should be fun. Too, she took well P-Pa mocking Harry Potter as Harry Potterdork. Of course, P-Pa has probably picked up the name P-Padork in her mind, at least!

Miss Cora remains a sensitive, kind-hearted young girl. She loves her little sister and little brother and speaks adoringly to them. P-Pa found one snippet of conversation particularly amusing when she was talking to her little brother. Said she, "Jackson, you're the cutest little thing, except for P-Pa. (Long Pause, Then) I don't know why I just said that." Neither did P-Pa, but he was sure glad he overheard it.

Miss Miriam has an answer for everything and is the most likely to come to P-Pa's defense for his mischief or the problems he throws at them, like at the birthday party. After the kids finished opening their gifts, he asked where his and Mema's birthday gifts were as they, too, had had birthdays. The others shrugged off the question, but Miss Miriam felt compelled to explain, "We didn't know we were supposed to buy you presents, and by the time we found out it was too late!" P-Pa loves the way she thinks!

Miss Carys is the baby girl of the bunch, but a clever little one, who picks up things very quickly, almost like a little mechanical engineer. When P-Pa showed all the young ones the trick of the disappearing wooden ball, she picked up the nuances better and was best able among all the girls to pull off the trick effectively. Even though she was the youngest of the girls, she was the best swordfighter of them all. P-Pa learned not to mess with her.

Then comes Mr. Jackson, who at four is either maturing or taking charge of things. The last night of camp he informed P-Pa as they went to bed that on his next visit he would be sleeping alone in their bedroom. P-Pa could only answer, "We'll see!" That aside, he's all boy and is amused by things the girls find gross. He came into the bathroom while P-Pa was using his sinus rinse and stood wide-eyed as P-Pa flushed out his nose. When P-Pa finished, Jackson just stood there wide-eyed, noting, "That's coooolllll!"

So was this edition of Camp Mema/Gulag P-Pa!

# CHAPTER ELEVEN

*"Before I formed you in your mother's womb, I
chose you," Jeremiah 1:5-
(New English Translation)*

A week after his birth we buried little Benjamin. The Thursday drive back to Houston for the funeral moved slowly because of the frequent rains. It was as if nature mourned with us. When we checked into the hotel near Scott and Celeste's house, the clerk said, "There sure are a lot of Lewises staying here." I couldn't tell her it was because of the Lewis boy that was not there. The tiny fellow that only his parents had met drew mourners from both coasts, my brother and his wife from Florida, Celeste's mother from California and her dad from Illinois and folks from everywhere in between.

After checking into the hotel, we drove by the funeral home where Benjamin rested and then found a florist where we bought a bouquet for our grandson. I don't remember the flowers we purchased, but I had the clerk add a yellow rose to the arrangement to be delivered to the cemetery for the graveside service.

After purchasing the flowers, everything is a

blur in my memory. At some point we joined up with my parents, my brother and his wife, and Melissa and her fiancé John. I know we saw Scott and Celeste at some point and that we must have eaten, but fifteen years later the details escaped me, except for the incessant rain. Memories of the graveside service and that heartrending day, though, remain burned in my brain. The rain continued all morning, a dark dreary March day. Scott and Celeste spent time with their son that morning at the funeral home, their final opportunity to be alone with him.

To pass the time, my dad, brother and I drove through the heavy showers to the cemetery, Klein Memorial Park. The place was a beautiful resting spot with verdant grass and tall pine trees, but the lawn was mushy from the rain, and we feared the precipitation would make a sad funeral even sadder. The canopy stood over the chairs where we would sit in the Garden of Innocence during Benjamin's graveside service scheduled for three o'clock. We returned to our spouses and waited. I remember telling Harriet of the cemetery's beauty, as I grasped for something positive out of the sorrow engulfing us.

By early afternoon, flight problems had developed with Celeste's mother, who had tried all Thursday into Friday to reach Houston from San Diego, but the weather spawned many cancellations. She would not arrive at the airport until less than an hour before the service. My brother volunteered to pick her up at the airport.

By late morning and into the afternoon, as if by a miracle, the sun broke through the clouds pushing the rain away. It was as if the heavens were welcoming Benjamin to his eternal home. It lifted our spirits knowing the sun would chase away the day's dreariness and shine on Benjamin's funeral. We left in multiple cars for the service, arriving an hour early. More flowers than I could've imagined awaited us under the canopy. Benjamin was loved by many. By the carpet leading to the canopy I found the bouquet that Harriet and I had purchased with the yellow rose amidst it. I picked it up and moved it beside the bench where little Benjamin would rest before internment. As I sat it down, I noticed another beautiful arrangement of blue flowers sent by dear friends from Lubbock, where Scott had been born twenty-eight years earlier and where I had delivered my first yellow rose under happier times.

We had reached the cemetery early so we would be there when the funeral home escorted Benjamin on his last earthly journey. The limousine arrived about thirty minutes before the service began. The suited and somber attendant removed the box holding little Benjamin and marched stiff-armed with the tiny coffin at chest level. I remember the little box had the sheen of expensive wrapping paper as the pallbearer marched toward the bench that would serve as a bier. Everyone stood silent and reverent as Benjamin passed us. Respectfully, the pallbearer placed the tiny coffin on the bench and covered it with a spray of flowers from his parents. Inside the little box slept our grandson. Scott and Celeste had selected his burial outfit and swathed him a baby wrap that my mother, his great grandmother, had crocheted for him. Alongside their son Scott and Celeste had placed the little Valentine teddy bear we had purchased for Benjamin. I couldn't help but stare at that little box, still in disbelief that it held my first grandson. I tried to comfort Harriet; she attempted to console me; and we both tried to reassure Scott and Celeste as did others.

By then other mourners began to arrive, including the pastor. Just moments before the service was to begin, my brother came with Celeste's mother.

At that moment, the grieving family was complete now that Benjamin's other grandmother had arrived. Harriet and I took our places on the front row of seats near our son to remember Benjamin's brief life. I remember little of what the pastor said or the music as I still couldn't believe we were burying our grandson. Harriet and I managed our emotions, holding and squeezing each other's hand. Scott remained stoic throughout and Celeste held up well, but our daughter sobbed at the loss of her nephew. I thanked God that John had accompanied Melissa to comfort her.

Besides the small butterfly that flitted around the flowers, what I remember most of the service came at its conclusion as Scott and Celeste stood up in front of the tiny coffin and held each other, silently praying. Seeing them in such grief brought tears streaming down my cheeks and heavy sighs so I wouldn't sob myself. Harriet was gently weeping, and I could not look at her for fear I would completely break down. I never felt so helpless in all of my life, wanting to help my wife, my daughter, my son and my daughter-in-law, but knowing nothing I could do would ease everyone's grief.

The pain of their sorrow overwhelmed me, and I looked away, my eyes focusing on the flowers in the bouquet from our Lubbock friends. I do not remember how long I stared at the arrangement, but as I did the little butterfly fluttered over and landed on the blue petals of a flower. I don't know where he came from after so much rain, but he lingered there until just before Scott and Celeste broke their embrace and returned to their seats. At that point, the butterfly flew skyward and disappeared. I took it as a sign from God that He had accepted Benjamin's soul, and we would all one day meet the little boy that we had awaited with so much joy and now bade farewell with so much sorrow.

In the program for the memorial service, Scott

and Celeste wrote the following message: "Our hearts are heavy with the loss of our son Benjamin, but we are comforted with the knowledge that he has gone to live with Jesus. We thank God for providing us with the grace and strength for each new day. We also thank our family and friends for the prayers and support that have given us peace during this difficult time. You have provided comfort in your own special way and we are grateful for each one of you. May the Lord's peace surround you. With Love, Scott and Celeste Lewis." They then quoted Jeremiah 1:5, the Bible verse they would enshrine on Benjamin's bronze grave marker. They showed much more eloquence and understanding than I was feeling at the moment.

After the benediction, the pastor announced that the internment would be for family only, but that a reception in honor of Benjamin would occur in the home of Sunday School friends. As the throng melted away after offering quick condolences, the family gathered around Benjamin as the pallbearer solemnly carried our grandson to the muddy grave where he would lie for eternity. As we walked toward his final resting place, I steered Harriet by our bouquet and pulled the yellow rose from among the other flowers. At the mounded dirt, two cemetery attendants used a scoop to bail rainwater from the earthen hole. When they finished, they slowly lowered the white box holding Benjamin and his teddy bear into the grave. Then they gently shoveled the sticky earth atop our grandson.

Once Benjamin had been covered, they carried flowers over and placed them upon his grave which bordered the perimeter of the plots for babies and children. When the attendants departed, we each made our peace with Benjamin, Harriet and I walking over and placing atop the grave the yellow rose for him, just as I had given one to his grandmother on the day his father was born. That yellow rose tradition which began with the birth of his father ended for me at Benjamin's gave. But I believe in family continuity and symbolism and sought some permanent connection between me and the grandson I never got to hold. On the way to Houston for the funeral, I stopped in Austin at a nice men's store. I bought an expensive red tie and wore it to Benjamin's memorial and burial. I have never again worn it, keeping it in a special place in my closet so I can wear it for my funeral.

We took a few pictures of family members with Scott and Celeste at Benjamin's grave, then drove to the reception in his honor. Our only consolation as parents who lived 350 miles away was knowing that Scott and Celeste had a supportive church family. The Lewises were showered with love and support at the reception by Sunday School class members, church friends and other acquaintances. When the function ended, we went to Scott and Celeste's home, took some more family photos in our funeral attire and returned to the hotel, all of us going our separate ways the next day. It was hard leaving Scott and Celeste behind, but we knew we could never work out their grief for them as it was something they together would have to do.

After we reached home, I remained at a loss and did what I have often done in life when I was saddened or perplexed, I turned to writing. On a Sunday two weeks and two days after his burial, I wrote a letter to Benjamin. It read:

*"Dear Benjamin,*
*"This, sadly, will be the only letter I ever write to you. In spite of the sadness of your brief existence on this earth, you brought the joy of anticipation into our lives, if only for 12 or so weeks. The mere thought of you always brought a mixture of smiles and tears to your Grandmamma, a look that I never tire of seeing on her face.*

*"Of you, I remember the excitement of knowing you were on the way and then the great sorrow of learning we would not have you long, if at all. I cried at your father's touching message to his Sunday School class that you were too precious for this earth. I treasure the moment on the weekend before you were born that your wonderful and loving mother allowed me to place my hand upon her stomach and feel your soft kicks while you lived within her.*

*"When Grandmamma and I returned to Houston for your memorial, it rained each day we were there, as if the whole world mourned with us. But late the morning of your service, the rains went away and the sun shone as the heavens welcomed you.*

*"We arrived at the cemetery before you did and looked at the many flowers that were left for you. You, Benjamin, were loved by many. Only after you arrived and were lovingly placed upon the Garden of Innocence bench did a yellow butterfly appear to kiss the blue flowers in an arrangement sent by some dear friends from Lubbock where your father was born. I noticed the butterfly periodically during the service, but not after the final prayer was said. Like the afternoon sunshine, the butterfly, to me, was a sign that you were in the arms of Jesus.*

*"Yellow was always my favorite color and on the day that your father was born, I gave Grandmamma a solitary yellow rose in his honor. In the bouquet that your Grandmamma and I sent you, I had one yellow rose included. After your internment, Grandmamma and I, hand-in-hand, tossed that yellow rose upon your grave, a small but symbolic gift until the day that we can meet you in heaven. We love you and will always remember the joy of anticipation that you brought us for those dozen precious weeks and the joy*

*of anticipation that you left us with in one day meeting you.*
   *Written with love,*
   *Your P-Pa*
   *3-21-04*

Though we had buried Benjamin, we had not forgotten him and we faced hard days ahead, simple everyday events bringing tears to our faces. Both of us cried in the shower more times than we like to admit. We took a long weekend to Ruidoso, New Mexico, where our kids had once spent time with their grandparents, and entered a Christmas store to look for ornaments. Harriet loves shopping at holiday stores, buying mementos and making each year's tree unique with ornaments celebrating our travels and adventures for the year. I was only in the store a few minutes before I realized how happy our last Christmas had been anticipating Benjamin and how sad this Christmas would be without him. I broke down and had to step outside and work through my grief.

Whether in this Christmas store or another I cannot recall, but Harriet found an ornament that she wanted to represent Benjamin on our annual tree. It was a little ceramic blue-and-white baby boy's jumper on a hanger. She thought the empty suit offered an appropriate representation for Benjamin so she purchased it, later writing his name and birthdate on the ornament in gold ink. She placed it first on our tree the Christmas after Benjamin's loss. And though she has since added ornaments for Benjamin's two sisters and his three cousins, each year Benjamin's is the first item she lovingly hangs from the tree, followed by the others in the order of their birth.

From the moment of his birth through the following Christmas, we faced many sad days, 454 to be exact. Then Hannah Alane Lewis arrived!

# CHAPTER TWELVE

## *YEAR SIX*

**Gulag P-Pa Diary/Pre-Camp No. 1:**

Demonstrating that their priorities are straight, both the White House and Pyongyang have confirmed with Mema that they will not schedule any U.S./North Korea summit meetings over the planned dates for the 2018 edition of Camp Mema/Gulag P-Pa. Reassured that neither government will upstage this year's extravaganza, Mema is pleased to announce that Camp Mema/Gulag P-Pa will run August 4-12.

The 2018 camp has the potential for being the most terrifying in history, especially for P-Pa. First, this year will welcome our first teenager. Yes, believe it or not, Miss Hannah just celebrated her thirteenth birthday. It's been more than two decades since Mema and P-Pa have had a teenager in the family and, well, the world has changed a little. Problem is, P-Pa hasn't. He can't adapt to those changes and is largely ill-equipped to deal with the challenges of post-modern teenagism. Another way of stating it is that P-Pa's antics no longer have Miss Hannah rolling in the floor with laughter. More likely, she is rolling her eyes in disgust. On top of that, she reads so much she has developed a vocabulary that allows her to talk over P-Pa's head to Mema. In other words, he's left in the dark, another way of saying he hasn't made the jump from the 20th century to the present.

The second scary factor is that for this camp, all campers will have had at least a modicum of education. Yep, Mr. Jackson has begun pre-K and already knows his A-B's and his 1-2's. But things get a little hazy when he gets to his C's and 3's. Let's just say that even lower education is not a high priority for Mr. Jackson with so many adventures to be lived. To put it in perspective, on his recent trip to Disneyland he wore a crocodile suit to meet Captain Hook, who was horrified that he might have to change his name to Admiral Twin Hooks! On top of that Mr. Jackson underwent Jedi training in the Magic Kingdom and actually beat Darth Vader in a light saber fight! If he can cut down the villainous Captain Hook with a crocodile suit and bedevil Darth Vader with a light saber, what chance does pudgy P-Pa have? After Jedi training at Disneyland, his mom caught Mr. Jackson standing at an automatic entrance stepping back and forth to watch the doors open and close. When his mom told him to please stop, he replied, "I can't. The Force is too strong in me!" P-Pa's only defense is The Farce, which is nothing compared to The Force.

On top of that, Miss Cora took Jedi training as well this spring and dominated Darth Vader, too. Then Miss Miriam and Miss Carys are a tag team of trouble always willing to plot against P-Pa and to side with Mema on everything. So, there's nothing but problems on the agenda for P-Pa during the first week in August.

Consequently, to minimize potential damage both to P-Pa and to Mema's domicile, we are planning to take some field trips this year. In the past, Camp Mema has pretty much been homebound for the primary reason that it takes a degree in mechanical engineering to install a 21st century child seat and an acetylene torch to remove it. Since Mema doesn't let P-Pa play with fire, removing car seats presented a problem. When we had four Grands in child seats it took two days to get all of them installed and another day to remove them. Now, everybody but the littlest Jedi can sit in a booster seat with a standard seatbelt.

So, we are looking at taking them to the lake for some cane-pole fishing, treating them to a live theatrical experience and making another movie, of course. Miss Hannah has volunteered to write the script, once school ends. Perhaps that's another reason for P-Pa to be terrified as he is very concerned about his screen image since he finally broke out of the villain mode last year and now fears Hannah will drag him back in! The saga begins where The Farce ends!

**Gulag P-Pa Diary/Pre-Camp No. 2:**

Preparations for Camp Mema/Gulag P-Pa are accelerating so intensely that the smoke alarm went off twice today as Mema feverishly cut out cloth for The Grands' summer outfits. It seems Mema works her sewing shears so fast that they heat up and start smoking, setting off the alarms. In spite of the hazards, Mema has all of the cloth cut and organized in trays with the appropriate patterns so she can start sewing after our next trip.

But despite Mema's ferocious shears, P-Pa claimed the record for setting off the smoke alarm as he triggered it five times while furiously typing the script for the next movie, a sci-fi space adventure called Star Stars. Miss Hannah decided she would rather be the script consultant instead of the screenwriter so it fell to P-Pa to complete the task. His word processor was steaming as his fingers pounded out a story that just seemed to come to him, interrupted only by his five trips to re-set the smoke alarm. His screenplay follows five intrepid interstellar voyagers whose craft, the Fillennium Malcon, a capsule for Imperial malcontents, runs out of gas because handsome hero Duke SkyTalker forgot to fill it up before beginning the Kessel run. Without gas, the Fillennium Malcon is forced to land on a forbidding planet of Sangelo where the Star Stars must face their fears.

So, P-Pa's putting out casting calls for actors to play Duke SkyTalker, Lincess Preia, Jay, Ern Jyso, Memoda, BooChacca, Dart Vapors and four Harm Troopers. It's amazing how P-Pa's creativity can come up with such unique characters out of thin air. On top of that, he must get the props and costumes in order. The costumes weren't a problem, but the props—particularly the Fillennium Malcon—were. It seems P-Pa had two options. The first was a LEGO Star Wars Ultimate Millennium Falcon building kit with 7,541 pieces for a modest $799.95. The second was a LEGO Star Wars Millennium Falcon microfighter building kit with 92 pieces for $8.99. P-Pa decided the 7,541-piece set, not the price, was much too intimidating so he opted for the $8.99 job. On the positive side, he got some bargain basement light sabers for the climactic battle between Dart Vapors and Duke SkyTalker. Now all P-Pa has to do is create a complete movie set of the infinite universe on a budget.

Mema also bought tickets for the Angelo Civic Theater production of Annie, which will be performed while The Grands are here. It has been years since we bought tickets for this many kiddos to a public function. As a result, Mema and P-Pa had this camp's first disagreement over the seating strategy. Mema was torn between two options: (1) all sitting on the same row or (2) half on one row and the other half on the next row. P-Pa, however, had a better option: Mema and P-Pa on one side of the theater and The Grands on the other. That way The Grands were somebody else's problem. Mema, however, vetoed that idea saying it was cruel and unusual punishment. Sort of like forcing P-Pa to see Annie in the first place, he countered. Mema did not smile, which is another way of saying the Force was STRONG with her. Consequently, P-Pa acquiesced, going for the two-row option. We bought so many tickets we got the group rate, which was actually cheaper than the senior rate.

So, the pre-adventure continues.

**Gulag P-Pa Diary/Pre-Camp No. 3:**

As preparations continue for Camp Mema/Gulag P-Pa, the front room sounds like a New England textile mill during the Industrial Revolution with all the whirring, spinning and clattering of machines as Mema scurries to finish the summer outfits for The Grands. She's working the schedule of a mill girl from sunrise to sunset without all the perks, like gruel for meals and cramped living quarters. On the positive side, she has a wonderful supervisor in P-Pa, just don't let her know he said so.

It's hard to know how far along Mema is on the outfits because the room looks like a tornado touched down inside. Even so, it's still in better shape than P-Pa's office where he's working on some writing projects and, well, let's just say he leaves a messy battlefield. As Mema explains her sewing process, some of the materials for the outfits are woven and some are knit. Consequently, she must reconfigure her machinery when she moves from one material to the other. Since some outfits have both woven and knit components she's not necessarily completing outfits one at a time, but partials, doing all the woven parts first and then the knits.

It's beyond P-Pa's mind to comprehend, even if he is her supervisor, again just don't tell her he said so.

When he's not supervising the textile mill, he's moving ahead on the production of Star Stars as there's a lot of pressure on him to save the franchise after the mediocre performances of this year's Soso and last year's The Last Dead Guy. Consequently, he has to make exceptional casting choices. After telephone casting calls, he filled all the screen roles, save one. The parts and actors are as follows:

- Duke SkyTalker—Mr. Jackson
- Ern Jyso—Miss Carys
- Lincess Preia—Miss Miriam
- Jay—Miss Cora
- BooChacca—Miss Hannah
- Memoda—Mrs. Mema
- Harm Troopers—Miss Cora, Miss Miriam, Miss Carys, Mr. Jackson

Dart Vapors, however, proved to be a difficult casting decision. First of all, it's hard to cast the perfect villain, especially one that is the stinkiest bad guy in that galaxy far, far away. Second, since P-Pa's sworn off villain roles, he didn't know where he was going to turn. Then one sweltering afternoon while P-Pa was away, a dark stranger came to the back door holding a sign "Will Act for Food." Mema realized that, in spite of his age, he was the ideal actor for the part, and she cast him without even consulting P-Pa. Mema thinks everyone will agree her choice seems perfect for the role.

Second unit filming on Star Stars begins next week and the actors are learning their lines. So the preparations continue for Camp Mema/Gulag P-Pa.

## Gulag P-Pa Diary/Pre-Camp No. 4:

Finally, P-Pa has found peace and quiet so he can remove the earplugs and protective sound muffs he has been wearing for the past three weeks. Yes, the roar of sewing machinery from the front room has ended. Yes, all is quiet on the western home front as Mema has finished her sewing projects for each of The Grands. She let P-Pa take a photo of the outfits folded and mixed up so as not to give away the designs and what goes to who. Next she wrapped the outfits in boxes so P-Pa wouldn't try to sort the pieces and determine which went to each Grand. Instead, he got a photo of her with the wrapped boxes next to the machinery that made all the non-stop noise over the past few weeks.

In the old days, at Christmas and the unified birthday party Mema gave outfits to The Grands after they had opened up their other presents (translation: toys), saving the best for last, she thought. But, The Grands never wanted to take time out from playing with their new toys for the obligatory group photo in their new outfits. Well, they weren't always happy with the interruption of their planned activities and made their displeasure known in some of the photos. Then P-Pa, who occasionally reeks of intellectual brilliance, decided Mema needed to reverse the order and have The Grands open their outfits first, then dress for the group photo. If they did that and everyone smiled, then they got to open and play with their gifts. If they didn't, then P-Pa got to open their gifts and play with them. Works like a charm. From the chronology of group outfit photos, Mema and P-Pa think everyone would agree that the new policy is working.

Sure, Mema's been busy, but it's not like P-Pa's just been holding his ears. He's been contacting the actors on their Star Stars movie roles and has been working with the bank and other entities to arrange financing for both the movie and camp. Generally, the movie script has been well received by the actors, though they have raised some issues.

First of all, the Kemp Girl Grands wanted to know how in the climactic Star Stars showdown between Dart Vapors and Duke SkyTalker, the villain was going to be able to lift the young Jedi off the ground by his ears without hurting their little brother, Action Jackson. Well, duh, anesthesia, of course! Generally, anesthetics are cheaper than special effects.

Second, Miss Miriam was curious how we could possibly shave BooChacca when the Wookie must face its greatest fear. Well, duh, again, just scissors and an electric razor. Seems kids these days don't realize there are gadgets out there other than iPhones and iPads that can accomplish a whole range of tasks if they just look up from their tiny little screens long enough to learn how to use them. Camp Mema will correct that deficiency.

Camp with its movie production, gourmet meals, field trips and medical expenses, not to mention liability insurance, has grown so much over the last five years that it is getting too expensive for Mema and P-Pa, who have no visible means of support, to fund activities. Consequently, P-Pa had to go to Stagecoach Bank, his financial institution of choice, to see about a loan.

To make a favorable impression, he dressed up in a suit and tie for the first time since he retired and set up an appointment with the Vice President of Questionable Loans. Figuring he should talk the nomenclature of the money men, he went in and asked for a quarter. The VP reached in his pocket and pulled out 25 cents for him, but P-Pa had to explain he meant a quarter of a million dollars. Well, the VPoQL had to see an itemized breakdown of the expenses. P-Pa was prepared, of course, and offered the following:

**Infrastructure:**
- $27,000—Railroad siding to the alley: (necessary to deliver supplies, remove debris)
- $9,500—Foundation Repairs (Camp takes a toll on P-Pa's and Mema's infrastructure)
- $5,000—Plumbing contingency (The pipes get a lot of usage)
- $3,200—Glass breakage (Obvious)

**Dietary:**
- $10,000—Spill proof cups and unbreakable glasses (P-Pa breaks and spills things when he's under stress)
- $7,000—Gourmet Chef (needed to accommodate every idiosyncratic dietary need)
- $6,003—Food They'll Eat (Breakdown: $1,800 for cookies, various; $1,500 for ice cream, $1,300 pancakes/waffles, $800 for birthday cupcakes; $500 for chocolate chips, and $3 for vegetables.)
- $19,000—Food they won't eat (But at least we tried!)

**Star Stars Movie Production:**
- $25,000—Costumes
- $19,000—Movie Sets (It's not cheap creating an alternate universe!)
- $11,000—Special Effects (Every successful movie these days has SFX, that's with an F not an E!)
- $38—Electric Razor
- $7—Anesthesia
- $5—Scissors

**Grooming:**
- $5,000—Manicures, pedicures and hair styling for female actors, including Mema
- $12—Haircut for P-Pa (He must look nice for

the movie premier)
- $9,000—Haircut for Mr. Jackson (He's got longer and thicker hair)

**Insurance:**
- $34,000—Liability Coverage (self-explanatory)
- $15,000—Umbrella Policy (covering what isn't covered under liability policy)
- $10,000—Umbrella Umbrella Policy Policy (covering what isn't covered under umbrella policy)

**Health:**
- $235—Sedatives (to keep P-Pa calm)
- $35,000—Psychiatric Services (post camp therapy for P-Pa, who keeps agreeing to do this each summer)

In spite of P-Pa's valiant efforts, Stagecoach Bank turned him down, saying they never ever at any time approve high risk loans to unworthy credit risks. The Stagecoach VPoQL suggested P-Pa seek a government subsidy or grant. So, undeterred, P-Pa contacted the offices of both Texas Senators and his U.S. Representatives. Unfortunately, he learned that the U.S. Government no longer has subsidy or loan programs for American-born kids, especially those coming from traditional, well-adjusted families who semi-voluntarily agree to spend time in the repressive regime that is Gulag P-Pa.

Undeterred, however, P-Pa has decided to raise the necessary funds online through a PleaseFundMe page. If you would like to make this year's Camp Mema/Gulag P-Pa a financial success so the sponsors don't have to spend their retirement savings just to amuse The Grands for 10 days, please give generously, preferably in small, unmarked bills in amounts under $10,000 so a certain Uncle we all love as long as he leaves us alone doesn't find out. So, if you care to donate to this wonderful cause, please go to YourAsuckerIfYouDo.com and help make this year's camp a success. Mema, P-Pa and The Grands, of course, thank you for your generous support of this American Institution.

**Gulag P-Pa Diary/Pre-Camp No. 5:**

Disaster Day minus 3: Well, the heavy loading for Camp Mema/Gulag P-Pa began yesterday, literally. P-Pa had to rent a forklift to unload all the groceries and supplies Mema picked up at the grocery store, and this was just the preliminary grocery run. She returns on Friday for the perishables, except vegetables, which are about as popular at camp as P-Pa when he tells them it's time to put up the iPhones, iPads or anything else they can use to record him to document their case for the authorities.

Because of the added stress of having Grands with snooping and recording capabilities, P-Pa suggested Mema add a defibrillator to her grocery list. She brought home a deluxe model with paddle electrodes, which are suitable for table tennis or corporal punishment, if P-Pa gets out of line around The Grands. It's amazing, the wonders of modern technology.

Today, Mema started cooking, beginning with the birthday cupcakes, forty-eight in all, half vanilla and half chocolate. It seems some of The Grands like one flavor and the others the opposite flavor, which is manageable. But, they don't all like the same icing combination. So Mema makes vanilla-chocolate, vanilla-vanilla, chocolate-chocolate, and chocolate-vanilla so every palate is satisfied. P-Pa thinks she should just blindfold them at cupcake time and simplify her life. Fact is, she makes everything too complicated like keeping count of the cupcakes. That is so unfortunate as it keeps P-Pa from honing up on his subtraction skills when she's not looking.

P-Pa finished setting up the western town this morning, a task that he started six weeks ago. Mema thinks P-Pa spent more time playing with the cowboys and Indians than building the town, but it kept him from practicing arithmetic—especially subtraction—in the kitchen.

Next he began the second unit filming for the Star Stars movie, doing the opening sequence of the Fillennium Malcon flying across the universe when it runs out of gas and has to crash land on an alien planet. He's got all of the props for the movies, including costumes and bargain basement light sabers in multiple lengths: two at four inches, four at forty inches and one at fifty-six inches. P-Pa's excited about Dart Vapors using the fifty-six-inch saber against Duke SkyTalker's four-inch saber. It'll make for great drama.

The birthday gifts for the unified party are all wrapped. P-Pa has observed over the years that as The Grands get bigger, their presents get smaller. Unfortunately, they don't get less expensive. He thinks he's nearing the end of The Girl Grands' princess period. He once thought nothing could be worse than princesses. Unfortunately, The Boy Grand is into superheroes, which are equally as nauseating, just not as cute as princesses. In the good old days, heroes wore cowboy boots and hats, not tights and masks. P-Pa misses those days.

Even so, the preparations are progressing, not the least of which is the doctor increasing the dosage for P-Pa's medications as he awaits the arrival of The Grands, now known by their code names Bookworm (Hannah), Songbird (Cora), Wordstar (Miriam), Saucepot (Carys) and Trainwreck (you guessed it, Jackson). As P-Pa puts it, these are our last three days of sanity for a while.

### Gulag P-Pa Diary/Pre-Camp No. 6: D-Day minus 1:

This was not a good day, finding P-Pa in tears and arrears, but not all is lost as he learned a valuable lesson: the new-fangled Internet is not all it's cracked up to be. In fact, it's downright disappointing. Last month, P-Pa started a PleaseFundMe page through YourAsuckerIfYouDo.com to cover the costs of 2018 edition of Camp Mema/Gulag P-Pa.

Well, today he checked his page and found he had raised exactly zero dollars from exactly zero donors. That's right, zero, zilch, nada, nothing. Even though he made no money and was reduced to tears, he did make dozens of new friends as he had that many offers from caring, magnanimous Internetters willing to show him how to raise more money if he would just pay them a modest fee. Thankfully, he didn't have a PayGal account so he couldn't partake of their generous offers, starting at $1,000 a pop.

To cover the mounting costs, P-Pa had to go to his savings and loan and withdraw enough money to handle the escalating expense of Camp Mema. The S&L folks were wonderful, commenting that this was the biggest certified check they had issued all year, and they were equally helpful. Then he went to Stage Coach Bank, the same institution that turned down his loan request to fund Camp Mema. P-Pa's teller was as surly as a TSA agent with a toothache. In fact, the teller wouldn't even deposit P-Pa's check in his own account without demanding to see P-Pa's ID. P-Pa tried to explain that the bank's policy was backwards, that they needed to see IDs when someone was making a withdrawal. The teller was intransigent so P-Pa had to prove he was P-Pa.

To make P-Pa's dealings with Stage Coach Bank even more galling, the bank yesterday agreed to pay a $2.09 billion fine from the federal government for making risky loans, when P-Pa could've funded Camp Mema/Gulag P-Pa on one-tenth of that and still had money left over to pay for The Grands' college education with enough left over for a round-the-world cruise for Mema and him to relax after the impending camp. He's still fuming over the ID request. After all, he didn't ask his PleaseFundMe donors to identify themselves before giving him money. Maybe that's why he didn't get any dough.

Meanwhile, Mema's too busy to fume. She's been cooking and prepping things for the impending disaster. Over the years she's learned a few tricks, like labeling a laundry basket for the kid's clothing. I guess you might say she got tired of collecting "dirds", as we call dirty clothes, from the floor, from under the beds, from the ceiling fans, from the trashcan, from the bathtub, from beneath sofa cushions, etc. It's like being on a fashion treasure hunt every day. The family dird baskets should make the collection and laundry chores a little easier.

Today Mema made her second grocery store run, focusing on the perishables or perhaps more accurately the meltables? Yep, she thinks a bag apiece for each camper is about right. So, she brought home five 100-pound sacks of chocolate chips. If you are a financier, the next ten days will be a good time to invest in chocolate futures or plastic sack futures as Mema also came home with twenty-eight plastic sacks of groceries.

Now, this missive has focused on Mema's and P-Pa's travails, but they've got to admit there's also pressure on The Grands as well. They have to remember to bring their sleeping bags and their Star Stars paraphernalia for the movie. Most importantly, they have to practice the goofy faces they insist on using whenever P-Pa tries to take the group photo.

Well, the invasion begins tomorrow at about P-Pa's bedtime. He's just hoping to survive.

**Gulag P-Pa Diary/Day 1:**

Unfortunately, Camp Mema/Gulag P-Pa got off to a horrible start this evening with an ophthalmologic and medical emergency. It seems P-Pa was totally exhausted from watching Mema cook, clean and prepare for The Grands, so about bedtime, he sat down in his easy chair, took off his glasses and dozed off.

Evidently, he was in REM sleep when the inmates arrived with all the subtlety of a brass band on the Fourth of July. He jumped up, rubbed his bleary eyes and put on the wrong pair of glasses. He was not only seeing double, he was seeing three or four times as many Grands as he was expecting. It was just too much of a strain on his declining constitution, and he just passed out there on the floor.

Mema, though, was prepared, quickly plugging in the defibrillator, grabbing the paddle electrodes and instructing The Grands to step back and yell "clear." Poor Jackson, bless his heart, misunderstood Mema's instructions and instead of "clear" yelled "STEER" at the top of his lungs. P-Pa suddenly snapped back into reality, not quite certain what was going on or what medical procedure Mr. Jackson had in mind. Of course, Mr. Jackson made a simple mistake, but it left P-Pa jittery. In fact, every time Trainwreck says "STEER," P-Pa jumps about two feet high and looks nervously over his shoulder to make sure Trainwreck isn't carrying a scalpel.

Prior to P-Pa's ophthalmologic emergency, things went pretty well with all the chores completed by late-afternoon. So being the magnanimous husband he is, P-Pa decided to take Mema out to eat since he didn't have the courage to ask her to fix his supper. After all, she had just finished fixing some 6,424 pre-meals for The Grands to consume in the days ahead. After supper at Cheddar's, it was back home to await the invasion.

The Grands arrived safely about 10 p.m. and after nursing P-Pa back to consciousness went to the western town and started playing. Mr. Jackson found one of the props for the movie and couldn't resist trying it on and having his picture made.

So, the adventure begins.

**Gulag P-Pa Diary/Day 2, Part 1:**

The terror resumed this morning when Scott and Celeste left The Grands alone with Mema and P-Pa. Mema handled it well, but P-Pa clung to Scott's legs all the way to the car, begging him and Celeste to stay. After Scott finally shed his dad, jumped in the car and sped away, P-Pa required additional medications.

Mema, however, was on the verge of needing sedatives by lunch time. Breakfast was a hit, chocolate chip muffins for all. One little lady code name Saucepot had three chocolate chip muffins, more than even P-Pa. Lunch, however, was a trial. The Lewis Grands are finicky eaters and requested sandwiches rather than pot roast, vegetables and mashed potatoes, while the Kemp Grands, well two of three, did well with the main menu.

Mr. Jackson, however, wanted to know why the Lewis Grands got a sandwich and he had to eat pot roast. P-Pa explained they were under medical orders. Jackson decided he wanted a sandwich, medical orders or not, so Mema obligingly got up and fixed him half of a peanut butter-and-honey sandwich, just as he requested. Trainwreck took one bite and said it wasn't as good a Mommy's and the bread, the peanut butter and the honey didn't smell the same as at home. After all the work Mema put into planning and fixing meals, P-Pa threatened to withhold Jackson's birthday cake if he didn't eat his sandwich.

At that point, Miriam became concerned and walked over to P-Pa and whispered in his ear, asking if he was really going to veto the cupcake for Jackson. P-Pa answered, "I don't know." Answered Miriam, "You could give him one, just to be generous." Later after she had finished lunch and Jackson was in tears over his meal, Miriam slipped up to P-Pa and announced, "If you need any funny faces for Jackson, I'll be in the next room."

So, P-Pa was faced with a dilemma and decided he wasn't going to be outfoxed by a five-year-old. So, he put the half sandwich in a baggie, then in a mailing enveloped and addressed it to Jackson with a return address from "Mommy." He then forged a letter from Mommy and enclosed it with the sandwich. He next hid the envelope with some other previous letters and walked out to the mailbox, returning with the day's "mail." P-Pa then distributed the mail to Mema and himself before giving Mr. Jackson his package.

Jackson was delighted to get mail until he opened up the envelope and saw the bagged sandwich and the forged note from Mommy. Miss Cora read the letter dated "today": "Dear Jackson: I miss you so, and I know you miss my cooking so I am mailing you a peanut-butter-and-honey sandwich. I hope you enjoy. Love, Mommy."

Jackson took the sandwich to the table, smelled the baggie and announced it smelled the same. Then he opened the baggie, took a sniff and next announced that it didn't smell as good as at home. Not only did Jackson foil his senile grandfather's ploy, he complicated matters by wanting to write a thank you note to his mom. Jackson then dictated to Mema who obligingly wrote down the following words:

*"Dear Mommy, I'm sorry, Mommy, the sandwich doesn't taste the same as Mommy's at Mema and P-Pa's house, Love Jackson."*

Then he drew a picture on the back of a stick-figure Jackson hugging his stick-figure Mommy.

So, P-Pa was outfoxed by a five-year-old after all, but impressed by his genuine social skills in wanting to write a thank you note and feeling guilty that his scam had led to such a magnanimous gesture. Final score, Jackson 1, P-Pa 0. Meanwhile, Mema's peanut butter-and-honey sandwich didn't stack up to Jackson's Mommy's pb&h sandwich, but after the unified birthday party, Mr. Jackson admitted Mema's store-bought ice cream was better than his Mommy's store-bought ice cream. Jackson's Mommy 1, Mema 1.

**Gulag P-Pa Diary/Day 2, Part 2:**

After the lunch standoff, Camp Mema/Gulag P-Pa got to serious business with the initial filming of Star Stars with all the actors. Due to technical issues (P-Pa pushing the wrong button), they'll have to re-shoot it tomorrow. P-Pa covered his blunder by saying it was just a rehearsal, then he invited the actors to see the second unit footage of the Fillennium Malcon flying across the universe. Everyone was laughing at the footage. P-Pa thought all the merriment was an expression of awe at his special effects on a budget until Miriam asked a simple question. "Is this a comedy?" Not intentionally, P-Pa responded, then called for rewrite.

While the movie didn't get off to a good start, the unified birthday party was a hit and The Grands got their summer outfits made by their Pennsylvania native grandmother from material she picked out visiting her hometown in State College back in May for her fiftieth high school reunion. The Grands loved their outfits and gleefully posed for the obligatory photos, knowing once they were done it was time to open up the rest of their presents. Misses Miriam and Carys got crop top blouses and shorts from the same pattern but in different materials in their favorite colors. Mr. Jackson got plaid shorts and a two-toned shirt. Miss Cora loved her blue-flowered slacks, yellow chemise and white camisole. Miss Hannah is a young lady now, almost as tall as Mema, and got leggings and a tunic top that looked great on her.

The best thing about the birthday party was the refreshments of cupcakes and ice cream. At past parties, the floor looked like city streets after a tornado, debris everywhere or in this case crumbs and splotches of melting ice cream. This year, P-Pa found only three crumbs on the floor attributable to The Grands and no ice cream splatters. Of course, it was a different situation under his chair since The Grands had to take him outside and hose him off. P-Pa apparently understands his feeding habits are getting messier as he ages. Last weekend when he was dressing for the church pot luck supper, he came out with a shirt and asked Mema if squash casserole would look good on it. Last time she took him out to eat, he asked if barbecue sauce would bring out the highlights in the shirt he was wearing that night. It seems The Grands are on the upside of the bell curve while P-Pa is faster and faster descending the downside.

Prior to the party, Mema asked Jackson, "Where's your water glass?" Replied Jackson, "It's not glass. It's made out of plastic and paint!" So there, Mema! Earlier, P-Pa asked Mr. Jackson if he knew his ABC's. "No!" responded Trainwreck. Then P-Pa asked him if he knew his 1-2-3s. Again, the response was "No!" "Do you know anything?" P-Pa asked. "Not right now," he replied confidently.

Don't let him fool you, though. He knows his Star Wars droids, thanks to the bedtime reading he forced on P-Pa last night. For instance, an astromech droid is a repair unit; protocol droids are intergalactic language translators; battle droids are warriors; surgeon droids are medical entities; bounty droids are hunters; probe droids are spies; magnaguard droids are protectors; and power droids are electrical units. Isn't it wonderful that there exists in a galaxy far, far away a genderless universe without himdroids! Or, even herdroids, for that matter!

The meal melees continued at supper when Mema served Jackson some grapes with his leftover peanut butter-and-honey sandwich. "It smells bad," Jackson announced. P-Pa's response drew a food-spewing laugh from the Girl Grands. "You don' eat it with your nose," he announced. Jackson then ate his grapes and a bite of his sandwich, announcing he wanted some chips. P-Pa told him he had to eat his sandwich first. After Mema cut the crusts off, he ate ALL of the sandwich and got his chips. New score: Jackson 1, P-Pa 1. These dinner dustups have all the excitement and scoring of a soccer game.

To cap off the night, P-Pa and Mema debuted LEGO Batman on their new ultra HD television set for The Grands. Unfortunately, The Grands just came in and out of the den and weren't available to explain the movie to P-Pa and Mema. In fact that's the main lesson from the first day of Camp Mema/Gulag P-Pa 2018. Last week P-Pa was attending his fiftieth high school class reunion and talking with folks who shared the same cultural references and anchors. This week he's with a generation that has to explain things to each other, like eating what's on your plate. The drama continues.

**Gulag P-Pa Diary/Day 3:**

Mema and P-Pa have been holding their own, actually winning a few battles as they enter another full day of pandemonium. The interior of the house looks like your typical freshman male dorm room with stuff everywhere. Getting around is as difficult as walking through a minefield, and even more challenging is holding your tongue to age-appropriate language when you step on a LEGO piece or an action figure.

After an uneventful breakfast of waffles with chocolate chips or syrup, everyone loaded into cars to go to the nursing home to visit P-Pa's mom, the great grandmother of The Grands. The little ones wore Mema's new outfits to show Gamma, as our son Scott named her some four decades ago. As P-Pa was trying to buckle Jackson into his car seat, young son gave him some advice: "Don't hurt yourself." So, P-Pa decided why risk injury by struggling against the car seat and decided it would be simpler just to put Jackson in the trunk, but fellow passengers Cora and Hannah convinced P-Pa to take Trainwreck out and put him back in the car seat or they would make P-Pa a YouTube superstar with the video they had recorded on their phones. That was the first eye-opening experience of the trip for P-Pa. The second was Hannah being old and tall enough to ride in the front seat without any type of car seat. That was a first, that and realizing it was less than three years that she could be driving.

The Grands had a great time visiting with their great grandmother, but not nearly as much as she had with them. They helped P-Pa put bird seed in the feeder outside her window, then waited for birds to show up. When none did, P-Pa said it was Sunday morning and they had gone to church. Miss

Miriam shot back, "No, they've gone to CHURP!" Miriam wins the pun of the day award. Each of The Grands got to push Gamma in her wheelchair and all was fine until Jackson was ticketed for pushing 35 mph in a 5 mph hallway zone.

Back home, we had a Sunday morning Bible story reading with Miriam volunteering to read the first story from a book of Bible Stories P-Pa read through multiple times as a child. Miriam read the story of the creation and closed it with a sweet prayer. She is a sweet young lady and made sure she brought everyone a little gift at Camp, giving everyone a little vase stone.

With the kids maturing, Mema and P-Pa this year have been trying to teach them proper etiquette about knocking on bathroom doors before entering them. Unfortunately, not everyone fully understands the concept. Did I hear someone say Trainwreck? Yep, Mr. Jackson hasn't fully grasped the idea. So when Miriam knocked, he told her to come in. This is how Miriam explained it to P-Pa: "When I opened the door, he was sitting on the potty with his shorts on his head." But a major tragedy was averted as Miriam confided in P-Pa, "I didn't see his ***** or I would've been scarred for life." Now you understand why she is nicknamed "Wordstar" around our house. Too, who knew Camp Mema could be so emotionally traumatic or that Miriam would know the proper terminology for the male anatomy.

After lunch, P-Pa had to re-shoot many of the scenes he shot yesterday because he flubbed up. Wordstar was most helpful in advising P-Pa, "You need to be extra careful to check the camera so you don't mess up again. We should all learn from our mistakes." Fortunately, P-Pa learned from his boo-boo and didn't flub up today. Cora always knows her lines and is willing to help the other petite performers say theirs. Hannah has been a real trooper in the filming. Though she's outgrown the Camp Mema film tradition, she sat patiently through the initial shooting and the re-shooting, wearing a BooChacca mask. In addition to re-shooting yesterday's footage, P-Pa shot new scenes today with Memoda, who performed her lines flawlessly. Let's just say Memoda is one hot swamp creature, and the director better mind his manners or he could get charged with harassment!

The buffet battles continue. Breakfast is never an issue as The Grands need the energy to battle P-Pa and Mema at the subsequent meals. For lunch Mema made tacos and two of the five Grands had them. Two years ago, four of the five ate tacos and one, Miss Carys, ate three tacos. This year only Carys and Cora had tacos, and then only one each. P-Pa made Jackson's peanut butter-and-honey sandwich and after some grandparental intimidation watched Jackson eat all of it. Updated scores: Jackson 1, P-Pa 2.

At supper P-Pa was proud to discover that Jackson has the listening and reporting skills that would qualify him to become a CNN correspondent. When Mema asked Miriam if she would like chips or Tostitos with her sandwich, Jackson yelled "mosquitoes" and started buzzing around the room, chasing his sisters with plans to bite them. In fact, Jackson may have CNN White House correspondent potential.

Finally, if the western town is a true sign of life in the Old West, it was carnage out there. Best P-Pa could determine, there were only three of the characters and a hat-wearing horse left standing in the streets after The Grands rolled through town. Cora did point out there were several kid characters in the saloon, raising the question of what kind of example is P-Pa creating for The Grands. The three younger girls figured out how to threaten Miss Hannah while playing with the western town.

They started calling her character a princess, and Hannah kept crying, "No, no, no!" It seems Hannah has long since outgrown the princess stage while the younger female trio are not letting her forget it. The carnage endures.

**Gulag P-Pa Diary/Day 4, Part 1:**

Even P-Pa's disposition was good this morning as everyone got a good night's sleep, thanks primarily to total exhaustion. Breakfast of Mema's chocolate chip pancakes was so well received that all five of the Grands played together. They moved from the totally demolished western town on the dining table to a desert they made on the carpet. Since no people survived in town thanks to their encounter with The Grands, four of them played with horses and while the fifth decided he would be the rattlesnake and bite all the horses. As always, rattler was tolerated for his cuteness.

Then it was time to shoot some of the outdoor scenes for Star Stars. This was a big day for the movie because Dart Vapors and his Harm Troopers made their debut. It was spectacular in 85-degree temperatures. The Harm Troopers complained about the heat. Dart Vapors didn't say a thing, just collapsing from heat exhaustion in his black uniform. Thanks to Mema and the defibrillator, which is getting more use than the western town, Dart has recovered after taking a shower.

The biggest challenges for the rest of the day are, of course, lunch and supper.

**Gulag P-Pa Diary/Day 4, Part 2:**

We are ashamed to say that the white flag of surrender flies over the shell of Mema's and P-Pa's former home and kitchen. Yes, The Grands have won the Meal Melee, the Buffet Battle, the Food

Fight, the Soufflé Scuffle, the Fricassee Fracas, the Caloric Combat, you get the idea. Armageddon came at lunch when Mema thought she had built up enough trust in The Grands by making them what they wanted for previous meals so that she assumed they would trust her to make a meal decision for them. Wrong! The green peas were a stretch, knocking Mr. Jackson out of the equation. Boiled chicken was the Waterloo for Miss Miriam. Rice was the demise of Miss Hannah. Misses Cora and Carys managed the Javanese dinner okay, but Misses Hannah and Miriam opted to starve when they were informed there would be no sandwiches today.

So, the Lewis Grands excused themselves from the table. After the others finished their meals, P-Pa broke and asked Wordstar if she wanted a sandwich to which she replied, "Not if you need to punish me." Game, Set, Match for Miriam. P-Pa made her and Hannah their standard sandwiches. For supper, P-Pa just gave them a credit card and called Uber to take them wherever when wanted to go for the evening meal. Mema and P-Pa stayed home and ate the bitter herbs of defeat.

Otherwise, it was a good day with filming going well on Star Stars, though the editing was a bit tricky for P-Pa. The youngest Grands seem to be enjoying the process. The main benefit of the movie is that it kills time, gives P-Pa something constructive to do and illustrates that you can't always believe what you see on TV.

Mema continued a Camp Mema tradition with Cora today. When each Grand turns ten, she offers to help show them how to sew an outfit for herself or her doll. Just like Hannah three years ago, Cora decided to make an outfit for her American Girl Doll. Mema helped Cora set the pattern, cut the material and begin sewing. Cora is anxious to finish the outfit for her doll Jennifer.

Mema even performed surgery today on the wolverine plush toy Miriam got for her birthday. It seems somebody tore the wolverine's hide and Mema had to sew it back together. She then issued the edict that only Miriam could play with the animal henceforth. Then one of The Grands asked who ripped it. To avoid a problem, P-Pa said he tore it. Replied Cora, "You may be mean, but you're not that mean." P-Pa appreciated the vote of confidence.

When she wasn't sewing or filming in the afternoon, Cora took it upon herself to rebuild the western town. In her honor, the town has now been named Coraville.

Tomorrow marks the halfway mark of this year's camp. The Grands will make it, though Mema and P-Pa remain uncertain about their longevity.

**Gulag P-Pa Diary/Day 5:**

Two catastrophes struck Camp Mema/Gulag P-Pa, the ecological disaster barely being averted and the cinematic cataclysm devastating what was shaping up to be one of the greatest science fiction films in history. The two calamities, oddly enough, were interrelated. It began with costuming for the day's shooting of Star Stars. When Dart Vapors was in costume, Mema reminded P-Pa today was trash day and the trash hadn't been taken to the alley. So P-Pa in costume rushed through the house, gathering trash, then putting it in the trash receptacle and rolling it out to the alley just as the garbage truck arrived. Seeing Dart Vapors hauling out the trash, the frightened driver braked, then passed out right there.

It all worked out for the best, however, as Mema ran out with the defibrillator, which appears to be the best investment she made this year for camp. While she was resuscitating the driver, P-Pa fired up the front-end loader and dumped six bucket loads of Camp Mema debris in the garbage truck. As the driver was coming to, Harriet sent P-Pa back into the house until she could explain to the driver that he was likely hallucinating from garbage fumes. After mechanically emptying the trash and recycle bins, the driver went on his way with a story to tell his kids.

Though P-Pa averted one crisis, he could not avoid the second calamity. It seems our Star Stars star actor got temperamental and didn't want to shoot the climactic scene where he takes on the villainous Dart Vapors. He went on strike and refused to let Dart Vapors show his powers by lifting Duke SkyTalker by his ears, even though they had done a run through just to show Mr. Jackson he would actually be lifted by a camera illusion rather than his actual ears. No matter! Mr. Jackson adamantly refused. Further contract negotiations, including offers of a cupcake, a gallon of ice cream, no more peas on his plate, a chance to spank P-Pa with a paddle, a pony, an all-expenses-paid trip to Disney World and a little brother, failed to change his mind.

So, while Mr. Jackson sat on the porch with his arms crossed over his chest and a pouty lip, Misses Cora, Miriam and Carys stepped in. It was a phenomenal light saber fight, but the three Star Stars ultimately vanquished Dart Vapors in the rectangular ring of death. Unfortunately, an unscripted remark about Dart Vapors' "butt crack" will force the rating to be elevated from a PG to an R. That's the price a director pays for hiring actresses at the pinnacle of their craft.

Early in the afternoon, Mema had to make a grocery run, which is code language for a sanity break. She actually saw and interacted with adults for the first time in three days since P-Pa can hardly be classified as mature. It was just a simple run for the essentials, more chips, more ice cream, more chocolate chips, and more muffin mix for The Grands and more sedatives for their keepers.

Now that The Grands vanquished Mema and P-Pa in the Meal War, it's on to the Bed Wars. They either don't understand the concept of staying in bed or have hearing problems and think he wants them straying. Night before last, P-Pa told Wordstar and Saucepot, code names for Misses Miriam and Carys, that they needed to stay on their bed. Then the conversation went like this with them alternating questions: "What if we need to weewee?" "Okay!" "What if we need to poopoo?" "Okay!" "What if we need a drink?" "Okay!" "What if we get sick?" "Okay" and "What if we have a national emergency?" "Okay!" By the time they were done, P-Pa had to admit there were a lot of valid reasons for getting out of bed. He resolved the matter by going to bed himself and covering his head with his pillow.

Then last night, he discovered Wordstar and Saucepot playing with their American Girl Dolls in bed at 11:15 p.m. "You girls need to quit playing," he told them. "We're not playing," Miss Miriam informed him. "I'm combing my doll's hair." Then Carys added, "I'm doing laundry." P-Pa just retreated to his own bed again and once again shut out the world with his pillow.

This afternoon the sewing lessons resumed and Cora proudly brought in her first completed piece for P-Pa to see. She's doing a great job as is Mema, who is a patient and loving teacher. By supper time, they had finished the dress for Jennifer. Cora was beaming. She didn't want to see the outfit on her doll until her mother could see what she had sewn. So we took a photo of Cora with the outfit she had sewn and Mema with her little sewing box, which just happened to be the first gift P-Pa ever gave her. She's kept and used it (and P-Pa) all these years!

At supper, Jackson was waving his apple slice in the air and P-Pa told him to quit using his apple as an airplane. "It's a boat," he replied.

The last two nights we've been watching the Yellowstone Live shows on the National Geographic Channel. It's as noisy as watching a football game with The Grands because every time a predator seeks prey, especially baby prey, the kids are screaming and yelling for the little one to escape. They almost lost it when a wolf was chasing a baby otter and his mother, but fortunately the otters found a snow slide and escaped into the water before the wolf could catch his breakfast.

As camp continues, P-Pa feels like the wolf as he can never stay up with The Grands, so he just retreats to his lair and hides his head under his pillow. His camp experience is best exemplified by this afternoon's conversation with the temperamental actor:

*P-PA: "Jackson did you say something to me?"*
*JACKSON: "No."*
*P-PA: "Don't you like me?"*
*JACKSON: "I do like you, but I like Mema the most."*

Just so Mema doesn't get a big head, P-Pa overheard Jackson telling Hannah "You're my favorite."

The journey continues.

### Gulag P-Pa Diary/Day 6:

In six years of hosting Camp Mema/Gulag P-Pa, Wednesday was the lowest day of them all, a day that will live in infamy in Camp annals. And the source of all the pain was Mema! That's right, Mema! Yes, Mema turned on P-Pa. Strike One against Mema. It seems that her regular hair appointment came up today and instead of doing the humane thing and re-scheduling, she kept her comb-and-scissors slot, leaving P-Pa alone with The Grands. That's right, ALONE with The Grands for almost two hours of pure...well, he would just call it intense.

To start with, P-Pa had to make breakfast for The Grands. Simple you say? Then, you don't know pressure until you have had to place one chocolate chip in every square and triangle in a round waffle. One mistake and breakfast is blown all to...well, you get the idea. It seems LEGOs and Eggos are valuable commodities at Camp Mema.

Somehow P-Pa made it through breakfast, but realized he had made a strategic mistake the night before by allowing The Grands to watch a National Geographic show on the wolves of Yellowstone. Barely had breakfast ended than the pack of Grands started howling and eyeing P-Pa like they were hunting for prey. After a half hour of looking over his shoulder everywhere he went, P-Pa had to get away and retreated to the shower for a little peace and quiet, leaving Miss Hannah in charge. When he finished, dressed and re-entered the wolf's lair, he was shocked to find the house immaculate with everything in its place and The Grands quietly reading on the sofa. Miss Cora decided she could no longer manage the suspense of having made a new dress for her doll and not seeing her in it, so she dressed up Jennifer with her handiwork and was justifiably proud.

Unfortunately, when P-Pa retook command from Hannah, The Grands went on a howling rampage of destruction. By the time, Mema returned The Grands had damaged so much of the house that they had actually established a tent city beneath Coraville to live out the rest of camp. When Mema entered the house, she found P-Pa babbling incoherently and shaking uncontrollably in the corner of the family room, uncertain about his future and the overall outlook for humanity.

Mema finally brought P-Pa back to reality, but then he got another blow to his movie. It seems Miss Hannah was no longer going to act in the movie as a show of support for Mr. Jackson's boycott of Star Stars. So, P-Pa was forced to change the script and re-edit the video to make it semi-coherent. He has to do two more scenes to provide transitions for the revised script and then it should be done. He debuted the preliminary edit, and The Grands seemed pleased with the first run-through. Impromptu highlights were Hannah as BooChacca giving the thumbs up sign when Cora orders her to repair the Fillennium Malcon and Miriam's light saber battle with Harm Trooper Jackson while she gives a fashion critique of his uniform "as so last year." The impromptu moments are what make the movie hilarious each year.

Even though things have not gone well with Star Stars, P-Pa is considering the movie for next year and thinks a musical is the ticket since all of the girls are wonderful singers. The working title is The Sound of Noise. If that's the name, Miss Miriam suggested that it be called a "noise-ical" rather than a musical. That's why she's our Wordstar.

After lunch P-Pa had about recovered from the shock of the morning when Mema announced that she, Hannah and Cora had decided they were going to the mall. What about, P-Pa inquired, the other three? Mema responded they were P-Pa's problem responsibility. Strike Two against Mema. P-Pa tried to convince Misses Hannah and Cora that the San Angelo mall was nothing like the malls they were used to in Houston and Austin and that the trip would be a great disappointment, but they insisted on going so P-Pa was left with Misses Miriam and Cora and Mr. Jackson. P-Pa, though, managed Mema's absence better this time. Though he wound up in the corner again, he wasn't shaking or babbling as the young Grands tied and gagged him.

P-Pa was relieved when the three older females returned, though it was a little bit disconcerting to hear Hannah say as she came in, "Do you think P-Pa survived?"

Women plus malls equals bank accounts minus deposits, and this trip was no different. Mema bought a stuffed puppy for Trainwreck, bracelets and friend necklaces for Wordstar and Saucepot, a shirt for Songbird and a "goal board" for Bookworm. P-Pa couldn't complain that he didn't get a gift since he was gagged, so Mema's gift to him was simply releasing him from his bindings and warning him not to cross The Grands anymore for his own good.

Then it was supper time and Mema announced she was going to church choir practice. Strike three against Mema. She informed P-Pa that if he behaved while she was gone, she wouldn't have to untie him when she returned. Mema came home from practice with a song on her heart while all P-Pa got was bruises on his legs, arms and buttocks. At least he wasn't tied and gagged this time when Mema returned.

To give you an idea of how the tables get turned on P-Pa, before one snack of cupcakes, he announced that anyone who dropped a single crumb on the floor would get some corporal punishment. Generally, after a cupcake snack the floor beneath the table looks like Broadway after a ticker tape parade. This time, though, the Grands were focused and succeeded in their first spotless snack in the history of Camp Mema. Then two hours later, Miss Carys happened to notice a crumb under P-Pa's chair. P-Pa thought it was part of a potato chip, but Miss Carys and her fellow female Grands thought it was a vanilla cupcake crumb since P-Pa was the only one that didn't have a chocolate cupcake. So, the issue was put to a vote. Mema, her conscience probably paining her for abandoning P-Pa with

The Grands for more than six hours on this day, and Mr. Jackson voted with P-Pa that it wasn't a crumb. However, the four girl Grands voted it was a crumb and proceeded to give P-Pa the spanking they would have gotten had the crumb been elsewhere. Since the election did not turn out the way P-Pa wanted it, he's claiming Russian interference and demanding a special prosecutor to investigate the matter.

By the end of the day, P-Pa was so exhausted that he didn't have the energy to post his regular daily camp update. So he retired to his bed with his roommate, Mr. Jackson. The plan was to take The Grands fishing in the morning so Trainwreck had a lot of fishing questions like "What color is fish peepee?" P-Pa told him that was a science question which he should ask Mema in the morning. The adventure continues as delirium sets in.

**Gulag P-Pa Diary/Day 7:**

It rained on the Camp Mema/Gulag P-Pa parade today. We got three-quarters of an inch of badly needed precipitation, but it and early morning thunderstorms delayed our fishing safari to Lake Nasworthy. We made it about ten o'clock well after the normal breakfast hours for fish in this part of Texas.

As for the success of our venture, let's just say the Kemp Girls are fishing pros as long as they don't have to touch a worm, bait a hook, touch a fish or return it to the lake. The others weren't so successful. Miss Carys was first to put a pole in the water, and she caught her first fish before P-Pa could bait the second pole. She was sure proud, as long as she didn't have to get too close to the fish. Consequently, she wouldn't hold the fish up for a picture, but she hauled in a monster. She named it "Miss Sparkles" as we returned it to the crystal clear waters of the lake. Miss Cora snagged one that got away, before hooking one she was able to lift from the lake. Once again, this fisherwoman was proud as long as she didn't have to get too close to her trophy catch. She named her fish "Shiney".

Mr. Jackson went next and kept his cork bobbing so much, I'm sure that any fish trying to nibble on his bait probably broke his back. It's a shame Trainwreck didn't get a fish because he planned to name the little thing "Ironman". Miss Miriam wasn't too much into the fishing game, but she gave it a try, unlike Miss Hannah who preferred to do her fishing on her iPhone. Miriam wanted to fish primarily so she could pull it from the water and give it a name, "Siren". So, thanks to "Miss Sparkles" and "Shiney" as well as "Ironman" and "Siren", wherever they are, for the fun adventure in the outdoors.

The fishing safari returned home right before lunch and P-Pa spent his time washing the mud off of The Grands' sneakers. Trainwreck had more mud on his than all the girls' sneakers combined. So by the time he finished with Jackson's sneakers, The Grands were done with lunch so P-Pa was able to have his share of chicken nuggets and French fries with Mema in relative peace and quiet until Jackson returned to the table. He asked P-Pa, "Do you know the Jackson tax?" Confused that he was misunderstanding his five-year-old grandson, P-Pa asked him to repeat the question. "Do you know the Jackson tax?" P-Pa shook his head and said NO. "It's when I grab a French fry from your plate," he answered, snatching the biggest fry on the dish and gobbling it down. Later during snack time, P-Pa asked Jackson if he knew about the P-Pa tax. Instantly, Jackson grabbed his bowl of Cheetos and hid it under the table. Isn't that just like a little progressive, wanting yours but not wanting to share his?

After lunch, the four Girl Grands played with all the toy horses from Coraville, setting up dates and talking about how cute the boy horses were. Mr. Jackson avoided the equine romances by playing with the buffalos. P-Pa thought he would give Mema a taste of her own medicine by running an errand to Walmart. When he got back the place was placid as could be and Mema had given the younger ones showers so they smelled springtime fresh rather than fisherman stale. Then Mema announced she was about to take her shower. P-Pa, still shaken by Mema's Wednesday absenteeism, told her that was fine as long as she remained within screaming distance.

Starved for more adult companionship, P-Pa went out to greet Pete the Mailman as he often does when he hears the mail truck. "Haven't seen you in a while," Pete said as he handed P-Pa the day's mail. Replied P-Pa, "I've got five grandkids in the house." Pete did a sign of the cross, said, "God bless you," and sped away to the next mailbox.

After supper, Mema continued a Camp Mema tradition by providing a cookie pizza. It's the only food item other than breakfast that they can all agree on. Mema makes a huge chocolate chip cookie on a pizza pan, then puts chocolate icing on it and gives the kids M&Ms to decorate their slices. It was smiles all around. Then Cora said that treats like this made Camp Mema special. P-Pa asked what's special about Gulag P-Pa, to which Cora replied, "Gulag P-Pa is the devil's playground." Where do these Grands come up with such? Afterwards, P-Pa regaled them with tales of how tough he had it as a child, only three TV channels and only a B&W television set at that. Rabbit ears were a foreign concept to them. They were not particularly amused or sympathetic to P-Pa's and Mema's deprived childhoods, though Mema and P-Pa were impressed that Hannah and Cora had at least heard of Roy Rogers. Unfortunately, they were oblivious to Captain Kangaroo.

After supper The Grands reverted to their primeval instincts instilled in them after the nature program on Yellowstone wolves two nights ago. They retreated to the front room and started howling and working on stalking techniques. P-Pa even got a photo of two wolves stalking and attacking another.

Unfortunately, P-Pa today realized his communication skills with The Grands are deficient, and he is not really getting through to The Grands. So, next year he's buying a bullhorn.

The endurance challenge goes on, but tomorrow reinforcements arrive. Will Mema and P-Pa last that long? Stayed tuned to your B&W TV to find out!

**Gulag P-Pa Diary/Day 8:**

It's been a week since the invasion began. Supplies are running low. Tensions are fraying. Everyone is on edge. Except for Mema, of course. She's the real trooper of Camp Mema/Gulag P-Pa. And, in her honor on Friday, The Grands decided to send P-Pa on a secret mission to buy her a card and flowers. After he smuggled the bouquet and card into the house, everyone signed the card.

Then The Grands had Mema sit in a throne, and they marched in with the yellow, green and orange flower arrangement. At that point they made her "Queen for a Second". Miss Miriam used her blanket to create a regal robe, and they gave her the card. The front of the card read, "Everyone has a Super Power!" The inside read "Yours is being Awesome! Thanks!!!" Then The Grands presented Mema the bouquet. P-Pa said he took up a collection from The Grands to make the purchase, but Wordstar set the record straight, "P-Pa bought them all." Then after

Mema's one-second reign, it was back to cleaning, cooking, negotiating, washing, arbitrating, scrubbing, translating and, most importantly, sedating P-Pa.

As this was the last full day of camp, it was cleanup time. Mema and P-Pa have learned that if they don't start the cleanup before The Grands depart, things get lost like socks, hair brushes, tops, bottoms, weapons and, heaven forbid, iPads and iPhones. Sometimes the missing items aren't found until months later. And even if they are found, Mema and P-Pa aren't always sure what the things are. So, the process began with the obliteration of Coraville. That toy has been a hit from the first year Jackson stayed for camp, and even Hannah still plays with it, as does P-Pa. That's why it took three hours to dismantle it as he says he has a certain way he wants to box the toys and that takes time, when in reality he's just playing with them all before he has to put them up for a year.

After P-Pa got the western buildings and characters boxed up, the dining table became the staging location for all the girls' belongings. Mr. Jackson is such a mess that it takes a whole room to organize his belongings for travel. Nonetheless, the packing and the house was in pretty good shape by the time Melissa arrived. P-Pa was the first to greet her, bolting out the back door to the drive way, falling on his knees and hugging her around the legs in grateful appreciation that she had come to save him and Mema. He just had one question: Why didn't she come five days ago? She didn't get a chance to answer that question as the Kemp Grands swarmed their Mommy with hugs and squeals. Barely, had she gotten settled than The Grands wanted her to see the Star Stars movie, which was a hit with the kids, though they were disappointed that the movie didn't have any special features or bloopers at the end. P-Pa, though, was too exhausted to do more than the movie this year.

After supper, it was time for the annual awards banquet. Camp Mema Awards went to Jackson for "Best Light Saber Warrior", Carys for "Best Fisherman", Miriam for "Best Commentator", Cora for "Best Seamstress" and Hannah for "Best Shopper". Gulag P-Pa Awards went to Hannah for "Best Silent Actor" for her role as BooChacca in the Star Stars movie; Cora for "Best Town Builder", Miriam for "Best Fashion Critic"; Carys for "Best Spaghetti Consumer"; and Jackson for "Best Tax Collector".

The culmination of Camp Mema/Gulag P-Pa was a trip to Angelo Civic Theater for the premier of the musical Annie. It was a delightful performance, and P-Pa was shocked how well ALL The Grands did. He wasn't concerned about the girl Grands, but a certain other Grand was potentially a problem. However, Mr. Jackson did quite well. The theater, however, was a shock for Miss Hannah, who was expecting the Hobby Center in Houston, where she had seen her first play. She thought bigger was better until P-Pa asked her if her seats at the Hobby Center were this close to the stage (and the girls were seated on the next-to-last row). Hannah said no and then admitted there maybe were some advantages to theater in San Angelo.

Annie was a fun experience all around, but when the lead character was singing *Tomorrow*, the signature song from the play, the lyrics that were going through P-Pa's head were: "Tomorrow, Tomorrow, They'll All Be Gone Tomorrow!"

**Gulag P-Pa Diary/Day 9:**

D-Day plus Rest: P-Pa was never in the military so he has not had training in hand-to-hand combat, but he took on three car seats this morning and won—eventually. The-high back booster seats in Mema's car for Misses Miriam and Carys only took 30 minutes apiece for P-Pa to figure out and remove. As for Mr. Jackson's seat in P-Pa's car, it took an hour and forty-five minutes to extricate. P-Pa was glad he got up at 5 a.m. to start the task because it would have been embarrassing to have to ask Melissa to show him how.

Melissa hoped to leave by 10 a.m. but everyone was so organized and so cooperative this morning that The Grands and their chauffeur were on the road by 9:20 a.m. P-Pa took the class picture with Mema before they left and then the annual make faces at P-Pa photo. Mema and P-Pa helped load The Grands up and sent them on their way.

As they drove off, and Mema and P-Pa stepped back inside what was left of their home, Mema had a flashback to the previous night and the musical Annie. Once the door closed, Mema started singing new lyrics to the tune of *Tomorrow*: "It's quiet, it's quiet, the house is so quiet. I thought this day would never come."

Then the recovery began as Mema and P-Pa called contractors to get estimates on the damage. An hour into the process, she texted all the parents: "All quiet on the western front. Melissa and The Grands left about an hour ago. Now the reconstruction begins."

As for the reconstruction, It looks like it'll run about $12.37 per square foot. That's a small price to pay for all the fun Mema and P-Pa had over the last week. So, adios until next year, if Mema and P-Pa are awake by then!

# CHAPTER THIRTEEN

.

*"The Lord will give grace and glory." Psalm 84:11-*
*(King James Version)*

I was prepared to deal with the grief of losing Benjamin, but not for the numerous ways that the sorrow manifested itself in the everyday events and encounters of daily life. Though I expected the pain to linger, I did not realize it would come up in so many unsuspected ways. At our age, it was common for folks to ask if we had grandchildren. How did you answer? If I replied no, I felt like I was diminishing Benjamin's brief time on earth. If I answered yes, I only opened up the conversation for questions with uncomfortable answers. Then if I responded that we had lost our first grandson, I created an awkward moment for whoever had inquired. I came to hate the question about grandchildren.

Mother's Day that following May was the hardest on us all. Harriet was a grandmother lacking a grandchild. Celeste, bless her aching heart, was a mother without a child. It was especially difficult on her after one unfeeling woman chastised her for claiming to be a mother when she had no child. How hurtful and insensitive could a person be, interjecting herself into Celeste's grief and stomping on her emotions so callously?

We both sent Celeste a Mother's Day Card with handwritten notes. I wrote of my bewilderment at the unfairness of life through the tragedy of Benjamin. "All I can do," I concluded, "is offer to you my love and appreciation on this bittersweet Mother's Day. Benjamin will always hold a special spot in my heart as our first grandson. I thank you for giving Benjamin the life that he had, and I thank God for giving you the strength to handle the loss, just as I have thanked him many times for bringing you into our lives as Scott's wife and companion. I took forward to future Mother's Days when Benjamin's brothers and sisters can bring you the joy you deserve. Until then, may God grant you peace and the knowledge that you are loved and honored by your mother- and father-in-law, who will never forget Benjamin! Written with love, P-Pa."

Harriet wrote, "Dearest Celeste, I am writing this letter to let you know that you are in my thoughts on this, your first Mother's Day. I wish with all my heart that you were the one rocking Benjamin instead of Jesus." Harriet reassured Celeste that she was a wonderful mother because of her sustaining faith in God; her love of her husband, our son; her love of all children as exemplified by her career choice in elementary education; and her care-giving and nurturing temperament.

"For these and many other reasons, you are a great mother. I look forward to the day when Benjamin's brothers and sisters will know you as their mother. What lucky children they will be. Love, Mom."

Until then I had thought of Mother's Day only as a sad occasion after the death of your mother. It had never entered my mind that the death of a child might cause an even sadder Mother's Day. But as the story of our loss spread, dozens of people acknowledged comparable losses. Our future son-in-law's parents lost a child, two of our college friends buried a son in the years after they graduated, a fellow employee at the university confirmed he and his wife had lost a daughter, and many others offered similar stories of losing a son or daughter, a granddaughter or grandson. Even the receptionist in Harriet's office had lost a child, and she was so helpful in telling Harriet what to expect. A lot more hurt than I ever realized simmered out there, and it gave me faith that I could go on as they had, tough though it might be for a while. In memory of Benjamin, Harriet wore on her blouse each day a little pin of an angel. That was a daily ritual for her for almost a year until she lost the pin at an airport during one of her academic travels. She cried over misplacing the little angel pin.

For months after the funeral when Harriet and I would go out to eat or for a walk, I'd see baby boys with their folks and wonder if that was how Benjamin might look or act at that age. It was a burden unlike any I ever carried before, and I was unsure how to handle it. We took weekend trips like a bluebonnet tour of the Hill Country. The bluebonnets blossomed with a magnificence we had never before seen. We attributed the glorious flowers to Benjamin, who was now embraced by the same Texas soil that gave life to the spring flowers. It was silly, I admit, but we kept seeking ways to rationalize the loss of our grandson.

Perhaps I should have sought grief counseling or a session with our pastor, but I had always been a contemplative introvert, careful to keep my problems to myself as I believed that ultimately I and I alone had to work them out with God's help. I found it difficult to accept what I had no control over and even had a hard time attending church, always sitting on the opposite side of the pews from where the elderly lady weeks before had pointed out the single father and his impaired son. My faith, it appeared, was not as strong as my son's and daughter-in-law's.

In June of that year, we had reason to rejoice as the young man who made our daughter laugh so much married Melissa in a beautiful ceremony in Austin. The family gathered again, this time to celebrate a wedding. The occasion marked the first time we had all been together since Benjamin's funeral. This time the flowers represented a joyous event. Our spirits and laughter soared not only at the wedding but also at the DVD scrapbook John created and debuted at the rehearsal dinner of childhood photos of himself and Melissa.

Then came Father's Day, another reminder of our loss and the grief that we were dealing with. Like we had done for the mother of our grandson, we each wrote a letter to his father. Harriet wrote:

*"Dear Scott, This is not the message I had hoped to write you on your first Father's Day, but I have some thoughts I would like to share with you at this time.*

*"As a mother I always wanted the best for you. To me that meant a happy life with a loving wife and children surrounding you. I never wanted you to be sad or hurt—I would do anything to shield you from that. I know that is not a realistic dream, but nevertheless it was my hope that you would never have to deal with such heartbreak as you and Celeste have endured with the short life of Benjamin Scott Lewis.*

*"But the birth and death of Benjamin have confirmed some things about you that I always knew were true and make me proud to call you my son. You are a strong young man with a faith that sustains you. Your sweet letter to your Sunday School*

*class shows that quality so plainly. You are the rock of your family. The way you have comforted all of us from the time we first learned about Benjamin is a mighty example of strength and comfort. You dearly love and cherish your wife, which was never more clear to me than the tender way you held her and spoke to her at Benjamin's funeral.*

*"Someday soon I pray that you will have the chance to teach these qualities of strength, comfort and love to your sons and daughters. The world needs more fathers like you are.*

*"Love, Mom."*

I wrote:

*"Dear Scott, For years I have known you were a man, but I never fully realized your strength as a man until the loss of Benjamin. You were the emotional anchor for the entire family in a difficult time. Perhaps the most enduring mental image of my entire life was watching you comfort Celeste in front of Ben's coffin. I know you offered her the support that only a husband can provide his beloved wife in a moment like that. You were a pillar to the rest of us as well from your poignant message to your Sunday School class to your loving care of Celeste. I only hope that you found a comparable source of strength so that you did not have to carry so much of the burden yourself.*

*"As we approach this, your first Father's Day, I hurt deeply that you will never have the opportunity to watch your Benjamin mature into such a man as I was able to watch my Scott grow. I pray that one day you will have another son, who will have the chance to grow up under your strong, yet loving hand and to mature into a fine Christian man such as you. This world needs more men like you.*

*"I wish I could offer you more than my love and*

*respect, which you always had. The curse of being a father is you can't always fix things for your children, and never was this more true than in this case. As for Benjamin, all I can do is remember his innocence and honor his memory. With love from your father on your first Father's Day, Dad."*

By that December flowers best summed up the past twelve months, and I started our annual Christmas letter:

*"For Preston and Harriet Lewis, this year was best represented by flowers—a bridal bouquet, a funeral garland and glorious Texas bluebonnets by the thousands." I concluded our annual holiday missive saying, "More than anything else, 2004 taught us that you should never take anything for granted. We realize how fortunate we had been up until February 27. Although we do not always understand things, we know there is a greater good behind all that God sends our way. We feel blessed that our children have each found a Christian spouse to share their lives with. We look forward to the day when they will have other little Lewises as well as little Kemps for us to spoil. May God bless you in 2005."*

We celebrated that Christmas with our children in our home. Benjamin's ornament hung prominently from the tree, but the celebration was subdued. Harriet placed her Willow Tree figurine of the angel holding a tiny baby on the dinner table for our traditional holiday feast. I blessed our food and family but broke down as I prayed for Benjamin on his first Christmas in the arms of the reason for all Christmases. It has been fifteen years since we lost our first grandson and my voice still quivers whenever I include him in our annual Christmas or Thanksmas blessing.

By the holidays that year, we had learned Celeste was pregnant again, but our excitement was muted. We would not let our emotions and dreams run wild again, only to be shattered by the greatest disappointment possible. We feared Celeste's every visit to the doctor might bring bad news and even when the sonogram showed a well-developed baby, we kept word of Celeste's pregnancy to ourselves, only sharing it with a few intimate friends and family. Harriet resumed the cross-stitch birth announcement she had started for Benjamin and began to finish it for his little sister.

In February of 2005 we returned to visit Scott and Celeste in Houston for Benjamin's first birthday, which fell on a Sunday. We shared Sunday School and church with them, then visited the cemetery. What shocked me most was the Garden of Innocence. While Benjamin's grave had been on the edge of the gravesites when we had buried him, other little graves now surrounded his spot. The children's section of the graveyard had grown by a third or more in the subsequent months. I thought of the all the heartbreak those additional little graves represented and the millions of tears shed over them. We were not alone in grief. We all greeted Benjamin, left little gifts and sang to him. Then Harriet and I headed back for San Angelo while Scott and Celeste returned to their home. We spent the night at a hotel where I wrote my second letter to my grandson.

*"Dear Benjamin,*

*"Today was your first birthday. Your Grandmamma and I went with your Mom and Dad to your church. The last time we were there with them, you lived in your mother's womb and our hearts were heavy because we knew you would not be long on this earth. Even though we know you are in heaven, our hearts were heavy today on your*

*first birthday. We miss you so much!*

*"After church we went to your grave. Your Momma left you three birthday balloons, one with fire trucks and police cars on it. Your Grandmamma left a candle in the shape of a "one". I left you a little Roy Rogers cowboy. I played with it when I was a kid and looked forward to playing with it again with you. I buried the cowboy beside your marker for you to play with as I wanted to leave you something from my childhood of 50 years ago. We all sang you Happy Birthday as best we could.*

*"Your Grandmamma and I started back for home after we left the cemetery. That night in the hotel, I heard her crying in the bathtub. She misses you so, as do I, but we think of you every day and await the moment we will be reunited with you. Happy First Birthday in heaven.*

*Love*
*P-Pa"*

On the way home, Harriet continued cross-stitching the revived birth announcement she had begun for Benjamin and now would complete for his sister. She aimed to finish everything but the dates so she could stitch them in upon your sibling's birth, then frame the elaborate artwork for her first present for father, mother and daughter. For three months, we anticipated Hannah's arrival with both excitement and fear, fear that something would go wrong again despite positive reports to the contrary.

Then on the last Thursday of May, less than a week after both Harriet and I celebrated our birthdays, Hannah Alane Lewis came into the world. She was an answer to so many prayers and brought such joy to our broken hearts that only then could begin to mend. Miss Hannah would be the first of five surviving grandchildren to bless Harriet's and my lives. We intended to have joyful times with them in the years ahead, but never forgetting little

Benjamin.

Twelve days after her birth, Hannah—with help from her mother—wrote the first letter of her life. It was addressed to her big brother.

> *"Dearest big brother Benjamin Scott,*
>
> *"I am Hannah Alane. I was born on May 26, 2005.*
>
> *"I weighed nine pounds and I was twenty-one inches long.*
>
> *"I wanted to tell you that I am proud to have a big brother, who lives in heaven with Jesus. I hope Jesus rocks you to sleep at night, reads your favorite Bible stories, and sings to you just like our mommy, daddy, and all of our grandparents do for me.*
>
> *"My mommy, daddy and grandparents miss you so much, but they have accepted that God had a different assignment for you that involved going to heaven on the same day you were born: February 27th, 2004.*
>
> *"Some day, after many years, I will join you in heaven. I want you to show me where you celebrated all your birthdays, where you walked with Jesus, and introduce me to all of our loved ones that went before us. I love you.*
>
> *"Admiringly, Your baby sister Hannah Alane Lewis*
>
> *"June 7, 2005*
>
> *"(Typed by Mommy)"*

# CHAPTER FOURTEEN

## *YEAR SEVEN*

**Gulag P-Pa Diary/Pre-Camp No. 1:**

Under growing pressure from his in-house seamstress, P-Pa is pleased to make the announcement the World has been waiting for, the dates for the seventh annual Camp Mema/Gulag P-Pa. Camp is in the books for July 26-August 3.

Unfortunately, we've already had our first casualty. It seems Miss Hannah, who will enter high school in the fall, has decided camp is a little too juvenile for her anymore and is opting to pass on the seventh edition. The public reason is that one participant is just too silly for her to deal with anymore. She's identified this miscreant only as "P". P-Pa thinks it's an encryption and has hired a cryptologist to decipher it. Deep down, P-Pa thinks the "P" is a code name for Mema. Mema, however, told P-Pa he was reading too much into it and to just go with the obvious. P-Pa informed her that Hannah was too clever just to go with the obvious. Mema just rolled her eyes, especially after P-Pa told her that as the official chronicler of camp, he would make the final determination, regardless of reality or facts, just like the mainstream media. If the cryptologist can't come up with the answer, then

P-Pa will hire a special investigator. He understands Robert Mueller has time on his hands now. Mueller is his first choice for special investigator. Bozo the Clown is his second.

While the mysterious "P" is the public reason for her passing on camp, the deeper reasons are the legal negotiations between Hannah's lawyers and P-Pa's legal team. Fact is, they just couldn't reach an agreement in spite of P-Pa's giving in on multiple points. P-Pa agreed to Miss Hannah's demands that (1) she could sleep as long as she wanted; (2) she could watch Anime, whatever that is, all day; (3) she didn't have to go fishing again; and (4) she could stay up as late as she wanted. P-Pa's legal team agreed to that and only asked in return that Miss Hannah (1) laugh at P-Pa's jokes; (2) stand in slack-jawed awe of his "moronic"—her word not his—magic tricks; and (3) put down her iPhone for a measly five minutes a day. Her legal team would accept those terms only if P-Pa agreed to read all the Harry Potter books and watch all the Harry Potter movies so he would become semi-literate on all things Hogwarts School of Witchcraft and Wizardry. P-Pa countered that she should read all fifty-eight books in the original Hardy Boys series so she could be conversant with his childhood heroes. The negotiations spiraled out of control after that until they completely fell apart last week, and Miss Hannah decided she would pass on the all-expenses-covered camp for 2019. So, no gruel, no manual labor, no incarceration for her this year.

Her contributions to Gulag P-Pa, however, will not go unrecognized. She's the one that named P-Pa "The Condamant", starred in the first movie Escape from Gulag P-Pa, figured out the criminal in The Cookie Thief movie and uttered such classic lines as "I can see the string" while P-Pa was making a dollar bill float in the air, much to the astonishment of the other inmates. P-Pa's favorite camp memory of Hannah is in the early years when she would sit in his lap while he was writing his Facebook posts, laughing or making suggestions to add to the humor. Mema's dearest memory came in later years with the way Jackson took to Hannah, and how she would hold hands with him as they walked to the park.

On the positive side, her absence means the female-male ratio is reduced from 2.5-1 to 2-1. Fact is, if attrition keeps up and only Jackson attends, the ratio will be reversed and the guys will prevail 2-1, assuming Mema will still cook for us. If not, us guys are in trouble.

Hannah's defection means Miss Cora will now be the senior camper. She was so good at sewing a doll dress last summer that Mema thinks the senior Kemp camper can make a dress for herself this year. During our last visit to Round Rock, Mema and Miss Cora went to the fabric store to pick out a pattern and material for her dress.

Misses Miriam and Carys are so close in age and so compatible that we call them the Bobbsey twins. Harriet has learned to sew them matching dresses, and they love it.

So, that leaves Mr. Jackson, who's all boy. When the Kemp Kids called to wish Mema a happy birthday last month, Misses Cora and Carys sang the verses to perfection while Jackson at the end of each line shouted "cha cha cha!" into the phone. It was quite special and ear-shattering.

Mema and P-Pa are disappointed to be losing Miss Hannah this year because they expected The Grands would want to continue camp well into their thirties, but it looks like Mema and P-Pa were wrong and will not only have to arrange for their own nursing home care but pay for it as well! The saga, though, continues.

**Gulag P-Pa Diary/Pre-Camp No. 2:**

If you've been experiencing brownouts, don't blame the growing summer heat or the utility company. Instead point your finger at Mema as she's been drawing down electrical power statewide as she scurries to finish the outfits for The Grands. The sewing machine has been screaming like a dynamo as she goes through yards of material and miles of thread. We figured she better get her sewing done before the heat of summer really sets in or she might cause a statewide power shortage.

On top of that, Mema and P-Pa have about three weeks of travel between now and camp so we had to accelerate the production schedule or she'd be sewing outfits until the moment they arrived, not a good option since it takes away some of the surprise, diminishes the magic of her sewing talents and eliminates any opportunity for gift wrapping.

As for P-Pa, he's been working on the script for the next movie, a musical called The Sound of Noise, but to be honest it's hard to think over the roar of the sewing machine and difficult to type on the computer when the screen keeps flickering because of the power draw of Mema's sewing engine. In a way, this is all Miss Miriam's fault as we had originally scheduled camp a week later, but it turns out her singing talents got her an invitation to sing in Minute Maid Park Stadium in another concert and we had to move up our schedule. So, the pressure's on Mema and P-Pa to get everything done, though it's worthwhile knowing Miss Miriam will perform in the largest venue ever for anyone in our family.

As for the musical, it was Miss Hannah's idea and she came up with the first line of the title song with P-Pa coming up with the others:

The house is alive with the sound of Jackson

With noises he has created since birth
The house bursts with the sounds of his action
And of peaceful silence there is a great big dearth.

Then P-Pa took a song from the Peter Pan musical and revised it slightly into a newly titled song, *I Won't Throw Up*. The lyrics so far:

> *I won't throw up,*
> *----I won't throw up*
> *Even if P-Pa cooks.*
> *---- Even if P-Pa cooks.*
> *I'll eat what's on my plate,*
> *---- I'll eat what's on my plate,*
> *And pretend that it's great.*
> *---- And pretend that it's great.*

Next, he's working on lyrics for *Some Enchanted Pizza*. So, the musical's coming along, but P-Pa has some writing competition on the horizon as Miss Miriam has decided she wants to write the script for next year. She gave P-Pa the first two pages of her script on our last visit to Spring. She's titled it Mother Mema's Messed Up Tales, a Mother Goose takeoff on three fairy tales: "Little Red Riding Hood", "Cinderella", and "The Brave Little Knight", a story P-Pa was unfamiliar with.

The writing is quite good, though P-Pa questions Miss Miriam's casting. Mema is the Fairy Godmother, of course. P-Pa is the Big Bad Wolf, the Bad Knight and, worst of all, the Ugly Stepmother, which will tax his acting skills. Here's a sample of Miss Miriam's dialogue:

*MOTHER MEMA:* "*I do have a few stories up my sleeve. Would you like to hear one, Jackson?*"
*JACKSON:* "*But you don't have sleeves.*"
*CORA:* "*It's a metaphor!*"

P-Pa's impressed. He's published novels and still doesn't know what a metaphor is. Of course, he's at the age now where he's uncertain if he ever knew what it was or has just forgotten it with the passage of time. Well, Mema's finished all but the hand-sewing, and the electricity is back on so P-Pa's got to get back to writing the script before Miss Miriam surpasses him.

**Gulag P-Pa Diary/Pre-Camp No. 3:**

Mema and P-Pa have a confession to make to all of our friends: We're horrible grandparents. Yes, it's true, Facebook friends. With five days to go until the beginning of the sixth annual Camp Mema/Gulag P-Pa, we've done absolutely nothing to prepare other than Mema sewing The Grands' summer outfits. The reason is Mema and P-Pa abandoned their grandparental duties to take a ten-day excursion cruising the Inside Passage in Canada and Alaska. Shame on us, though it was pleasantly cool up north.

Or adventures included battling mosquitoes the size of hummingbirds, dodging humpback whales during a feeding frenzy, running from a brown bear (Mema escaped, but P-Pa fell and the only thing that saved him was that the grizzly was on a low cholesterol diet and opted for healthier food!) and facing on the last day of the vacation the most vicious and mean creatures on earth—TSA officers at D/FW International Airport. Mema and P-Pa, it turns out, are suspected terrorists.

We made it through Canadian security without taking off our shoes, belts and watches or removing our electronics from our carry-ons or losing our dignity. Apparently, our good old American TSA doesn't trust Canadian TSA so we had to go through a more intense search process because we apparently fit the profile of potential terrorists. So,

Mema placed all her belongings on the conveyor and went to the body scanner while P-Pa was unloading all his stuff from four pants pockets, six shirt pockets, a brief case and a roller bag (P-Pa doesn't travel lightly). By the time he had removed his shoes, taken off his belt, laid out all his electronics flat in a tray, cleaned out his earwax and sent his belongings down the conveyor belt, six other people had gotten in line between him and Mema.

When he next saw her, she was standing outside the full body scanner with her arms in the air while a burly TSA agent frisked—as in fondled—her. It seems her body scan showed she was carrying two bundles of explosives in her bra. Now P-Pa has always thought Mema was dynamite, but this was the first time a government agency had confirmed it in his presence. After the TSA found nothing in her bra other than what was supposed to be there, the agent determined Mema wasn't wearing a suicide vest after all. To cover for their ineptitude, TSA officials blamed the false positive on her new blouse with its metallic design. At least she got an explanation, if not an apology.

As for P-Pa, he stepped into the full body scanner and thought everything was fine until he exited, and a TSA agent told him the scanner had spotted unusual activity in the groin area. At his age, P-Pa was uncertain whether to be proud or insulted. Nonetheless, P-Pa was informed he would receive a pat down, including the suspect region. Being the patriot that he is, P-Pa offered to drop his pants and drawers right there for a visual search, sacrificing his dignity for the higher good of national security.

The agent, however, said he preferred a manual pat down, but we could go to a private room if P-Pa preferred. P-Pa declined and told him to get on with it, while the agent explained the procedure for a proper and legal manual search. P-Pa told him to dispense with the explanations and get on with the groping. But the agent said he was required by law to give P-Pa the whole spiel. Then the agent asked an odd question: "Do you have any sore spots?" Replied P-Pa, "Not unless you squeeze them too hard." The agent was not amused, so P-Pa shut up for fear he would be doing ten-to-twenty years in San Quentin if he did not take this matter as seriously as this representative of our federal government.

Not satisfied when the manual search turned up empty, the agent then swiped a pad over P-Pa's hands and ran it through an analyzer, looking for traces of explosives, P-Pa assumed. Since P-Pa had done no hunting or fishing, there were no traces of gunpowder or stink bait on him, so he escaped the clutches and groping of the federal government.

But now that he and Mema are on a suspected terrorist list, P-Pa is concerned that this year's camp may be under surveillance as a potential training site for little jihadies. The worries of running a successful camp never end.

**Gulag P-Pa Diary/Pre-Camp No. 4:**

P-Pa is not a scientific scholar, but he thinks the biologists are wrong. Sure, there are carnivores, herbivores, omnivores, piscivores, and even insectivores, but nowhere in his extensive biological research has he found any references to somenivores and nonenivores, the most apt descriptions for The Grands and their eating habits. Some of The Grands are somenivores, eating some of the foods some of the time. The others are nonenivores, consuming no food much of the time. In fact, Camp Mema menus are so controversial that one year, Miss Miriam prayed for "food we like."

That's the problem, there's no food they all like, save maybe chips, but even that is iffy depending on the flavor or brand, unless they are chocolate chips. So, Mema has a challenge whenever she tries to buy groceries for The Grands. Her weekly trip to the grocer usually takes forty-five minutes. This week it took her two-and-a-half hours to purchase the food, an hour to unload the U-Haul trailer with the non-perishables, and another hour to hide the goodies—as in chips of any kind—from P-Pa. She's still got to return to the store on Friday for perishables. P-Pa's depressed because he can't find the chips, can't afford all these specialized diets and will likely have to buy a new home with more counter space to hold all the groceries for future camps as The Grands and their appetites grow, at least in theory.

Mema bases her menus on the foods that went over well at the last camp, but The Grands' little appetites are so variable that her approach is like typing blindfolded. She baked two dozen chocolate chip muffins for breakfast. Previously, she baked a dozen chocolate chip and a dozen blueberry muffins, P-Pa's favorite. However, The Grands avoided those muffins, blueberries being too close to vegetables to risk it. So, P-Pa no longer gets his favorite muffin. As he doesn't view anything with chocolate chips in it as a proper breakfast food, he is left to figure out his own breakfast while The Grands are partying on CCMs.

Probably the best training P-Pa ever got for Camp Mema/Gulag P-Pa came in the summers before and after his senior year in high school. He worked for Curry Motor Freight in Midland, delivering packages and equipment throughout the Permian Basin, handy experience for bringing in all the LEGOs and other toys from the barn or Library Annex, as Mema calls it. While Mema was cooking, P-Pa was moving Grands' freight and then setting up the western town, or Coraville as it is now known in honor of Miss Cora, who always puts the town back together after the others wreck it. As a result of a Coraville zoning change, P-Pa moved the saloon to the opposite end of the street from the school. In past years, he's set them up next door to each other, but he now realizes that was not a positive influence on the young ones. Now the school is adjacent to the jail.

Things are getting tense here as Camp is just three days away, and Mema and P-Pa, especially him, have been swamped with a lot of unrelated tasks. They're uncertain if they can get all their Camp chores done ahead of the arrival of the inmates on Saturday and, if they do complete them, whether or not they will have the energy left to stand guard over the finicky eaters. The challenges continue.

**Gulag P-Pa Diary/Pre-Camp No. 5:**

While Mema kept slogging away inside the house with pre-camp chores, P-Pa moved outdoors to mow the lawn, trim the edges, sharpen the concertina wire, and test the alarm system, just in case any of The Grands try to escape. P-Pa focused on the back yard, which he tries to keep functional for Grands' playtime. The front yard is a combination of xeriscape, thinning grass and ineptitude, while the back has a fine, thick turf. While the world may judge P-Pa by the front yard, he's more concerned about judgment of The Grands so he focuses on the back, which was handsome enough last year to attract five out-of-this-world visitors from a galaxy far, far away. Again, this year, the back yard looks pretty good for a homeowner with a brown thumb in a semi-arid environment, though P-Pa fears opening his next water bill, which may exceed the grocery bill for The Grands.

In addition to the yard, he got out the two wading pools that have been a feature of every camp to date. Always safety conscious, P-Pa also retrieved his rescue pole in case any of the little ones get in water trouble. The pools, though, have less appeal as The Grands grow older. P-Pa thought he was anxious for The Grands to outgrow the pools so he could dispose of them, but he's not sure anymore. Senior Grand Hannah gave up on the pools two years ago and is skipping camp this year as she prepares for her freshman year in high school. Yep, all kids grow up, well, all of them except P-Pa, who keeps sneaking into the living room when Mema's not watching so he can play with the western town.

Mema is vacuuming and dusting, as paranoid about the house being clean as P-Pa is about the yard looking spiffy. She spent most of her time working in the front room, which doubles as her sewing room and the dorm room for the Giggle Twins, as Melissa has named Misses Miriam and Carys. As Mema will be spending extra time in the sewing room helping Miss Cora sew an outfit, she wanted it to look especially nice.

So, what's a little dust on a shelf or a weed in yard, you say? Well, this is the age of social media. The Grands come armed with electronics and the knowledge of how to use them, unlike Mema and P-Pa. So, they can take videos, post them on social media and destroy P-Pa's reputation for a single brown spot in the yard or Mema's for a solitary dust bunny in the corner. Cell phones, tablets and other electronic devices have also made discipline a real problem at Camp Mema as P-Pa is old-fashioned, believing a swat on the bottom solves all childhood problems. Mema says that approach is old school, as in the Neanderthal School of Parenting. Mema says modern parenting involves empathy, emphasizing good behavior, seeking out the why behind misbehavior, avoiding a power struggle, keeping your cool (Uh oh! P-Pa's in trouble there!) and remaining patient (Ditto! P-Pa's in BIG trouble!)

Strategies behind those principles include creating diversions, rewarding good behavior, never expecting perfection, establishing consequences, presenting alternatives and introducing timeouts.

Wow, P-Pa never realized grandparenting was as complicated as international diplomacy. Being old school, he preferred swat-and-go parenting as Scott and Melissa will confirm. Sure, it could get noisy as those little lungs could really wail, but it was quick and saved on endless negotiations. P-Pa was, after all, an honor graduate of the Neanderthal School of Parenting.

Tomorrow is the last full day of camp preparation. P-Pa was so busy today that he missed the mailman and will have to go to the Post Office tomorrow to pick up a registered letter from Zip Code 20002.

**Gulag P-Pa Diary/Pre-Camp No. 6:**

The eve of destruction. Yep, that's how Mema and P-Pa felt when they retired after midnight following an exhausting day of final preparations for Camp. Things got off to a horrible start when P-Pa went to the Post Office to retrieve his registered letter. It turns out the letter was a cease-and-desist order from the Federal Department of Health and Humor Resources to cancel camp for the well-being of all involved. It seems the bureaucrats in Washington fear that sexagenarians Mema and P-Pa cannot keep up with The Grands, much less handle all the fun without seriously endangering their health.

P-Pa thinks it's federal retribution after his commentary on his experience with the TSA. There seems to be a little cross-pollination or cross-retribution between federal agencies. P-Pa and Mema have survived six previous Camp Mema/Gulag P-Pas and weren't going to take this sitting down in their wheelchairs. So, they hired legal representation and filed for an emergency injunction against the Department of Health and Humor Resources with the Ninth Circuit Court of Appeals, the most humorless court in the country, but the only one open when their lawyers completed the paperwork. At first the court rejected our request, saying it was the federal government's job to wring the fun out of everyone's lives in the name of greater safety for all.

For a moment, P-Pa was stunned until he realized he could make this a win-win situation. He said if the court allowed Mema and P-Pa to conduct camp, they would allow the media to come in to shoot video of kids in cages. When the court realized such images could embarrass the President and his administration, the judges voted unanimously to allow the camp to continue as originally planned. Whew!

So, watch for us on the national news next week, likely on FNN or MSDNC! Mema and P-Pa have a long history of caging our children. Scott and Melissa spent a lot of quality time in a playpen, but by the time we became grandparents, the name playpen was out of vogue, "pen" being too insensitive and demeaning for young egos, creating the possibility of a lifetime of shame and insecurities for the inmates. "Play yard" became the appropriate new term. Being progressive grandparents, Mema and P-Pa decided they would not inflict such lasting mental anguish and pain on their grandchildren, so they stopped using the term "playpen" and settled on "The Slammer" as the best term. The first time we kept Hannah after she could talk fairly well, we kept her in The Slammer when she misbehaved or when we needed to keep her out of the way. The afternoon before we were to take her home, we folded up playpen while she was napping and put it away. When she got up from her nap, Hannah walked into the family room, stopped, did a double-take and looked up at P-Pa. "Where's The Slammer?" she inquired.

When he wasn't fighting legal battles to keep Camp Mema/Gulag P-Pa open or planning on incarcerating the little ones, P-Pa was straightening his office. He hadn't planned on it, but he kept coming back to a conversation he recalled from last year's camp when the Giggle Twins ventured into his office and looked at each other, proclaiming their rooms NEVER looked that messy.

The stress of meeting the little ones' expectations has gotten to P-Pa, who has taken to drink, as much as a six-pack an hour. Mema's uncertain what kind of damage all that Diet Mountain Dew will wreak on P-Pa's fragile physique, but she has noticed his t-t-ta ta-lk-ing and ty-ty-p-p-ing have grown e-e-ra-ra-tic. Now she's stressed that she'll have to commit P-Pa to treatment and manage camp all by herself. Consequently, she's enrolled P-Pa in her two-step abstinence program: First Step—STOP Drinking; Second Step—OR ELSE! Her sensitive approach to addiction has worked because P-Pa's talking and typing have suddenly improved, if not his attitude.

As the invasion nears, the tune of Barry McGuire's 1965 hit Eve of Destruction keeps playing in P-Pa's mind. Is that a foreshadowing or merely the worries of a feeble mind? Only time will tell, and that time is just hours away.

**Gulag P-Pa Diary/Day 1:**

D-Day! Mema's and P-Pa's tranquil world disappeared at 10:51 a.m. today when The Grands arrived and then exploded at 2:09 when Melissa, their chauffeur, headed back to Round Rock, leaving Mema and P-Pa on their own. Their arrival was an insidious almost sinister beginning as The Grands entered not in a rush, but one at a time like infiltrators on a search-and-destroy mission.

The cloak-and-dagger atmosphere was heightened when Miss Miriam came up and hugged P-Pa, saying "I love you, P-Pa..." So far, so good, until Miriam finished her sentence, "...but we shall never speak of this moment again." Another instance P-Pa prefers to forget started out well and ended poorly. He was excited when Miriam told him she had a cap for him. His excitement died when he put on the headgear and realized it was a unicorn cap.

After the greetings and the unpacking, The Grands gravitated to Coraville to play with the western town and figures. Miss Carys came up with a new rodeo event—windmill riding—and P-Pa has the photos to prove it. Miss Cora, the city's name sake, happened to be playing with the fort cannon when it went off and accidentally shot the western groom that Miriam was playing with. In the great tradition of the Old West, Miriam vowed revenge and armed the jilted gal, calling her, "The Outlaw Bride." A light popped off in P-Pa's head: That's the name of a good western novel. He checked Amazon, but at least three different authors had already used it. It's just as well, as P-Pa would likely have had to pay Miss Miriam royalties for her intellectual property.

Mr. Jackson played with Coraville for a while, then set up the train track and began a little engineering. He has a unique way of laying track and his etiquette is impeccable. At the lunch table, Trainwreck told Mema "Thank you" for everything she'd done. Said Cora, "That's called manners, P-Pa!" Touché!

Even though they are still kids, The Grands have matured a lot since last year. For instance, Jackson picked up toys without being told once he was finished playing with LEGOs. And then The Grands had cupcakes at two meals. In the past, there were so many crumbs under the table that it looked like a mini-tornado had struck a pastry factory. The floor under the table this time was immaculate, save for where P-Pa ate. Mema still had to hose down his spot. Other changes from last year included Miriam in glamorous glasses and Cora in unglamorous but effective braces.

At supper we almost had a historic first as Miss Miriam came close to finishing her meal ahead of Miss Carys. Miriam eats with the blazing speed of a glacier and is always the last to finish. Despite a close call, Miss Miriam is still undefeated when it comes to finishing last.

The persistent question of the day was "when can we open presents?" Yep, everyone was excited about the unified birthday party, though Mr. Jackson admitted it wouldn't be the same without Hannah. So, we stacked Hannah's presents at the end of the table and placed a photo of her atop them so she could be there in spirit. Harriet's outfits were the hit of the party, everyone loving her/his outfit. Miss Cora looked so mature in her sundress and Misses Miriam and Carys loved their matching skirts and tops in their favorite colors. Jackson was excited about his "superhero" shirt and matching tie, which P-Pa knotted for the photos. When the Giggle Twins were dressed in their new outfits, they decided they looked like professional businesswomen and Jackson decided his tie made him a businessman with superhero tendencies.

Because of a busy schedule over the past month, P-Pa failed to complete the script for the musical, which excited The Grands because they could help write the screenplay. They decided they would have four songs in The Sound of Noise. Miss Miriam was particularly concerned about the performances for the song The House Is Alive with the Sounds of Jackson. Said Miriam, "I really believe we should put some personality in it so people will believe how noisy Jackson really is." P-Pa couldn't agree more.

We ended the night watching *The LEGO Movie* 2. It was cute and terrifying at the same time as P-Pa remembered watching the first LEGO Movie back five years ago and hearing The Grands marching around the house after that singing "Everything is awesome". He got tired of hearing everything was awesome even if you're part of the team or even if you're living the dream. LEGO Movie 2 brought back those horrors, though the terrors were partly assuaged by Miss Miriam who brought popcorn P-Pa popped for everyone. Even so, it looks like another five years of therapy for P-Pa if he survives the night.

**Gulag P-Pa Diary/Day 2:**

Everything is awesome after a good night's sleep. The Grands were in bed by 9:15 last night and asleep by 9:45, even the Giggle Twins who share a bed and are known for giggling into the wee hours of the night. Mema and P-Pa hit the sack by 10:15 and were asleep even quicker. Carys arose first, then P-Pa, Jackson, Miriam, Cora and Mema. P-Pa, who bunks in the same room as Jackson, thought everyone got a great night's sleep until breakfast when Mr. Jackson said, "P-Pa, it's hard to sleep when you snore!"

It was chocolate chip muffins for breakfast, P-Pa providing the service while Mema woke up and showered. P-Pa reminded the kids to eat over the table, and Jackson took the command to new extremes, plopping his chin on the table and continuing to munch on his muffin. No floor crumbs again, at least under The Grands' and Mema's places.

By mid-morning The Grands were having wolf training in the living room, howling at the moon and having mock wolf fights. Scary! P-Pa fears they are training for an attack on him in the night if he snores again. Whether it's coincidence or not, P-Pa doesn't know, but after wolf training The Grands drew first blood of the camp, Jackson wolf stubbing his toe and drawing a drop of blood around the nail. Fortunately, P-Pa upped his umbrella insurance policy to $40 million for this week so he is covered financially. Unfortunately, he forgot to add a wolf waiver to the policy so he could be at some financial risk, though it's something the attorneys will have to work out.

Even after a good night's sleep, P-Pa was exhausted by mid-morning and tried to take a family room nap in his easy chair while The Grands played in the living room. Just as P-Pa dozed off, The Grands came into the family room and started yapping. Without opening his eyes, P-Pa called for them to quit squawking. "We're not squawking," replied Carys. "We're playing babysitter." So much for the nap. Later they quit playing babysitter and started rummaging through the boxes of LEGOs, looking for just the right piece. P-Pa would've had an easier time napping by a rock crusher in an echo chamber.

Miss Miriam gives the sweetest and best prayers you've ever heard over meals. She also dispenses solid advice to her fellow campers. At lunch she gave a precocious prayer, well above her age. Then later during the meal when you-know-who was trying to con Jackson, Miriam offered some sage advice: "Jackson, don't give in to his P-Pa-ness!"

For the afternoon, Mema and P-Pa planned on treating The Grands to a San Angelo Broadway Academy production of *Peter Pan*. When P-Pa announced they would have to go in two cars, Miriam and Carys shouted, "Mema!" followed by Jackson with the same appeal. Sweet, wonderful Cora said she would ride with P-Pa if no one else would, saving him from a severe case of Traumatic Grandparent Stress Syndrome.

Everyone enjoyed the musical. Though Mema and P-Pa had no worries about the Girl Grands, they weren't sure about one, but the little fellow did pretty good overall and picked up a new nickname: "Wiggle Wand." He was all over his seat and P-Pa before the program began, but then climbed on P-Pa's thigh, leaned back and was very calm while the performance progressed. Though hyper at halftime or intermission, as Miriam corrected P-Pa, Mr. Jackson was great once the musical resumed. Until the performance started, though, he was like a pogo stick on Red Bull.

As soon as they got home, The Grands wanted iPad time. So, P-Pa set them up at the table with their electronics while he popped them some of Miriam's popcorn. The look on Jackson's face was priceless when P-Pa gave Wiggle Wand a bowl with one kernel of popcorn inside. P-Pa filled Mr. Jackson's bowl, and everything was fine after that until Miriam freaked out on Minecraft because she had four chances to get a little pony and failed each time. We've had a digital disaster on our hands and neither P-Pa nor Mema could help Miriam navigate the Minecraft world.

To make matters worse, Miriam got up from the table and started counting. P-Pa asked what she's doing, and she replied playing hide-and-seek. P-Pa told her she must be the only one because all the other Grands were still sitting at the table. "Hide and seek on Minecraft," she replied to P-Pa. Then she turned to her fellow hide-and-seekers who weren't hiding in P-Pa's world and said, "Wouldn't it be easier if we just went in there (living room) away from P-Pa?" After they marched off, Mema and P-Pa sat peacefully alone in the family room in the real world, enjoying everything but the odd noises coming from the virtual-world hide-and-seek iPads in the front room.

Camp this year initiated the Blue Ribbon Award

to be voted on by the campers for the outstanding accomplishment of the day. After discussing various award options ranging from the best insult of P-Pa to the most helpful camper, the inmates deciding on awarding the Blue Ribbon for the Good Deed of the Day. In the biggest upset in Award history since Shakespeare in Love beat out Saving Private Ryan for the 1998 Oscar, P-Pa received the Sunday Blue Ribbon for taking The Grands and Mema to see Peter Pan. P-Pa was struck speechless at the honor and decided to retire the award for the rest of camp.

However, a half hour later one inmate likely would've revoked the Blue Ribbon Award. The Grands wanted to play "Scared by P-Pa" where he hides (not an easy task for someone his size and age) somewhere in the house. The Grands search for him and then he jumps out and startles them. Well, P-Pa hid in the entry closet by the vacuum cleaner, and they searched five or six minutes, finally standing right outside his cracked door, wondering where he was. He leaped out and screamed. The girls shrieked and ran while Jackson took to bawling as he was terrified. Only Mema could ease his fears. End of that game.

Later after everyone calmed down, Jackson got his feelings hurt in a game with the girls, so fine grandparents that they are, Mema and P-Pa called the disputants in and tried to get an explanation. The best the elders could make of it, Jackson didn't think the girls had done something they thought they had. Mema and P-Pa couldn't understand. Jackson informed us that "it's difficult to explain." Then Miriam, also known as WordStar, came to her boy cousin's defense. Said Miriam, "It is kind of tricky to explain to someone who's not a kid."

The only way Mema and P-Pa could counter that logic was to send them all to bed!

## Gulag P-Pa Diary/Day 3:

Screams of terror echoed through the house when The Grands learned P-Pa was cooking breakfast today. Only after they saw that P-Pa was pulling waffles from a bag did they calm down and realize things weren't as bad as they thought, especially after he found the sack of chocolate chips Mema had left on the counter. As Miss Miriam explained to P-Pa, "You didn't really cook it. You just warmed it up and somehow knew what was the right temperature." Or as Jackson said, "P-Pa wouldn't intentionally poison us." Only Miss Cora ate waffles the traditional way with syrup while the three younger ones inserted a chip in every waffle square and expected P-Pa to melt them in the microwave. To his credit, P-Pa again knew the right temperature to get the chips squishy without making them too hot to eat, good enough for Miss Carys to consume two waffles with chips.

Mema took Cora to the grocery store after breakfast to purchase items for Cora to cook everyone's lunch the next day. Cora's menu will include teriyaki chicken, rice and broccoli.

Mr. Jackson approached P-Pa and asked, "You know what you need to do now that we are all grown up?" P-Pa had no idea how to answer his grown up six-year-old, but before he could respond Wiggle Wand continued: "You need to get us all new LEGOs. These are baby LEGOs." It was the biggest LEGO con since Misses Miriam and Carys hoodwinked P-Pa into buying the Cindewelly Castle and then the Cindewelly Carriage with Prince Charming.

P-Pa went to get a paper mid-morning and when he returned, Miriam and Carys were listening to Miriam's iPad and dancing to Korean pop music, a girl group called Blackpink, a new one on P-Pa, who pretty much lost track of popular music at the end of the 1960s. There's a lot of contemporary American singers and groups P-Pa's not familiar with, much less Korean groups. It could be that Kim Jong-un and his South Korean counterpart are winning the culture war with the U.S. P-Pa checked with the CIA (Culture International Agency) for intelligence on the group and found out the four members were named Jisoo, Jennie, Rosé and Lisa, who debuted in 2016 with their Square One album, which included hits Whistle and Boombayah, neither of which P-Pa has ever heard, nor was he familiar with their unpronounceable Ddu-Du Ddu-Du. P-Pa misses the time in pop music when all he had to know was American and British groups to be pop-culturally literate. Ah, for the good old days!

Mema helped Miss Cora lay out the pattern for her dress, then let her cut out the fabric. Cora was most attentive to her task, and Mema overheard her talking to herself, saying, "I've got a pair of sharp scissors in my hand, and I'm not afraid to use them." P-Pa hopes she's just talking about cutting fabric rather than settling scores with him! Mema thought she and Cora would be lucky to get the fabric cut out, but because Cora was so diligent, they not only got the pieces cut, but completed three of the nine sewing steps. Mema's descriptions coming from the sewing room were "perfect," "terrific" and "good job," though Mema did come rushing out one time saying, "Holy, moley. She's sewing a straighter seam than I do."

As for P-Pa, he had a score to settle. For the last ten years he thought nothing could be worse than the Princess Stage, which he has endured for more than a decade with his four granddaughters. He was wrong. There's the Super Hero Stage that Jackson's been in the last two years, and it's much worse than the Princess Stage. According to P-Pa's CIA connections, there are 227 known fairy tale princesses. According to the same source, there are 6,434 superheroes and villains. Say there's two villains for every superhero, that means there are still 2,144 superheroes, almost ten times as many as there are princesses. It's enough to send P-Pa's mind a spinning, like Spiderman's web.

There are so many superheroes that P-Pa gets confused, referring to Captain Marvel as a man when Miss Carys corrected him that Captain Marvel is now a "girl", her word not his. P-Pa was stunned but didn't pursue it because he was uncertain if Captain Marvel was really a woman or just self-identifying as a girl, Carys's word not his, or whether he/she/Captain/Captainess had had a surgical transformation. Anyway, P-Pa is old school, thinking they were super he-roes not super her-oes, his words, not Miss Carys's.

Consequently, P-Pa was so tired of super he- or her-oes he decided to fight Jackson's superheroes (Spiderman, Iron Spider, Ironman and Captain America) action figures with his real heroes (members of the 101st and 82nd Airborne and the 29th Infantry Division) action figures. So, the boys did battle and could not agree on who won, P-Pa insisting the real heroes won and Jackson arguing that his ersatz heroes prevailed. Rather than argue, they decided to join forces and fight the real villains, Princesses or Nazis, otherwise known as Republicans to Progressives. Since the girls were offended by the references to Princesses as villains, P-Pa and Jackson decided to take on the Nazi action figures, quickly whipping them, good triumphing over evil as it always should. Satisfied that their princesses were no longer in danger, Carys and Miriam retreated and put together a 100-piece jigsaw puzzle.

The Grands got together and decided that since P-Pa didn't have the script completed when they arrived for this year's movie, The Sound of Noise, he should write himself out of the musical, since he can't sing anyway. As a result, P-Pa has no spoken lines even though he put words in everyone else's mouths. The best he can hope for is a cameo in this year's movie. On the positive side, at least he is not the villain. Filming begins tomorrow.

The evening ended with Miriam's popcorn and the 2015 movie Descendants, a DVD that Cora got for her birthday. Now from what P-Pa understands, Descendants is a story of the offspring of fairy tale villains and how they try to adapt to the world of fairy tale heroes when given the chance to live in Oregon, at least that's what P-Pa thought they said. The Grands corrected him that it was Auradon instead or Oregon, though some of the characters could pass for Portland Antifa members. Descendants is sort of a princess redux and now P-Pa wishes he and Jackson had triumphed over princesses as well as the Nazis in the battle of the action figures. Unfortunately, P-Pa couldn't follow the story very closely as he was having to complete the script in which he has no lines. Hollywood's a tough town, sort of like Everafterville.

After the movie it was bedtime for The Grands and recovery time for the Grandpars. Two full days down, three to go. Will The Grandpars still be standing at the end? Stay tuned.

**Gulag P-Pa Diary/Day 4:**

Never in the history Camp Mema/Gulag P-Pa have we had a surprise celebrity visit—until today. Yes, Camp Mema/Gulag P-Pa Alumna Hannah dropped by the concentration camp for a quick visit after lunch, during a trip with her parents from San Antonio to Midland. There's a backstory about this trip that P-Pa will go into after camp, but for the time-being Miss Hannah is the story, spending more than two hours with the gang before heading on with her parents to Midland.

Mr. Jackson was delighted to see his senior cousin as he had been asking when she would arrive. He was jumping up and down when Hannah entered. We had thought Friday afternoon would be the earliest she would get by when she came with her parents to relieve Mema and P-Pa of their inmates, but Miss Hannah had been following her sister's and cousins' adventures on Facebook and decided she wanted to make a guest appearance. The Grands, Mema and P-Pa were thrilled to see her, and it was just like old times when she sat down at Coraville and started playing with the other four at the western town. Hannah got to open her birthday gifts, including the romper Harriet made for her. Hannah said rompers were very popular with her set now, and Celeste said Hannah would look sexy in the outfit, drawing a smile from Hannah and Mema and a frown from her protective father. Before heading on to Midland, Hannah actually begged her folks to stay at camp, but she had an appointment in Midland that precluded more than a brief visit. Mema and P-Pa and the other Grands, especially Jackson, were delighted to see her, even if briefly.

Cora continued her sewing with Mema, getting through seven of eleven steps in her dressmaking and took time away from seamstressing to fix our lunch of teriyaki chicken, rice and broccoli. She did everything about lunch from the shopping to the cutting to the cooking, well everything but the cleaning up. P-Pa got stuck with that chore, though it was worth it after such a delicious meal.

While waiting for Miss Hannah and her parents to arrive, Carys, Miriam and Jackson worked on their own Tower of Babel, first creating the tallest LEGO tower ever built in Mema's and P-Pa's house, then building a shorter but sturdier one which could stand on its own. The fun came in watching them assess blame whenever the tower collapsed.

Hannah's impromptu visit pushed back filming

of The Sound of Noise and uncovered a huge problem that required a major rewrite. P-Pa assumed all The Grands were familiar with such classic show tunes as Some Enchanted Evening and Hello, Dolly, which were revamped into Some Enchanted Pizza and Goodbye, P-Pa. The Grands didn't know the tunes to those Broadway standards, and P-Pa complained about their musical illiteracy until Hannah asked P-Pa if he was familiar with BTS. Well, duh, P-Pa was familiar with the second, nineteenth and twentieth letters of the alphabet. Hannah just rolled her eyes, informing him that BTS, also known as the Bangtan Boys, was a seven-member South Korean boy band with multiple international hits. "They're hot guys," Miriam chimed in, drawing a frown from her father and a shrug from her grandfather. What is it with South Korean bands these days, P-Pa wanted to know? He could understand South Texas, but South Korea? So, Hannah made her point and P-Pa had to revamp the songs for the movie. The score now includes four songs, The House is Alive With the Sound of Jackson, and I Won't Throw Up, salvaged from the original script, plus new songs He's a Pest, styled after Be My Guest, and These are a Few of Our Favorite Things. P-Pa learned the hard way he needs to ask the singers first the tunes they are familiar with.

After supper they played Cootie, where you build a bug. You always know trouble's brewing when one of them says that's not fair. Sure enough, the Kemp Grands began to argue fairness until Miriam whipped out the rules, skimmed them and found the applicable paragraphs and read them to the entire crew. It might not have been fair, but it was the rules, so the issue of fairness was put aside and the game continued until Carys finished building her Cootie first.

For movie time, P-Pa took the biggest personal risk in Camp Mema/Gulag P-Pa history by introducing The Grands to the wonders of the classic television show Green Acres, P-Pa's favorite television series of all time. Mema is much less enthusiastic about the artistic merit of Green Acres, thinking it banal or, in P-Pa's words, corny. Much to P-Pa's delight and relief, The Grands for once, sided with him. They loved it, sitting in rapt fascination, especially liking Arnold the Pig. As a bit of cultural history, Green Acres was the final answer to the last Carnac the Magnificent question on the Tonight Show with Johnny Carson. The question was what does Kermit the Frog get when he's kicked in the groin.

P-Pa retired to bed ecstatic that The Grands enjoyed his old TV show, though Mema is a bit worried about her grandchildren's cultural tastes. As for P-Pa, he is the first lyricist in history to rhyme the word "Mema" with "Hee Haw", another classic television series. Mema could only roll her eyes at his eloquence with language.

**Gulag P-Pa Diary/Day 5:**

It was P-Pa's delicious waffles for breakfast again and The Grands managed okay until P-Pa told them Mema was leaving. They panicked until Mema explained she was just going to the grocery store to pick up a few supplies. "P-Pa," Jackson said, "sometimes your jokes are disturbing."

Sometimes Jackson's LEGO creations are disturbing to P-Pa, like the little fellow's airport. Rather than a control tower or a runway or a hangar, Jackson came up with a security line, complete with luggage line, security gate as Jackson called the scanner and a manager. How he came up with that aspect of airport travel perplexed P-Pa and gave him flashbacks of his recent TSA experience in the DFW Airport. Was Jackson a TSA plant?

Then Wiggle Wand made a LEGO music player where you slip the disc or USB drive into a slot and adjust the volume with a dial. Fortunately, Jackson didn't play any songs from South Korean bands. Mr. Jackson certainly has a nonlinear imagination.

On top of that, he's grown enough that he can reach the faucets on the lavatory. Consequently, we no longer need the bathroom stepstool that has served us for a decade with The Grands. Sure, it's a little step toward maturity, but it is another reminder of how quickly The Grands are growing up now that the littlest one can manage more things on his own.

Taping started—and finished—today on The Sound of Noise, destined to be a classic movie that is bound to make feminists everywhere happy, assuming they have a single happy bone in their bodies. Sure, it was written, filmed and directed by a man, but he was written out of the script and in a show of solidarity, Mr. Jackson decided to stand with P-Pa in the shadows and refused to read his parts. Power to the oppressed men of this household! But once you get past the politics, it's a sensitive portrayal of women with a chip on their shoulders because of the male oppression at Camp Mema.

The GGs (Girl Grands) each had a solo and then joined in with Mema on another song. Cora started it off with a Camp Mema anthem, The House is Alive with the Sound of Jackson, the song title and idea credited to the Missing GG, Hannah. Cora sang with sensitivity the opening lines: "The house is alive with the sound of Jackson/With noises he has created since birth/The house bursts with the sounds of his action/And of peaceful silence there is a great big dearth."

Mema plus the GGs next sang I Won't Throw Up, a tune the Sunday performance of Peter Pan prepared them for. Mema crooned and the GGS echoed: "I won't throw up/I won't throw up/Even if P-Pa cooks/Even if P-Pa cooks/I'll eat what's on my plate/I'll eat what's on my plate/And pretend that it's great/And pretend that it's great." Mema will definitely confirm there's a lot of wishful thinking in those lyrics, especially the fifth through eighth lines.

Then Carys performed a touching rendition of These Are a Few of My Favorite Things. The crew was in tears as she kicked the patriarchy in the teeth with such touching lyrics as: Bruises on P-Pa and flowers for Mema/Classic T-V Shows, Especially Hee Haw/Hot cookie pizza that inspires us to sing/These are a few of our favorite things." P-Pa doesn't mean to brag, but the opening two lines rhyming Mema with Hee Haw is certainly deserving of Oscar and Grammy consideration.

From the beginning of the movie process, Miss Miriam insisted on singing the rousing finale and she got her chance with He's a Pest, sung to the tune of Be Our Guest. She performed the tricky song with aplomb, including these concluding lyrics: "He can't sing, he can't dance/Miriam calls him poopy pants/And P-Pa's mentally un-bal-anced/So don't give the guy a chance/Check him out and you'll shout/He's a pest!/He's a pest!/He's a pest!"

Editing began tonight with the goal to have the movie debut tomorrow night. P-Pa has learned from past Camp Mema/Gulag P-Pa Productions not to write long scripts. This one was six pages. He's done one as long as twenty-two pages and the editing drove him crazy.

Progress continued on other fronts, too, as Cora continued making strides on her dress. At supper The Grands asked P-Pa if he knew about the Avengers. P-Pa replied he wasn't into the Marvel Parthenon of characters. They started making fun of his cultural illiteracy. To change the subject, he asked them what their superhero names would be, but they decided to counter by coming up with his superhero name. Carys wanted to be known as Gemmastone with the power to teleport. Miriam decided her name would be Any Girl with the power to change into different animals. Blackphobia was the name Cora chose with the power to control minds and fly. Jackson preferred to be Krakan, the legendary cephalopod-like sea monster that could attach to things and make them sink.

Then The Grands turned to P-Pa and started thinking about the possibilities. Sensing a disaster, Cora came up with Captain AmeriPa. Miriam modified the name, coming up with Captain Poopy Pants. We put it to a vote and Captain Poopy Pants won, 3-2, with Mema and Cora dissenting in a failed effort to preserve P-Pa's dignity. As for Captain Poopy Pants's superpower, let's just say it's not his shield he flings. Hey, don't blame P-Pa as it wasn't his idea for a superpower but rather that of the terrible trio. Well, it's signoff time as Captain Poopy Pants has a world to clean up, not to mention his superhero tights, while The Grands watch Descendants 2 and eat Miriam's popcorn.

**Gulag P-Pa Diary/Day 6:**

This was the day all the inmates have been waiting for, the day that made enduring P-Pa's harassment worth it in the end. Yes, this was Mema's Famous Cookie Pizza Day. A mid-afternoon snack that draws rave reviews each year, Cookie Pizza starts with a base of chocolate chip cookie dough (what else?), slathered with a sauce of cake icing and then sprinkled with Plain M&Ms in the individual style of the diner. There's the regimented style of M&M design, the haphazard style and the I-ate-most-of-my-M&Ms-before-I-got-to-the-pizza style. Regardless of the topping style, food critics everywhere agree that it is amazing. Chef Boy R

Jackson says, "It's good, and I like it, and I like to eat it." The Gourmet Giggle Twins call it "yummy, delicious and fun to make and eat!" And Chef Cora labels it "chocolaty, crunchy heaven."

Even without the Cookie Pizza, this would've been a red-letter day with the events of lunch and Miss Cora's fashion show after supper. First of all at lunch Miss Miriam did not finish her meal last for the first time in Camp Mema history. She actually finished FIRST, ahead of everyone. After Mema gave P-Pa smelling salts to revive him from shock, they both congratulated their little Alaskan for a job well done.

Then after supper Cora finished her dress. As Mema was doing a few final touches, Cora slipped out of the sewing room and told P-Pa that when Mema came out of the room, he was to get his camera and be ready to take pictures as she wanted to surprise her fellow campers. She scampered back to the sewing room and shortly Mema came out. P-Pa got his camera and corralled the three younger Grands and sat them on the couch with the promise of a surprise. Jackson figured it out that it was Cora's dress, and the Giggle Twins got excited. Then the door to the front room opened, and Cora came out just beaming in her new dress. It was hard to tell whether she or Mema had the biggest smile. Cora did a great job not only of sewing but also of modeling her custom-made dress. The other Grands were impressed with Cora's pink dress. It was a Camp memory for the ages.

Earlier in the day, pangs of conscience struck P-Pa today, and he decided maybe he needed to learn more about the Marvel Pantheon of superheroes when he saw Jackson's book on the Avengers. He asked to read it, but Mr. Jackson nixed his request, saying "You can't read my diary." P-Pa asked what he had written in it and he answered, "Nothing but it's still my diary, and you can't read it." So much for enhancing his Marvel sense.

P-Pa caught Carys, Miriam and Jackson playing Simon Says in the hall. They had shut all the doors and P-Pa asked them why. They explained they shut the front room door to keep out the light, the bathroom door for safety sake and the middle bedroom door for consistency. They didn't explain why they shut P-Pa's office door. When P-Pa asked, they looked sheepishly at one another and stood silently for a moment. Miriam finally broke the silence. Said Miriam, "Jackson says creepy things come out of there." P-Pa didn't pursue the matter further.

It can be a little disconcerting when you walk in on The Grands playing on their iPads and overhear the conversation. When P-Pa entered the living room during electronics hour, Cora announced, "I've got tons of gunpowder." P-Pa turned around and walked out in case she was planning on going after creepy things.

P-Pa left the stepstool that Jackson no longer needs by his hat rack. Jackson spotted it, climbed atop it and asked P-Pa if he needed it to reach his hats. P-Pa could only nod.

The other big event of the day was the debut of The Sound of Noise. It drew critical raves after P-Pa spent most of the day editing and finalizing it. He showed it to The Grands on the computer and tomorrow will convert it for DVD player with plans to have the first Camp Mema/Gulag P-Pa Film Festival tomorrow night with all the movies they've produced since the start of camp. It and the awards presentations will provide a big gala to end camp Friday night.

As for this night, The Grands wanted to end it watching Green Acres, much to P-Pa's delight. They got to watch three episodes before heading off to bed.

**Gulag P-Pa Diary/Day 7:**

After six years and six days of Camp Mema/Gulag P-Pa, The Grands finally found an important task for P-Pa—emergency plumber. Mema gets all the attention for feeding them, cleaning up after them, tending their scrapes and bruises, being patient with all their problems and keeping P-Pa in line. On this day, though, only P-Pa could solve their problem. It seems that Misses Carys and Miriam had showered together and, unfortunately, created a problem that sent Captain Poopy Pants to the rescue. While poor, innocent P-Pa was sitting in his easy chair dreaming of the next day when peace and quiet would supplant pandemonium, the Giggle Twins approached like little angels, their wide eyes overflowing with love and innocence. Then they spoke: "We knocked Carys's toothpaste in the commode and you need to get it out." P-Pa suggested they retrieve it since they had created the problem. "Eeeeewwwww," they answered. As this was a plumbing problem the equal of P-Pa's skills, he took on the challenge, fetched a pair of channel locks, even though Miriam kept insisting he use tongs, and pulled the contaminated toothpaste tube from the bowels of the commode, then dropped the tube in the trashcan. P-Pa earned the Giggle Twins' undying gratitude for about 15 seconds, though both refused to shake his proffered hand, even though he had never touched commode water and had washed his hands five times, just to be on the safe side. It seems like P-Pa's popularity took a dive once the odious task was completed.

The creative Mr. Jackson cross-pollinated Coraville with his superhero fixation and devised a new villain—Dr. Obvious Cactus. His saguaro cactus flew through the air attacking and knocking over the innocent residents of Coraville. The only thing that saved Coraville was a sharp-eyed, rifle-toting belligerent eagle that was able to fill Dr. Obvious Cactus with lead. P-Pa doesn't know if that makes the eagle a superhero, but that's more his style than those dysfunctional Marvel freaks Mr. Jackson is enamored with.

Over the years, Mema and P-Pa have figured out that cleanup starts the day before The Grands leave, not after they're gone. So, the afternoon was spent dismantling the western town and picking up a zillion LEGO pieces and corralling all The Grands' clothes, electronics, books (yes, they still use that outdated technology) and uncontaminated toothpaste. It's obvious The Grands are maturing as you don't have to remind them to pick up things like previous camps when they would get sidetracked and start playing instead of gathering playthings.

While they were cleaning up, Mema was folding all The Grands' previously dirty clothes. Mema is so considerate that she launders all their clothes the final day so their Moms don't have to do it. After cleaning up the toys, The Grands got to put on M&M toppings and finish the Cookie Pizza and one fellow had to clean up after the cleanup.

Their growing maturity makes things easier all around on the camp superintendents. On the one hand, it's better. On the other hand, it means the childhoods we have enjoyed all these years are gradually slipping away toward adulthood as exemplified by Hannah, who returned with her parents to deliver The Grands back to their homes. Hannah is maturing into a fine, intelligent young woman, who begins her freshman year of high school in a few weeks. That's hard to believe!

When Hannah returned, everyone got in their new Mema outfits, and we took pictures again. And, we had another camp first as Cora, after posing in Mema's outfit, changed into the dress she sewed, and we got another group picture. She was proud as was her Mema.

After supper, it was time for the awards show, a longstanding camp tradition. Mema and P-Pa were pleased that Miss Hannah even asked if she was getting any awards this year. We told her to wait and see. The awards this year were as follows for Camp Mema: Cora, "Best Seamstress and Chef" for achievements in the sewing and culinary arts; Miriam, "Best Puzzle Provider" for achievements in sharing her jigsaw puzzles with everyone; Carys, "Tallest LEGO Tower Engineer Award" for achievements in structural engineering; Jackson, "Most Innovative LEGO Engineer" for achievements in LEGO lunacy; and Hannah, "Best Surprise Guest Award" for achievements in making everyone happy on a special day at camp.

Gulag P-Pa awards went to: Cora, "Best Mayor of Coraville" for achievements in keeping order in the western town; Miriam, "Meal-Time First Award" for achievements in finally finishing a meal ahead of everyone else; Jackson, "Most Bashful Actor" for achievements in avoiding a speaking part in The Sound of Noise; Hannah, "Missing in Action Award" for achievements in missing most of camp; and Carys, "Best Toothpaste Manager Award" for achievements in commode splashing.

Then it was time to premier on the big TV screen the new movie The Sound of Noise, a seven-minute epic that had the crowd on their feet and cheering. After the debut of The Sound of Noise, everyone hung around for the retrospective of Gulag P-Pa movies. The classics included Escape from Gulag P-Pa, The Good, the Bad and the Cutely, The Cookie Thief and Star Stars. The Grands loved seeing their impromptu lines, their bloopers and how they had grown over the years. One poignant moment was Jackson settling in beside Hannah and holding her hand throughout the screenings.

After the film festival, the curtain came down on another successful camp and everyone retired to awake for getaway day.

## Gulag P-Pa Diary/Day 8:

Mema and P-Pa survived seven days, twenty-one hours, nineteen minutes and forty-seven seconds of unabated anarchy with most of their senses intact. It's obvious to us why you have kids when you're young and grandkids when you're mature, well at least in Mema's case. The physical energy of young adulthood more than offsets the lack of wisdom that comes with aging. And P-Pa could've used a little more of the patience he exhibits with his grandkids on Scott and Melissa. It's a testament to P-Pa's parenting skills that many of his most memorable parenting moments have the word "incident" at the end of them like "The Tea-Ball Incident" or "The Barton Creek Mall Incident".

Shortly after Scott married Celeste, she asked him to describe his mother in a single word. He came up with the word "perfect". When she asked the same thing of him about his father, he paused, then answered with a grin and a single word, "adequate". Melissa needed two words to describe P-Pa's parenting skills: "He tried!" Their lukewarm reviews were the main reason that P-Pa decided last year to go ahead and buy his tombstone so he'd control what the inscription was.

Getting The Grands on the road is sort of like organizing an armored division to move as it takes a lot of cooperation and coordination. Fortunately, Scott was here to load the eighteen-wheeler and Celeste was able to herd the inmates to the vehicle and get them on the highway for the return trip to Round Rock and Spring. They pulled away at 8:30 a.m., and Mema and P-Pa had cleared the rubble and collapsed into their easy chairs by noon, spending the afternoon and evening recovering and thinking about all the new memories we made over the last week.

For the first time in years, we didn't use the kid table and chairs, nor the stepstool previously mentioned. Yes, they are growing up. In Hannah's absence, Cora was proud to be the senior camper and was a good level-headed leader. We had to leave her in charge for about twenty minutes while Mema drove P-Pa to the auto dealership to retrieve a vehicle. Cora was proud to be in command and handled her responsibilities without incident. The highlight, though, with Cora was the look of awe and pride on her face when she came out in the dress she had sewn with Mema. Priceless!

Hannah's guest appearances were special for everyone. She hasn't totally outgrown Camp, and the cousins loved having her here, especially Jackson who has bonded with her ever since his first Camp stay. It's hard to believe Hannah will be in high school in a couple weeks. She looked so grown up in Mema's outfit.

While Jackson is all boy, he's got a sensitive side. Nothing's sweeter than him coming up and giving you a hug and telling you he loves you. He's now six and in the first grade. It's hard to believe he's school-age now. Jackson has a vivid imagination and listening to his stories or to his explanations about his LEGO creations is fun. His favorite shirt he brought with him was a Texas A&M tee. He likes the back of it better than the front, so most of the time he wears it backwards.

The Giggle Twins are a hoot and work together well. Miss Carys is spunky. Hard to believe she is the same girl that was so shy a few years ago that she could barely utter her lines for the early movies. The thing about her is that she loves to change outfits over the course of a day. She may wear two or three outfits a day. So, half the laundry Mema did probably belonged to Carys.

Miss Miriam tends to be a pleaser, but she's outspoken as well. She's unfiltered in what she says and can leave P-Pa chortling with some of the answers she gives to his manufactured questions or crises. Mema came up with the nickname "Word-Star" for Miriam and it fits because she has a way with words that can be both innocent and naively insulting at the same time. However, you won't find a more finicky eater anywhere than Miriam.

The day before they returned home, Miriam asked P-Pa if he and Mema were going to hold Camp Mema/Gulag P-Pa forever. P-Pa answered, no, that one day we would have to stop it as The Grands would outgrow Camp, much like Hannah. She thought a moment then said, "Don't stop it until after I outgrow it."

P-Pa gave her his promise and began to look forward to next year, once he and Mema get rested up, which should take about six months. Until then, adios from Camp Mema/Gulag P-Pa.

# CHAPTER FIFTEEN

*"Children are a heritage from the LORD,
offspring a reward from him." Psalm 127
(New International Version)*

Hannah came as such a blessing, a source of joy and comfort, diminishing the sorrow of losing Benjamin and helping us look toward the future rather than fixating on the past. The November after her birth, we visited Houston for Hannah's church dedication where our granddaughter's name was listed with its Biblical meaning, divine grace, or by some interpretations that God has favored me with a child. How appropriate!

Hers was the first of five dedications we would attend for our grandchildren. Three years later in June came Cora Belle Kemp, the daughter of our daughter and John. Two years later two more granddaughters, Miriam Faith Lewis in January and then Carys Anne Kemp in December, blessed us. Three years after that our second grandson Jackson Josiah Kemp arrived in April. For all the joy each pregnancy brought, the thought lingered in our mind that something might go wrong again. Fortunately, nothing did, and we loved and valued each precious child all the more because we had lost our first.

As they grew, we shared many visits and holidays with them, but later decided we wanted to do something special before they escaped the magic of their childhood years. Thus, we came up with the idea of a camp as we neared our retirement and had more flexibility with our time and careers. As a family we always looked to have fun with our children as they grew and matured, whether it was playing games, going camping, reading books or visiting historical sites. After her first extended stay with us before she married Scott, Celeste came up to me and said, "Your family sure does laugh a lot." I had never thought about it, just assuming laughter was a normal part of every family's life.

I always believed love of God and of each other was the key ingredient to a successful family, but laughter came a close second. In my mind, laughter helps overcome the various challenges all families face, whether economic, religious, cultural or personal, though that belief was challenged by the loss of Benjamin as there was no humor in what Scott and Celeste endured, nor in the sorrow we all felt.

Consequently, we wanted to immerse ourselves in our surviving five grandchildren once a year with seven to ten days of fun, laughter and activities so we would have time with them, and the cousins would spend extended time with each other. Too, we remembered how much we enjoyed the break from child-raising when my parents would keep our son, daughter, niece and nephew. More than that, we recalled the great memories our children had with my parents, either on the farm or in the mountains of New Mexico.

As we approached grandparenthood, Harriet and I both decided on names we would want our grandchildren to call us. I settled on P-Pa since my father was known to his grandkids as "Pa" and P-Pa would pay homage to him as well as the first initial of my given name. Harriet liked the idea of being called Grandmamma. While my grandparent alias was easy to say, Hannah had trouble pronouncing Grandmamma. The best she could do was "Mema," which was how Harriet would forever be called by The Grands. That continued a family tradition as Scott could not say Grandmother for my mother and called her "Gamma" instead.

Each year we held camp, we tried to come up with different ideas and activities for The Grands as we grew to call them. LEGOs and the Playmobil western town became a Camp tradition. We created a movie five of the first seven years of camp, a good way to laugh. Each year we now have the Camp Mema/Gulag P-Pa Film Festival where we re-watch all the old movies and laugh again at ourselves. And, I did the Facebook posts to poke fun at us all, though I was most often the butt of the jokes, most times deservedly so. In many cultural folklores and mythologies, there is the character of the trickster, who disrupts the societal norms by his chicanery. While Mema was the nurturer, I was the trickster, always looking for ways to trick or challenge The Grands to think or outsmart me. I loved playing tricks on Scott and Melissa as they grew to see how they reacted and to gauge how they thought. I remember one time when I pointed to something in the back yard while Melissa, maybe 18 months old, was eating a cookie with a sippy cup of milk. I took her cookie when she wasn't looking. When she turned around, she had this perplexed look on her face like she knew a cookie had been there. Then she picked up her sippy cup with both hands and looked under the bottom to see where her cookie had gone. She laughed when I returned to her the missing cookie.

So, at camp when something is missing or askew, all The Grands point their finger at P-Pa as the culprit, even when I am completely innocent. In fact, they've even been known to set things up to make me the fall guy so I would get in trouble with Mema. Ah, the joys of grandparenting. We've had serious activities as well, such as the year I put on various disguises and drove the car by the house and attempted to get the kids to go with me to find a lost puppy, to get some candy or to go to a movie, trying to train them never to go with strangers. It's a shame we have to think like this in modern society, but there are so many dangers out there that we feel obligated to try to protect them from. In some ways, that is one frustration of grandparenthood: Life is more complicated (and dangerous) in today's world than in the era Harriet and I or even our son and daughter grew up in.

Despite those complexities, we look forward to every visit we get with our children and The Grands, and we especially relish the fun and alone time we spend with them each year at camp. But always in my mind is one child missing, little Benjamin. His loss remains the greatest tragedy of mine and Harriet's life. Yet, had he lived, we might not have been blessed by Hannah, who as of this writing began her freshman year in high school. Little Benjamin would've been a sophomore or junior as of this writing. It's hard to imagine that for him, though not for the other Grands as we have watched them grow each year.

As much as we love his five successors, not a one of them is perfect or without sin. Only little Benjamin is. I can imagine him as an infant and even a toddler, but not much beyond that, certainly not as a high schooler. As the other Grands mature, little Benjamin remains our eternal grandson, the little baby that was perfect spiritually, if not physically. He was the tiny boy we were blessed to love, but never to hold. His absence always left an empty seat—in our minds at least—at our gatherings. We know that one day The Grands will all outgrow the silliness of Camp Mema/Gulag P-Pa and they will start lives and families on their own. Hopefully, their camp experiences will remain with them like our memories of little Benjamin.

Our first grandson is memorialized with his name in bronze on the marker at his grave. As we recently addressed our own earthly mortality, Harriet and I purchased a granite tombstone for our local gravesite. We had the usual information about ourselves engraved on the front and listed our family on the back: Scott and Celeste, Melissa and John.

Then we had the names of The Grands engraved. Benjamin came first. Now he is memorialized in both bronze at his gravesite and in granite at ours. At least on our tombstone our family is complete.

## *IF YOU LIKED THIS, CHECK OUT: MOMENTS OF GRACE*

Written in a friendly, conversational style, Moments of Grace, provides seniors with encouragement and inspiration. It reflects the authors firsthand knowledge of what it means to be a senior and what it means to draw strength from the Lord. Readers will identify with the personal and often humorous anecdotes. They will find the Scripture quotations meaningful and uplifting. Moments of Grace brings hope to those who despair and refreshing assurance of wellbeing to those who fear the future. For every senior who reads this book there is evidence of God's unfailing love.

**Available on Amazon**

# ABOUT THE AUTHOR

Growing up in West Texas and loving history, Spur Award-winning author Preston Lewis naturally gravitated to stories of the Old West and religiously read his father's copies of True West and Frontier Times. Today he is the author of more than 30 western, juvenile and historical novels as well as numerous articles, short stories and book reviews on the American frontier.

Preston Lewis is a past president of WWA and WTHA, which in 2016 named him a fellow. He has served on the boards of the Ranching Heritage Association and the Book Club of Texas. He and his wife Harriet live in San Angelo, Texas.

Find more great titles by Preston Lewis at https://wolfpackpublishing.com/preston-lewis/

www.ingramcontent.com/pod-product-compliance
Lightning Source LLC
Chambersburg PA
CBHW020924090426
42736CB00010B/1027